Conflict, Security, Foreign Policy, and International Political Economy

MILLENNIAL REFLECTIONS ON INTERNATIONAL STUDIES

CONFLICT, SECURITY, FOREIGN POLICY, AND INTERNATIONAL POLITICAL ECONOMY

Past Paths and Future Directions in International Studies

Edited by

Michael Brecher and Frank P. Harvey

Ann Arbor

THE UNIVERSITY OF MICHIGAN PRESS

Copyright © by the University of Michigan 2002
All rights reserved
Published in the United States of America by
The University of Michigan Press
Manufactured in the United States of America
⊗ Printed on acid-free paper

2005 2004 2003 2002   4 3 2 1

No part of this publication may be reproduced, stored in a
retrieval system, or transmitted in any form or by any
means, electronic, mechanical, or otherwise, without the
written permission of the publisher.

*A CIP catalog record for this book is available from
the British Library.*

Library of Congress Cataloging-in-Publication Data applied for
ISBN 0-472-08860-2

Acknowledgments

The editors would like to thank the distinguished scholars who contributed to this project for their gracious response to our demands over an extended period. We are very grateful to Jeremy Shine, political science editor of the University of Michigan Press, for his encouragement and support; to the International Studies Association for the opportunity to organize the millennial reflections panels at the Los Angeles conference in March 2000; to Ann Griffiths and Graham Walker for their excellent editorial assistance; to Kevin Rennells, of the University of Michigan Press, and to Impressions Book and Journal Services, for steering this multivolume project to publication with skill and empathy; and to Sarah Lemann for valuable word-processing assistance in the preparation of the typescript.

Frank Harvey would like to thank Michael Brecher for the privilege of serving as ISA program chair in 1999–2000 and for his truly outstanding contribution to the intellectual quality of the final manuscript, the Social Sciences and Humanities Research Council of Canada, the Centre for Foreign Policy Studies (Dalhousie University), and the Security and Defence Forum (Directorate of Public Policy, Department of National Defence, Canada) for supporting various stages of the project. Michael Brecher wishes to thank Frank Harvey for his selfless and invaluable role as coeditor of the Millennial Reflections Project. He also appreciates the reduced teaching load accorded by McGill University for the autumn term of 1999, which facilitated the organization of the millennial reflections panels and, more generally, the ISA's Los Angeles conference in March 2000.

Contents

The Essence of Millennial Reflections on International Studies: Conflict, Security, Foreign Policy, and International Political Economy   1
Michael Brecher and Frank P. Harvey

Foreign Policy Analysis

Foreign Policy Analysis: Steady Progress and a Half-Empty Glass   27
Yaacov Y. I. Vertzberger

Beliefs and Foreign Policy Analysis in the New Millennium   56
Stephen G. Walker

Public Opinion and Foreign Policy Analysis: Where We Were, Are, and Should Strive to Be   72
Ole R. Holsti

Simulation and Experimentation in Foreign Policy Analysis: Some Personal Observations on Problems and Prospects   91
Jonathan Wilkenfeld

International Security, Peace, and War

Security Theory: Six Paradigms Searching for Security   113
Edward A. Kolodziej

Security and Peace: Understanding, Production, and
  Work Style   141
  Davis B. Bobrow

Convergences between International Security Studies
  and Peace Studies   160
  Louis Kriesberg

Accounting for Interstate War: Progress and Cumulation   177
  J. David Singer

Notes from the Underground: A Tale of Three Perspectives   198
  Linda B. Miller

International Political Economy

Reflections on the Field of International Political Economy   207
  Helen Milner

Some Thoughts on International Political Economy in
  the Context of Public Policy Education   224
  Robert T. Kudrle

International Political Economy: From Paradigmatic Debates to
  Productive Disagreements   244
  Lisa L. Martin

Contributors   253

The Essence of Millennial Reflections on International Studies

Conflict, Security, Foreign Policy,
and International Political Economy

Michael Brecher and Frank P. Harvey

When Michael Brecher was introduced to international relations (IR) at Yale in 1946, the field comprised international politics, international law and organization, international economics, international (diplomatic) history, and a regional specialization. The hegemonic paradigm was realism, as expressed in the work of E. H. Carr, Arnold Wolfers, Nicholas Spykman, W. T. R. Fox, Hans Morgenthau, Bernard Brodie, and others.[1] The unquestioned focus of attention was interstate war and peace.

By the time the other editor of this collection, Frank Harvey, was initiated into international relations at McGill in the late 1980s, the preeminent paradigm was neorealism,[2] but there were several competing claimants to the "true path": institutional theory,[3] cognitive psychology,[4] and postmodernism.[5] And by the time he received his doctoral degree, other competitors had emerged, notably, critical theory,[6] constructivism,[7] and feminism.[8]

The consequence, at the dawn of the new millennium, was a vigorous, still inconclusive, debate about the optimal path to knowledge about international studies (IS), most clearly expressed in the views that it is a discipline—international relations (IR) or world politics—like economics, sociology, anthropology, history, or that it is a multidisciplinary field of study; the "big tent" conception of the premier organization, the International Studies Association (ISA).

It was in this context that the Millennial Reflections Project was conceived. The origin and rationale of the idea may be found in the central theme of Michael Brecher's presidential address to the ISA conference in Washington in February 1999: "International Studies in the Twentieth Century and Beyond: Flawed Dichotomies, Synthesis, Cumulation." The next stage was the creation of a set of ten millennial reflections theme-panels by Michael Brecher, then ISA president, and Frank Harvey, the program chair for ISA 2000: these panels served as the highly successful centerpiece of the Los Angeles conference in March 2000. Soon after, we enlisted the enthusiastic support of the University of Michigan Press for the idea of publishing revised and enlarged versions of these conference papers. Most of the participants in the Los Angeles panels readily agreed to revise and enlarge their papers. A few other papers were invited. The result is this volume and the accompanying set of four shorter, segment-focused volumes, prepared for the benefit of teachers and students of IS in colleges and universities everywhere.

Whether a discipline or a multidisciplinary field of study, IS has developed over the last half century with diverse philosophical underpinnings, frameworks of analysis, methodologies, and foci of attention. This diversity is evident in the papers that were presented at the panels at the 2000 Los Angeles conference and revised for publication in this state-of-the-art collection of essays on international studies at the dawn of the new millennium.

In an attempt to capture the range, diversity, and complexity of IS, we decided to organize the forty-four "think piece" essays into eight clusters. The mainstream paradigms of realism and institutionalism constitute the first two concentrations; critical perspectives (including critical theory, postmodernism, and constructivism); feminism and gender perspectives; methodology (including quantitative, formal modeling, and qualitative); foreign policy analysis; international security, peace, and war; and international political economy make up the remaining six.

The raison d'être of the Millennial Reflections Project was set out in the theme statement of the Los Angeles conference, titled "Reflection, Integration, Cumulation: International Studies Past and Future." As we noted in that statement, the number and size of subfields and sections has grown steadily since the founding of the International Studies Association in 1959. This diversity, while enriching, has made increasingly difficult the crucial task of identifying intrasubfield, let alone intersubfield, consensus about important theoretical and empirical insights. Aside from focusing on a cluster of shared research questions related, for example, to globalization, gender and international relations, critical theory, political economy, international institutions, global development, democracy and peace, foreign and security policy, and so on, there are still few clear signs of cumulation.

If the maturity of an academic discipline is based not only on its capacity to expand but also on its capacity to select, the lack of agreement *within* these communities is particularly disquieting. Realists, for instance, cannot fully agree on their paradigm's core assumptions, central postulates, or the lessons learned from empirical research. Similarly, feminist epistemologies encompass an array of research programs and findings that are not easily grouped into a common set of beliefs, theories, or conclusions. If those who share common interests and perspectives have difficulty agreeing on what they have accomplished to date or do not concern themselves with the question of what has been achieved so far, how can they establish clear targets to facilitate creative dialogue across these diverse perspectives and subfields?

With this in mind, our objective was to challenge proponents of specific paradigms, theories, approaches, and substantive issue areas to confront their own limitations by engaging in self-critical reflection within epistemologies and perspectives. The objective was to stimulate debates about successes and failures but to do so by avoiding the tendency to define accomplishments with reference to the failures and weaknesses of other perspectives.

It is important to note that our call to assess the state of the art of international studies was not meant as a reaffirmation of the standard proposition that a rigorous process of theoretical cumulation is both possible and necessary. Not all perspectives and subfields of IS are directed to accomplishing cumulation in this sense. Some participants found the use of such words as *synthesis* and *progress* suspect, declaring in their original papers that they could not, or were not prepared to, address these social science–type questions. We nevertheless encouraged these individuals to define what they considered to be fair measures of success and failure in regard to their subfield, and we asked them to assess the extent to which core objectives (whatever they may be) have or have not been met, and why.

Our intention obviously was not to tie individuals to a particular set of methodological tenets, standards, assumptions, or constraints.

We simply wanted to encourage self-reflective discussion and debate about significant achievements and failures. Even where critiques of mainstream theory and methodology are part of a subfield's raison d'être, the lack of consensus is still apparent and relevant.

As a community of scholars, we are rarely challenged to address the larger question of *success* and *progress* (however one chooses to define these terms), perhaps because there is so little agreement on the methods and standards we should use to identify and integrate important observations, arguments, and findings.

To prevent intellectual diversity descending into intellectual anarchy, the editors set out "guidelines" for the contributors, in the form of six theme questions, or tasks. The panelists were requested to address one or more of these tasks in their essays:

1. Engage in self-critical, state-of-the-art reflection on accomplishments and failures, especially since the creation of the ISA more than forty years ago.
2. Assess where we stand on unresolved debates and why we have failed to resolve them.
3. Evaluate the intrasubfield standards we should use to assess the significance of theoretical insights.
4. Explore ways to achieve fruitful synthesis of approaches, both in terms of core research questions and appropriate methodologies.
5. Address the broader question of progress in international studies.
6. Select an agenda of topics and research questions that should guide the subfield during the coming decades.

The result, as is evident in the pages to follow, is an array of thought-provoking think pieces that indicate shortcomings as well as achievements and specify the unfinished business of IS as a scholarly field in the next decade or more, with wide-ranging policy implications in the shared quest for world order. Readers will no doubt derive different conclusions from the various contributions. Some will observe that divisions within and across subfields of international studies are so entrenched that constructive dialogue is virtually impossible. Others will conclude that there is much more consensus than might have been imagined. In either case, the need for self-critical assessment among IS scholars is imperative as we enter the new millennium.

Foreign Policy Analysis

The cluster of millennial reflections on foreign policy analysis comprises papers by four authors: Yaacov Y. I. Vertzberger, Stephen G. Walker, Ole R. Holsti, and Jonathan Wilkenfeld.

Vertzberger

The essence of Yaacov Vertzberger's sweeping critique, "Foreign Policy Analysis: Steady Progress and a Half-Empty Glass," is evident in his introductory "panoramic reflective view of the FPA [foreign policy analysis] landscape since the 1950s. . . . There has obviously been steady progress . . . in . . . theoretical and conceptual development, in . . . empirical richness and availability of both case studies and aggregate data analysis, and in increasing methodological diversity, rigor, and sophistication. Yet . . . we are still facing a half-empty glass." The reasons for "straitjacketed progress" are "overlearning by imitation, decontextualization, oversimplification, and biases toward precision, conservatism, and risk aversion," shortcomings that "represent a general malaise" in IS and, more broadly, political science.

In a discussion of "the nature of progress," Vertzberger ranks theory as most important, followed by empirical data, with methodology a distant third place in the research enterprise, and the logic of discovery as far more important to social scientific innovation than the logic of verification. He notes two types of progress: horizontal, an expansion in the amount of knowledge; and vertical, a qualitative change that is "more likely to be transformational." Progress takes five forms, which are, in ascending order of significance, expansion, verification/falsification, integration, contextualization, and at the apex, extrapolation. These "may take place serially or simultaneously." In foreign policy analysis, progress has centered on the first two of these forms.

One of Vertzberger's intellectual bêtes noires is the unthinking adoption of norms and standards from the natural sciences, notably decontextualization, parsimony, precision, and methods—what he terms "scientificity": "Once adopted, they acquired a life of their own and became difficult to unlearn."

Another major weakness of foreign policy analysis, in his view, is "excessive conservatism," that is, confining its scope to diplomacy and security. Areas where it could have made a contribution include: IPE, specifically, foreign economic behavior by decision makers for states; institutionalism/neoinstitutionalism; the role of accountability and policy acceptability in decision making and implementation; public policy; extending foreign policy analysis from a two-level to a three-level game, that is, domestic, international, and supranational, as with the EU; and systematic prescription so as to make foreign policy analysis policy-relevant, assessing the success or failure of policymakers' judgments and decisions.

For Vertzberger, the grave methodological error of decontextualization in foreign policy analysis leads to "cognitive and motivational biases [that] are built into the parsimony imperative." They are limitations on memory ("we have turned our natural cognitive limits into a normative scientific merit, . . . a search for a 'do-it-all' paradigm . . . such as neorealism, rational choice theory, and their derivations that respond well to our biocognitive limitations"); the aggregation and sample bias; multiple causations and causation loops; the actor's motive bias; and slow integration.

Turning to methodological progress, Vertzberger acknowledges "steady but major improvements and increased diversity." However, these have been offset by three other serious shortcomings: the overvaluation of numbers—"numbers don't lie"; the "precision imperative," part of "the drive toward scientificity"; and the high price in cost-effectiveness, the flawed assumption that costly methodologies pay off. Formal modeling, too, is assessed as a promise unfulfilled, without any important contributions to foreign policy analysis.

Vertzberger concludes his reflections with a skeptical cognitive psychologist's view of theory and science: "Theory building in the social sciences in general, and international politics in particular, is the art of the possible. It does not always converge with the pure truth; at best it represents a practical truth. Evangelical scientificism and methodologism only stand in the way of creativity." He closes the circle by reaffirming his respect for "the immense amount of accumulated knowledge since the late 1950s." But, on balance, the foreign policy analysis glass emerges as much less than half full.

Walker (Stephen)

The core concept of "Beliefs and Foreign Policy Analysis in the New Millennium," beliefs, is used by Stephen Walker "generically to refer to the various conceptualizations for the products of cognition in the human mind—for example, schemata, attitudes, perceptions, images ... all part of the 'cognitivist' research program in world politics." Walker surveys the literature on beliefs and their impact on foreign policy behavior starting with the "seminal" work by Snyder, Bruck, and Sapin, which he identifies as the first serious challenge by the decision-making approach to realism's explanation of state behavior.

He poses the question "Are beliefs merely epiphenomenal?"—that is, "merely doctrinal expressions of more fundamental bureaucratic interests, organizational structure, or institutional history"? He sums up the arguments of the critics thus: first, the influence of beliefs on foreign policy behavior is important and independent "only under a restricted range of conditions"—external crises; second, they constitute only one variable in a larger explanatory constellation; third, their effects are "indirect and general rather than direct and specific; fourth, they serve as an intervening variable only; fifth, they are "extraneous variables in foreign policy and world politics and [are] best ignored except ... [for] deviant cases." This is a formidable critique, to which he replies at the end of his paper, beliefs "are pivotal variables with mapping, steering, and solution effects within a dynamic interactive causal model rather than being simply intervening or dependent variables."

On the follow-on question "Are beliefs important causal mechanisms?" Walker cites Goldstein and Keohane's affirmative view that there are three types of causal role for beliefs: as "worldviews" for leaders, exerting mapping effects; as "principled beliefs," exerting normative influence on behavior; and as "causal beliefs" in problem representation. The reasons for the resurgence of interest in beliefs, Walker writes, were the failure of scholars to anticipate the end of the cold war and a growing dissent from rational choice theory.

He notes that "more recent work by rational choice theorists ... recognizes beliefs as important intervening variables" and cites the distinction between "thin" and "thick" models of rationality, in which beliefs are relatively unimportant and relatively important, respectively. On that basis, he sketches "a strategy for synthesis," with two lines of inquiry—beliefs as micro-level and as macro-level mechanisms of choice.

The second half of Walker's millennial reflections paper sets out "a research agenda for future progress": it emphasizes the analysis of initiatives toward peace as well as toward war, more specifically, the de-escalation phase of an international crisis—for example, the Sadat initiative to Israel in 1977. Such a "reconceptualization of the conventional crisis model expands the universe of cases [and permits viewing] military initiatives and diplomatic initiatives within the same general analytic framework." His "interaction game ... integrates threats of conflict and opportunities for cooperation, thereby synthesizing a focus on [explanations by the realist and liberal schools of thought]." These are the benefits of what he terms "a bidirectional, strategic approach with a two-level, psychological approach."

Holsti (O. R.)

The primary focus of Ole Holsti's millennial reflections paper, "Public Opinion and Foreign Policy Analysis: Where We Were, Are, and Should Strive to Be," is "some main currents of theory and research." He begins by noting the dominant view of public opinion held in the 1950s, the result of influential writings by realists and American scholars, reinforced by the early findings of scientific public opinion polls. In Holsti's words, "Ill-informed, emotion-driven, short-sighted, and self-absorbed publics constitute a major obstacle that threatens to prevent the United States and other Western democracies from playing a constructive role in an increasingly dangerous international system."

It took several decades to dethrone that harshly critical assessment. The catalyst for change was the Vietnam War, which generated a plethora of studies, including large-scale survey projects on U.S. foreign policy, like the quadrennial surveys by the Chicago Council on Foreign Relations since 1974, along with works by U.S. scholars, many of whom are cited in Holsti's comprehensive survey.

The upshot was a successful challenge to the earlier negative view, with "some convergence on two points of relevance to foreign policy analysis: First, even... rather poorly informed ... attitudes about foreign affairs are in fact structured in moderately coherent ways.... Second, there is growing evidence that the single internationalist-to-isolationist dimension ... is inadequate."

This was replaced by the Chicago Council's three perspectives—conservative internationalism, liberal internationalism, and noninternationalism—which Wittkopf transformed into "two faces of internationalism," militant and cooperative, yielding four foreign policy belief systems: hard-liners, accommodationists, internationalists, and isolationists. Nonetheless, observes Holsti, there has been more progress on description of trends in public opinion than on analysis of its impact on the foreign policy process.

Holsti also assesses the three methodologies that have been used in this field—quantitative-correlational analysis, case study, and interviews. The "impressive" findings from the first of these methods reveal very little difference in the extent of congruence between public opinion and foreign policy (62 percent) and the public opinion–domestic policy nexus (70 percent). The results from case studies are mixed, indicating that "the impact of public opinion varies according to the type of issue, the stage in the policy process, the decision context, and policymakers' beliefs about and sensitivity to public opinion. . . . Public opinion had a direct impact on getting the issue on the agenda and on ratification of the agreements, but only an indirect effect on negotiations and implementation."

Turning to the future, Holsti suggests three major areas of research to improve our understanding of the public opinion–foreign policy process linkage. The first takes the form of specifying eight questions that should guide future research—such as the indicators of public sentiment relied upon by leaders; the purpose for which this information was used (to gain public support or to manipulate/ influence public attitudes); and whether the timing of decisions and the choice of means to implement them were influenced by beliefs about what the public would accept, not accept, or demand, among other pertinent questions. The second recommendation is to engage in cross-national studies, for, he notes, "even among democracies, the nature and impact of public opinion may vary across countries and political systems." And the third is the need to standardize questions for polling on foreign policy issues.

Holsti concludes that much progress has been made since the 1950s and that public opinion "remains a vibrant area of inquiry." However, he expresses concern about the danger of leaders using increasing survey data to manipulate the public and the evidence of "persistent poverty of international knowledge, despite the information revolution."

Wilkenfeld

Of the value of experimentation in foreign policy analysis in general Jonathan Wilkenfeld has no doubt: "Experimentation allows researchers to isolate a crucial independent variable by providing the means to control extraneous factors. . . . It is the most reliable means of examining and understanding the nature of a causal relationship, of demonstrating the internal validity of a theory in political science," he writes in "Simulation and Experimentation in Foreign Policy Analysis: Some Personal Observations on Problems and Prospects." The essay contains a brief survey of experimental work in IR, followed by a report on the Conflict and Negotiation (CAN) Research Group, which is designed to enhance understanding of how humans and machines negotiate in crises to attain mutually beneficial outcomes.

Wilkenfeld notes three features of CAN research that distinguish it from other experimental work in foreign policy analysis: an exclusive focus on behavior in crisis; the reliance of its subjects on decision support systems (DSSs); and the conduct of all communications in controlled network environments. The project has addressed five broad research issues so far, namely, "the impact of the use of DSSs on the utility-maximizing behavior of crisis negotiators"; "the impact of the dynamics of crisis negotiations on their outcomes"; "the relationship between the level of cognitive complexity of crisis negotiators and the outcomes of crisis negotiations"; the impact of the same mix, with the addition of crisis mediators, along with the link between crisis negotiators' level of cognitive complexity and crisis outcomes; and "the impact of the mix of cognitive complexity levels among crisis negotiators on the outcome of the crisis."

Wilkenfeld puts great emphasis on the analytical value of merging empirical and experimental approaches to foreign policy analysis. His "merged research design"—using data from a large-N empirical study, the International Crisis Behavior (ICB) project, and the findings from experimental work on mediation in international crises—is the focus of the rest of his paper.

While a consensus definition of mediation remains elusive, there seems to be agreement on its three roles in negotiation—the mediator as communicator or facilitator, as substantive contributor, and as manipulator. Two issues were addressed using ICB data: the circumstances in which mediation is most likely to occur and the most likely types of outcome from mediation.

Wilkenfeld reports both empirical and experimental findings on mediation in international crises. The former relate to threat, polarity, system level, ethnic origins of crisis, geographic proximity, and types of outcome—content, form, extent of satisfaction, and escalation or reduction of tension. On outcomes he notes: "Clearly, . . . mediation makes a difference"; it is more likely to lead to compromise outcomes, agreements, mutual satisfaction by the parties, and a reduction of tension over time.

The experimental findings are summed up thus: "mediator as manipulator produced higher utility outcomes for both parties, while mediator as facilitator produced greater mutual benefit.... [the former led to] shorter elapsed time to outcome in general, [the latter to] shorter elapsed time to agreements.... all parties were dissatisfied with mediation.... [and] there were no discernible differences in satisfaction with outcome resulting from the two forms of mediation."

Wilkenfeld has no illusions about the prospects for experimental work in foreign policy analysis. This is partly because the transition from simulation to an experimental lab is not simple, partly because most subjects, students, are relatively uninformed and often indifferent or hostile to the rigorous task of experimentation, and partly because of the expense and time required for design and execution of experiments. Yet he views experimentation as a valuable supplement to cross-national and in-depth case studies; and to that end, he urges proper training of future scholars in foreign policy analysis.

International Security, Peace, and War

Papers by Edward A. Kolodziej, Davis B. Bobrow, Louis Kriesberg, J. David Singer, and Linda B. Miller make up this cluster of millennial reflections.

Kolodziej

Edward Kolodziej's comprehensive survey, "Security Theory: Six Paradigms Searching for Security," is divided into two sections: a brief discussion of the concept of security and a much longer assessment of realism, neorealism, economic liberalism, institutionalism, behaviorism, and constructivism, noting key differences and their implications for security theory.

He acknowledges the existence of diverse views on the meaning and scope of security, from "preservation of the state and the nation-state system" and "physical security of individuals within civil society" to these conceptions enlarged to include "economic welfare" and/or the avoidance of anxiety.

As a starting point, he opts for the traditional view that identifies security with power and violence, deriving from Thucydides and sustained by Machiavelli, Hobbes, and the modern exemplars of realism. However, "security theory ... [must] be principally concerned with explaining both peace and war"; that is, it "may begin with Hobbes, but it must end with Kant and the possibility of perpetual peace if it is to be comprehensive and coherent." The bulk of Kolodziej's paper takes the form of an analysis of the central tenets of each of the six competing IR paradigms and of their failure to anticipate the collapse of the Soviet Union and the concomitant peaceful end of the cold war.

Realism's and neorealism's ex post facto explanation emphasizes the growing economic and technological disparity between the two superpowers; this compelled the USSR to adopt a (failed) domestic reform program and retrenchment abroad; and this in turn generated an increasing imbalance in military power. Under the impact of that growing pressure the Soviet Union could no longer compete with the United States, and its imperial domain, external and internal, crumbled.

Economic liberalism, too, had an ex post facto explanation for the pressures leading to Soviet attempts at economic reform; but "neoclassical economic theory has no theory of power" and could not explain the two related transforming events in world politics at the end of the 1980s. Liberal institutionalism describes actor behavior more effectively than realism, argues Kolodziej; however, by sacrificing parsimony to complexity, it too failed to anticipate or explain either of these seminal developments.

For behaviorism, the end of the cold war and the collapse of the Soviet Union were "instances of a larger set of actor actions and reactions relevant to a pattern of behavior of interest to the researcher"; this preoccupation with methodology prevented any contribution to an explanation of these events. As for constructivism: some adherents emphasized cognitive reformulation (learning) by Gorbachev and his colleagues, recognizing their inferiority in military power and technological and economic sources of growth vis-à-vis the West; others focused on structural constraints, like resurgence of nationalism and the delegitimization of communist ideology and regimes throughout eastern Europe. Like all the other paradigms, these were belated, after-the-fact attempts at explanation.

The findings for security studies, notes Kolodziej, are both negative and positive. No single paradigm can explain security behavior fully. No single methodology can lead to a definitive theory of state behavior. No single policy prescription can overcome the security dilemma. And there is no consensus on which actors have a crucial impact on security. At the same time, each of these paradigms "provide useful, if not fully satisfactory, theoretical tools" in search of a theory. In conclusion, one might despair over an array of competing paradigms. However, "pluralism serves us better than we might believe—or wish."

Bobrow

In "Security and Peace: Understanding, Production, and Work Style," Davis Bobrow presents a wide-ranging, critical assessment of the state of this subfield of international studies. His reflections begin with "The Good News," followed by "The Darker Side," "Some Lessons (We Should Have) Learned," and "Some Suggested Emphases."

The bulk of this millennial reflections paper takes the form of a positive and negative evaluation of six expansions in this domain. These are identified as (1) "a cornucopia of 'prisms' for considering security and peace" beyond realism and idealism, namely, rational choice, institutionalism, critical theory, gender, power transition, domestic politics, failed state, democratic peace, and ideationalism; (2) "issue domains" beyond the political-military, including economic, environmental, demographic, public health, sociocultural continuity, and fundamental political forms; (3) "generic types of actors inside and outside of governments," comprising civil departments of central governments, subnational authorities, multinationals, NGOs, and IGOs; (4) "relevant specific actors with asymmetric agendas and assets," notably lesser powers on the periphery of the dominant system; (5) the revolution in technology, leading to a proliferation of independent and intervening variables in the security-peace nexus; and (6) a vast increase in information resources.

The positive aspect, notes Bobrow, is "a period of 'riches' with respect to concepts, phenomena, information, and human capital." At the same time, there is a "darker side," for two reasons: first, "the first five expansions involve resurrection and relabeling rather than genuine discovery and innovation"; and second, "the improvements may not have kept pace with the challenges posed by the . . . expansions." Thus, for example, while more prisms are welcome, this does not ensure a wise synthesis, as is evident in two high-visibility current theories, power transition and the democratic peace: the U.S. policy community seems to subscribe to both simultaneously, but "international audiences may instead see a realist draped in an idealist democratic cloak." His reservations about the benefits of the other five expansions are outlined. "The more fundamental difficulty is that the truth often is hard to know about recent and current security and peace matters."

The general lesson for Bobrow is that "security and peace are and will remain contested or captured concepts," without a consensus on content, sufficient conditions, and a reliable indicator as to when, and to what extent, they exist. The operational lesson is that the six expansions do not provide a reliable guide for policy analysis and prescription; rather, "we should accept a continuing need to adapt to them."

In his concluding reflections Bobrow urges the security-peace research community to display humility and modesty and notes the merit of pluralism—a recognition that each element of his noted prisms, issue domain, or generic type of actor is relevant, but none "tells the whole story." He also recommends three practical changes: "in the education of security and peace specialists," who must acquire literacy in science and technology; better use of available resources, including non-American peace and security analyses; and the adoption of Wohlstetter's applied systems analysis approach, both "opposed systems design" and "end-to-end analysis," for explanation, prediction, and prescription, because they "are well-suited to accommodating and indeed being strengthened by the six widely recognized expansions."

Kriesberg

A clearly articulated goal permeates Louis Kriesberg's "Convergences between International Security Studies and Peace Studies": to enhance cooperation between these two subfields of international studies. The paper divides into three sections: "Earlier Relations," "Contemporary Developments," and "Future Developments."

In the past, notes Kriesberg, there were several significant differences between these subfields: their IR intellectual sources for one—realism for security studies, liberal-idealism for peace studies; the latter was also influenced by the feminist perspective in IR, the impact of religion and culture on war and peace, the role of transnational social movements, and the critical perspective on global political economy. In addition, security studies focused on one primary actor, the analysts' own state, military means, and the avoidance of war—that is, negative peace—while peace studies concentrated on global and systemic concerns, nonviolent methods, and justice and equity—that is, positive peace.

Moreover, the former relied on foundation and government funding, while the latter concentrated on social movement organizations. These differences in theory, research, and practice were more evident in the United States than in Europe. There were, however, some bridge-building foci, notably, a shared interest in the causes of war, crisis management, and foreign policy decision making.

During the four decades of the cold war, security analysts concentrated on the military dimension, including nuclear and general deterrence, while peace analysts focused on the peace movement and the military-industrial complex. Neither group anticipated the end of the East-West conflict, and each offered a different ex post facto explanation. According to the security analysts, the West's containment of the Soviet Union and the arms build-up forced Moscow to yield; the peace analysts placed credence in the Western policy of reassurance as embodied in the 1975 Helsinki Accords and the legitimacy given to post–World War II borders in Eastern Europe. Finally, the two groups tended to ignore each other's work.

In short, they differed on the questions they posed, methodologies, the answers they provided, and their underlying values and goals. Rapid global changes after the end of the cold war—growing economic integration, vast improvements in communication, and the reduction of state sovereignty as a result of the increase in number, size, and resources of multinational corporations, transnational organizations, and intergovernmental institutions—moved the two subfields closer together.

Norms of international human rights, including the necessity of international military intervention in extreme cases, are increasingly shared. So, too, is a commitment to extend the ambit of international conflict resolution, the prevention of large-scale violence, and the building of stable peace.

Turning to the future, Kriesberg anticipates—and welcomes—the emergence of new subfields focusing on substantive issues. One "is likely to relate increasingly to different conflict stages: prevention, limiting and interrupting violent conflict escalation, terminating violence, and postconflict peace building," as well as extending the role of mediation and negotiation as instruments of conflict termination. Other new subfields will concentrate on early warning and preventive diplomacy, interrupting and stopping violence, peacekeeping, creating institutions to reduce intercommunal conflicts, extending democratic processes and institutions, and enlarging the scope of civil society to sustain them. Kriesberg also expects a convergence between peace and security studies in their common attention to the link between democratic polities and foreign intervention and to the task of achieving reconciliation between conflict adversaries. He concludes on a note of optimism about the continuing convergence of the two subfields. And he views this as being aided by the increasing involvement of women in both subfields, along with the growth of centers of conflict resolution in the Third World. But he also notes the risk of peace research being co-opted by political authorities to serve their end; and he expects the time frame of the two fields to continue to differ—short term for security studies, long term for peace studies: "Such differences in approach . . . are needed."

Singer

The raison d'être of J. David Singer's millennial reflections paper is the need "to get more serious about trying to explain, and perhaps reduce the incidence of, that brutal, stupid, and destructive form of collective behavior known as war." To that end he begins "Accounting for Interstate War: Progress and Cumulation" with a blunt critique of what he terms the illusory view that "such a process is already underway."

Singer's criticism is directed at many in the world politics community. Citing the optimism of Mueller and Levy, he contends that "the indicators to the contrary are difficult to ignore"—landmines in many parts of the world, "the steadily increasing worldwide trade in light weapons, the obscene U.S. military budget, and the presence of more than thirteen thousand strategic warheads on high alert among the nuclear powers." He also dismisses the "Kantian peace" school and Axelrod's "evolution of cooperation" as "week reeds": "there is not much hard evidence to support the alleged expansion of democracy"; and "how often in history have we seen most states . . . behaving in a cooperative fashion. . . . So much for peace on the cheap."

Singer's wrecking operation is also evident in his later discussion of "Premises: Epistemological and Empirical." One object of disdain is "the posties"—postmodernism, poststructuralism, postbehaviorism, postpositivism, and constructivism—which, denying the existence of any empirical reality, consider a science of human behavior as "mission impossible." Another is Alker who calls "for more hermeneutics and less exegesis." Still another is followers of Bull, who "assure us that the classical methods of the historian will do just fine." There is also a "variety of dubious epistemologies . . . [that] lead to . . . increasingly ambitious 'theories' that are, in truth, little more than speculative models that rest on problematic and far from operational and thus testable premises." He cites two variants—the "analytic narrative" approach and "the so-called 'structured, focused, comparison,'" whose individual case studies result "in something only weakly structured, focused, and comparative." Singer also castigates the "doomed effort to ascertain/demonstrate 'causality,'" as well as "evolutionary epistemology." And he finds some major works in the philosophy of science—Hempel, Popper, Harre, and Lakatos—"not very helpful."

A negative tone also permeates Singer's extensive discussion of "semantic problems." He rejects "international relations/IR" in favor of "world politics"—"international misses a lot." He criticizes the "archaic" concept of nation-state—he prefers "territorial state"—and the misuse of "bipolarity" and "multipolarity"; the use of "collective defense" and "collective security" as synonyms; the facade of terming "military spending" a "defense budget"; and especially, the misunderstanding of "theory" and "data." He also is harsh on "the pernicious distinction between positive theory and normative theory."

In a more positive vein, Singer sets out his four-stage reading of the quest for an explanation of war: (1) pre–World War I—a literature that was "interesting, diverse, and insightful, but resting largely on assertion, speculation, and anecdote"; (2) 1920 to 1960, notably the work of Richardson and Wright, which "illustrated the possibility of utilizing scientific method in our quest"; (3) his Correlates of War Project, ongoing since the early 1960s, the "natural history" stage, "combining a rigorous methodology with an explicitly agnostic, multitheoretical orientation", and (4) the current stage, just beginning, testing more formal models with the results of the Correlates of War's "systematic historical empiricism."

Much later in his paper Singer spells out the "empirical-epistemic assumptions" underlying his project. The "central axiom" is the presence of "highly regular and thus recurring patterns" in the global system, along with a recognition of "plenty of exceptions" and an inherent randomness, leading to "statistical distributions rather than deterministic and perfectly uniform law" and erratic advances in the search for large regularities. He concludes with a reprint of a summary of his 1975 article to highlight the continuing "bad habits" that thwart cumulative progress in 2000.

Miller

Linda Miller's reflections on international security take the form of personal "Notes from the Underground: A Tale of Three Perspectives": the "underground" refers to her career as teacher of mostly female undergraduates at U.S. liberal arts colleges; and her "perspectives" are those of student, teacher-researcher, and editor.

Her preferences are indicated forthrightly. She lauds Wolfers's notion that security is "an ambiguous symbol"; the "important role of history as the database for international relations rather than the hard sciences . . . a self-evident truth"; "the interplay of domestic and international factors in . . . analyses of security and insecurity"; and political theory as a "rich source of complex questions" relating to security. These are "bedrock views."

Miller is no less blunt in her criticism of much of the IR literature—theory, methodology, and research findings. Waltz's *Theory of International Politics* "threaten[s] to distort . . . [IR] by narrowing the agenda of acceptable questions to investigate more than twenty years after publication"; the democratic peace findings "might be limited to the North Atlantic–North American region, rather than constitute a law of global politics in the twenty-first century"; the "self-styled 'great debates'" in the security field often bury "the organic connection between theory and practice."

She also decries the application of "'scientific' methods" to the social sciences; the denigration of ideas in explanations of transforming events such as the end of the cold war; the "primacy of theory" ("we know that these intellectual constructs are just that. Theories do not and cannot on their own delineate the range of choice and consequence, let alone the sequence of cause and effect"); the hazards of relying on other disciplines, notably economics—"that unfortunate deformity"; the "infatuation with natural science models" and the clinging by political scientists "to obsolete hard science methods"; and "a professoriate that is increasingly specialized and doctrinaire." All this earns the opprobrium, "this dreary trend."

As for "the way forward," Miller strongly recommends multidisciplinary cooperative research: "groups of scholars brought together by a belief that each of their disciplines has something needed to complete an empirically rich picture of the phenomena." She cites as a model the Borderline series of the University of Minnesota Press. She also lauds the growing interest in normative "theories" and the ethical dimension of IR, concluding, "our studies must try to repair the world."

International Political Economy

Three millennial reflections papers on international political economy (IPE) are offered—by Helen Milner, Robert Kudrle, and Lisa Martin.

Milner

Helen Milner's "Reflections on the Field of International Political Economy" presents a sweeping survey of IPE since its emergence in the early 1970s under the impact of the first wave of oil shocks experienced by the developed parts of the world economy—Europe, North America, and Japan. "What is IPE?" Milner asks, and she first draws attention to the two competing views of its proper scope. One embraces everything in IR other than security studies; that is, it includes all aspects of international institutions, the environment, human rights, gender, minorities, and international cooperation writ large, as well as the economic domain of IR. In this context, Milner cites, but emphatically rejects, Susan Strange's extreme formulation: "Far from being a subdiscipline of international relations, IPE should claim that international relations are a subdiscipline of IPE."

The second view, to which Milner subscribes, limits IPE to the "interaction of politics and economics, or more narrowly markets and states.... Without an economic component, I would argue, ... phenomena are not properly part of IPE." And to those who propose expanding the field even beyond Strange, she responds: "the role of norms and values, 'critical' theory, reflectivity, methodology, epistemology, and ontology ... are not intrinsically or largely the domain of IPE." At the same time, any international issue or topic with an economic dimension, such as the economic causes of war and peace and the economic consequences of conflict, fall within the domain of IPE.

Milner considers IPE not merely a subfield of IR but rather as extending beyond, with strong links to economics and comparative politics. Regarding the first of these disciplinary links, she notes that some IPE scholars rely heavily on economic models and tend to fuse the two fields, while others insist that economists should add political variables to their explanations. As for IPE and comparative politics, "Integrating the two fields seems to be an important avenue for future progress.... It is imperative to a better understanding of IPE topics ... to use models of domestic politics that explain how policy is made.... It is difficult today to distinguish the fields of comparative and international political economy."

In contrast to security studies, where a consensus exists on the centrality of war, IPE lacks a single focus of attention. She notes three crucial foci: "economic development and differential growth rates"; "the impact of the international economy on domestic politics and vice versa"; and "conflict and cooperation among states in the international economy."

The IPE research agenda has changed over time, notes Milner. During the 1970s and early 1980s there were five key issues: economic sanctions versus military force as a means of achieving foreign policy goals; hegemonic stability theory; the role of domestic politics; dependency theory and development; and international institutions. By the late 1980s, two of these—hegemonic stability theory and dependency theory—had become passé, overtaken by events. Others had shifted their focus under the influence of globalization. In 2000, she specifies the main IPE topics as the effect of regime type, especially democratization, on development; globalization; and, with an altered focus, the role of international institutions, as well as the effects of domestic politics on economic integration.

Milner cites two methodology debates in IPE: the merits of rational choice models and the value of large-N versus small-N studies. Formalism helps sometimes, she writes, if one wants to communicate with economists; but rational choice does not explain everything about IPE. As for aggregate data versus case studies, she shares the view expressed by many, namely, a preference for a combination of the two. She concludes by calling for a response to the increasing penetration of IPE by economists: either a drastic break with economics, that is, establishing the autonomy of IPE, or "taking on the economists on their own ground ... by doing more economically sophisticated work in the field ... [and fostering] an interdisciplinary brand of IPE."

Kudrle

Robert Kudrle's "natural starting point" for "Some Thoughts on International Political Economy in the Context of Public Policy Education" is William Riker's definition of political economy as "the application of microeconomics to political phenomena." In contrast to Milner, he stresses method, rather than substance, to explore the sources of foreign economic policy. He treats this "as a species of public policy," linked to comparative politics, though from an economist's perspective.

Kudrle identifies three fundamental goals in international affairs—autonomy, security, and prosperity. The first is "akin to common definitions of nationalism." The second is operationalized as "protection from foreign violence." And the third is "the maximization of national wealth because modern nation states command redistribution policies." A fourth goal, though less universally important, is cited: "standing," that is, "international rank and influence upon, or regard from, those in other states"—"[but] the valuation [of these goals] cannot be directly observed."

In the section "Basic Approach," Kudrle distinguishes between preferences and constraints: the latter include "the structure of the international system and the place of the state in it, the levels of income and technology of system members, and the degree of congruence of purpose in various dimensions of the state in question."

The presentation of his approach is followed by a lengthy survey of recent research relevant to IPE. This includes the role of ideas, game theory, "policy networks" in framing public policy, constructivist and rational choice literature, and works on the "new institutional economics." And he expresses the novel view, for an economist, that "qualitative analysis remains essential in careful political analysis, including IPE . . . for the indefinite future."

In "Looking to the Future," Kudrle focuses on globalization. He is skeptical about its threat to key areas of national policy, notably growth and taxation, though he acknowledges its increasing effect on attitudes and identities relevant to national goals. He cites approvingly Rodrik's notion of a political economy "trilemma"—of the nation-state, mass politics, and integrated national economies. And he notes some obstacles to further European integration, including the role of cultural differences in inhibiting labor mobility and looming fiscal tensions.

He concludes with remarks about the three categories of international economic interaction: exchange, which has little effect; penetration, highlighted by the role of international corporations; and constraints on the operation of domestic policy by the forces of globalization. And he notes the increasing relevance of public finance, labor economics, and environmental economics in the study of policy aspects of IPE.

Martin

In "International Political Economy: From Paradigmatic Debates to Productive Disagreements," Lisa L. Martin dissents from the editors' assumption that the task of identifying intrasubfield consensus is difficult: IPE, she asserts, "is today characterized by growing consensus on theories, methods, analytical frameworks, and important questions.... disagreement today generally takes the form of productive, theoretically and empirically motivated claims, rather than the paradigmatic clashes that characterized IPE as an early field of study."

In a brief discussion of the development of IPE as a field of study, Martin acknowledges Gilpin's contribution, which viewed IPE as divided into three paradigms: realism, liberalism, and Marxism. However, she notes "an alternative organizing device," a dual focus on the explanatory role of interests or institutions, at the domestic or international level. This, in turn, after "a deep divide between IPE and international economics," led to "intense interaction between economics and political scientists," with a growing shift from an IR to a political economy orientation, especially in the area of international trade. Specifically, "Much of the debate today over interests on trade policy revolves around applications of Stolper-Samuelson versus the Ricardo-Viner model." Similarly, the analysis of domestic institutions benefits from input from both disciplines.

According to Martin, IPE is characterized by "productive research ... in all four of the boxes" of the interests/institutions and domestic/international framework in IPE. Overall, "IPE is a mature, exciting field of inquiry.... Current research agendas provide the tools and point the way; but a multitude of challenges remain," notably "breaking down the barriers between interests and institutions and between the domestic and international levels of analysis ... [in] an exciting and tractable research agenda for the future."

Notes

1. E. H. Carr, *The Twenty Years' Crisis, 1919–1939: An Introduction to the Study of International Relations* (London: Macmillan, 1939); E. H. Carr, *Conditions of Peace* (London: Macmillan, 1942); Arnold Wolfers, *Britain and France between Two Wars: Conflicting Strategies of Peace since Ver-*

sailles (New York: Harcourt, Brace, 1940); Arnold Wolfers, *Discord and Collaboration: Essays on International Politics* (Baltimore: Johns Hopkins University Press, 1962); Nicholas J. Spykman, *America's Strategy in World Politics: The United States and the Balance of Power* (New York: Harcourt, Brace, 1941); W. T. R. Fox, *The Super-Powers: The United States, Britain, and the Soviet Union — Their Responsibility for Peace* (New York: Harcourt, Brace, 1944); Hans Morgenthau, *Scientific Man versus Power Politics* (Chicago: University of Chicago Press, 1946); Hans Morgenthau, *Politics among Nations: The Struggle for Power and Peace* (New York: Knopf, 1948); Bernard Brodie, ed., *The Absolute Weapon: Atomic Power and World Order* (New York: Harcourt, Brace, 1946).
2. Kenneth N. Waltz, *Theory of International Politics* (Reading, Mass.: Addison-Wesley, 1979); Robert Gilpin, *War and Change in World Politics* (Cambridge: Cambridge University Press, 1981).
3. E. B. Haas, *The Uniting of Europe* (Stanford, Calif.: Stanford University Press, 1958); E. B. Haas, *Beyond the Nation-State: Functionalism and International Organization* (Stanford, Calif.: Stanford University Press, 1964); Robert O. Keohane and Joseph S. Nye Jr., *Power and Interdependence: World Politics in Transition* (Boston: Little, Brown, 1977).
4. Robert Jervis, *Perception and Misperception in International Politics* (Princeton, N.J.: Princeton University Press, 1976); Robert Jervis, Richard Ned Lebow, and Janice Gross Stein, *Psychology and Deterrence* (Baltimore: Johns Hopkins University Press, 1985).
5. Richard K. Ashley, "The Poverty of Neorealism," *International Organization* 38, no. 2 (1984): 225–86.
6. Robert W. Cox, "Social Forces, States, and World Orders: Beyond International Relations Theory," *Millennium* 10, no. 2 (1981): 126–55; Robert W. Cox, *Production, Power, and World Order: Social Forces in the Making of History* (New York: Columbia University Press, 1987).
7. Alexander Wendt, "The Agent-Structure Problem in International Relations Theory," *International Organization* 41, no. 3 (1987): 335–70; F. V. Kratochwil, *Rules, Norms, and Decisions: On the Conditions of Practical and Legal Reasoning in International Relations and Domestic Affairs* (Cambridge: Cambridge University Press, 1989).
8. Jean B. Elshtain, *Women and War* (New York: Basic Books, 1987); Cynthia Enloe, *Bananas, Beaches, and Bases: Making Feminist Sense of International Politics* (Berkeley: University of California Press, 1990); V. Spike Peterson, ed., *Gendered States: (Re)Visions of International Relations Theory* (Boulder, Colo.: Lynne Rienner, 1992); J. Ann Tickner, *Gender in International Relations: Feminist Perspectives on Achieving Global Security* (Minneapolis: University of Minnesota Press, 1992).

Foreign Policy Analysis

FOREIGN POLICY ANALYSIS

Steady Progress and a Half-Empty Glass

Yaacov Y. I. Vertzberger

The Domain of Foreign Policy Analysis

Foreign policy analysis (FPA), broadly defined, is a field of study that describes and investigates the structures, processes, and outcomes of the purposeful policy initiatives and responses that are conceived by sovereign political entities and directed toward other political units (not necessarily sovereign states) *beyond* their borders. The boundaries of the FPA domain are porous and cannot be strictly drawn, and thus it is not uncommon for some of the literature to belong in more than one field of study (e.g., security studies and FPA). Furthermore, FPA as a field of study emerged over the last four decades unbound by a single paradigm, containing multiple and diverse approaches, and *should not* be associated with (as some do) and conceived to be narrowly wedded to one or another variant of state-centric realism. In a nutshell, it is claimed here that while FPA has been a lot more vibrant than some observers are inclined to believe,[1] it has also delivered substantially less than one would and

---

An earlier version of this paper was prepared for presentation at the forty-first annual convention of the International Studies Association held March 14–18, 2000, at Los Angeles, while the author was a fellow at the Netherlands Institute for Advanced Study (NIAS). I would like to thank NIAS for its generous hospitality and support. A revised version was prepared during the period I spent as a visiting scholar at the Peace and Governance Program, the United Nations University (UNU), Tokyo. I am grateful to UNU for this unique opportunity. The author also thanks Michael Brecher and Miles Kahler for useful comments and suggestions.

could have hoped for; hence the proverbial half-empty glass metaphor. The discussion in this paper does not intend to dwell on and review all aspects of FPA[2] but to address critically the most salient weaknesses in the current state of FPA and their implications for the agenda, methods, and priorities of future directions that FPA studies should take.

A panoramic reflective view of the FPA landscape since the 1950s leaves an observer with mixed feelings. There has obviously been steady progress that is expressed in extensive theoretical and conceptual development, in the growing empirical richness and availability of both case studies and aggregate data analysis, and in increasing methodological diversity, rigor, and sophistication. Yet, at the same time, there are reasons to believe that there is in FPA a lot less than what meets the eye and that in spite of progress we are still facing a half-empty glass. What is missing in the current state of our knowledge and understanding may occasionally outweigh, or at least equal, the weight of what we claim to know. It cannot even be taken for granted that faster and more dramatic improvement and progress in the state of the art are around the corner. Scientists, especially social scientists, are after all not only socialized by the norms of their trade to open-mindedness, curiosity, and changes; they are also products of their societies and are exposed and socialized to the norms of stability, risk aversion, and, in general, a preference for continuity over change even in the face of negative feedback. As such, they are driven by both cognitive and motivational biases and fallacies that too often have resulted in little, or skewed, learning; they tend to follow the dominant intellectual fashions of the time less critically than they should, and in the process overestimate the value and contributions of these fashions to actual progress in their respective fields. The following discussion identifies and elaborates on how and why FPA progress has been less than adequate. In brief, it is claimed that the causes for this state of affairs include overlearning by imitation, decontextualization, oversimplification, and biases toward precision, conservatism, and risk aversion. It is argued that these have seriously straitjacketed progress in the field of FPA.

Two qualifying comments on this assessment of the state of FPA research should be made at this point. One is that an evaluation is not independent of the observer's initial expectations. Against lower expectations current achievements may look more impressive than against higher initial expectations.[3] Second, some of the more general criticisms of FPA that follow are not unique to this research domain but apply to other fields as well; they represent a general malaise in the study of international politics and more broadly the political science discipline.[4] The following sections set out the nature of progress and the multiple forms it could take, on the one hand, and discuss in detail areas of inadequacy of progress and missed opportunities in FPA research, on the other hand.

The Nature of Progress: Unpacking and Repacking the Research Enterprise

A meaningful discussion of progress in a research domain requires that it should be ontologically unpacked and its constituent elements individually examined, and then repacked for an overall progress assessment. In essence, a research domain consists of three constituent components, or building blocks: theory, which requires systematic conceptualizing and generalizing toward theory building; empirical data, which result from comprehensive search, collection, and organization of relevant data; and methodology, which requires applying a set of transparent and explicit rule-based methods and techniques for the transformation of data into theory-relevant information and then relating the transformed empirical data to the theory for hypotheses-testing and theory-validation. The premise underlying my argument is that progress does not necessarily occur simultaneously and to the same extent across all of the three constituent building blocks of the research enterprise, nor can progress be synchronized to achieve that effect. Hence, identifying where and to what extent the most progress took place, whether in theory, empirical data, or methodology, is important for a holistic assessment of progress. It is also important to recognize the trade-offs between progress in one constituent block compared with another and the cost-effectiveness of progress. I would argue that in the social sciences in general, and international politics research in particular, the most salient condition for substantial progress is advances in theorizing; the second most salient is improvement in data availability and quality; and the least prominent factors for progress are methodological innovations, which are also the most vulnerable to diminishing returns. Implied in this argument is the notion that progress in each of these constituent elements of research can have overall regressive effects, when more is less, for reasons that will be further explained.

The logic of my argument for a three-tiered, ordinally-layered salience of improvement in knowledge is simple and self-explanatory. Knowledge and its qualitative improvement is first and foremost the product of ideas and concepts. In the absence of ideas there is no coherently meaningful and generalizable knowledge across time and space. Furthermore, since in the social domain information is often not readily available, theory plays an important role in going beyond the information given. Although data are indispensable stimulants of important research questions and puzzles, in the absence of theory data produce merely descriptions and at best ad hoc explanations. Whether theory is produced inductively or deductively is of little importance in this context and is mostly a matter of researchers' preferences. Advances in methodology improve the logical quality and validity of theory, allow for the efficient transformation of data into information, and verify the validity of the knowledge that results from the coupling of theory with data (history). But in and by itself methodology does not produce knowledge; it is merely an instrument for scientific progress and not an integral part of it. To put it concisely, in the social sciences important scientific innovations are more likely to be driven by the *logic of discovery* than by the *logic of verification.*

Herbert Simon is correct in criticizing the preoccupation with the logic of verification in the social sciences,[5] and he traces this bias to the practices of the philosophy of science, on which social science epistemology heavily depends. "The history and philosophy of science have been excessively formulated with the drama of competition between theories. . . . Researchers in psychology and some of the other behavioral sciences, where there is often a severe deficit of good candidate theories, have sometimes been misled by the literature on philosophy and methodology to exhibit in research and publication an exaggerated concern with verification, accompanied by uncritical application of statistical tests of hypotheses to situations where they don't properly apply."[6]

Whether a scientific investigation is discovery-driven or verification-driven will have decisive ramifications for the research questions that should and can be asked—and which variables can be applied and will be salient to answer these questions. Taking into account the relative limitations of alternative methodologies across variables and data sets, a verification-driven approach to research seriously limits the type of explanation that can be offered, while a discovery-driven approach has a much more open and wide horizon for the range of what are considered testable and acceptable explanations. This makes progress more likely and more broadly based. In other words, preference for one orientation—discovery or verification—over the other will have substantial agenda-setting implications for research.[7]

Looking now at the substance of progress, it can heuristically be categorized as either horizontal or vertical. Horizontal progress expands the amount of knowledge and is largely incremental, but not exclusively so. Vertical progress represents a qualitative change at a deeper level and is more likely to be transformational. The crossover line between horizontal and vertical progress is not always sharp and clear, nor is it obvious when a quantitative increase in available knowledge becomes a base for qualitative change in the state of knowledge. More specifically progress may take one or more of several forms. *Expansion* represents a quantitative increase in knowledge on particular subjects. *Verification/falsification* produces metaknowledge that tells us how valid our knowledge is about an issue. *Integration* implies combining segments of knowledge that were originally produced independently into a whole, where the whole is more than the sum of its parts. Integration can take place within a single issue area and level of analysis boundary or across issue areas and levels of analysis. *Contextualization* goes beyond mere integration by providing contingent knowledge. Unlike unconditional propositional statements that tell us something that is supposedly unconditionally true about the social environment, contextual propositions tell us what is true (or false) on a conditional base, and what will be true should these conditions change. *Extrapolation* reflects going one step further in the integration and contextualization processes by extending knowledge beyond the porous boundaries of an issue area or a discipline and integrating it with knowledge from other disciplines to create interdisciplinary theories (e.g., important progress in this direction was made in theories of cognition, theories of markets, and theories of institutions). These five forms of progress are not necessarily mutually exclusive and may take place serially or simultaneously. As more of these forms of progress are experienced in any particular research field, it can be said that progress is more extensive.

It is important to note that this ordinal scale of progress is not meant as an ordinal evaluation of the research produced by individual scholars (microbehavior) but is intended to provide a long-term perspective and evaluation of the state of a discipline or subdiscipline. In other words, I am talking about the macroconsequences of microbehavior. This is then not a recommendation to individual scholars concerning what line of research they should pursue. In fact, only by allowing individual scholars to make the most efficient individual choice as to how best to apply their interest and talent is the aggregate research product likely to be maximized and progressive. It results from a self-regulatory mechanism that drives aggregation and complementarity of individual, narrowly focused research efforts to the end consequence of disciplinary progress. How and why this happens is well beyond the subject of this paper, and we shall therefore black box this mechanism without explaining it.

To illustrate my point consider the contributions of Margaret Hermann on the role of personality in foreign policy behavior, those of Morton Halperin to the understanding of bureaucratic politics, the work of Charles Hermann and his associates on international crisis behavior, or the research of Stephen Walker and his associates on role-related foreign policy behavior.[8] Each of these authors has been involved in expanding knowledge in a relatively narrow issue area. But it is unimaginable to have an integrative view of foreign policy behavior in crisis without integrating their building blocks into a comprehensive perspective that would take into account the cumulative pushes and pulls in coping with a foreign policy challenge, of personality attributes' effect on preferences, role-framed objectives, and bureaucratic structural constraints within which the former two motives have to be played out. Whether this level of integrative contextualized progress of individually produced knowledge and theory will actually take place depends on the incentives offered and impediments posed, such as the nature of the research agenda and the norms dominating the profession, as well as the effects that common motivational and cognitive biases have on scholars. As will be argued throughout this paper, FPA has not achieved the extent of progress that it should and could attain because the incentives for progress were not vigorous enough to cope with and overcome impediments to progress that are specified in the following sections. Consequently, innovative individual-level research was not regularly translated and integrated to result in the anticipated broad, progressive macroconsequences in FPA.

It can be argued that most FPA research advances focused on the first two types of progress, expansion and verification. We obviously know now, by far, more and with a greater degree of confidence about an increasing variety of subjects and issues concerning international politics than we knew four decades ago. But much of this knowledge lacks coherence and can metaphorically be described as an archipelago consisting of islands of knowledge, between which travel and communication tend to be irregular and nonsystematic. On the other hand, the types of progress that are conspicuously less visible are integration, and even more so contextualization and extrapolation. By focusing on the parts, and so often missing a holistic vision, we often misread the salience of specific instances of progress by exaggerating it.[9] In the absence of integrated contingent knowledge, small advances in specific, sometimes even esoteric issues loom much larger than they would had they been perceived within a broad holistic background— against which the actual value of small advances is more correctly assessed.

The Emperor's Ill-Fitting Clothes and the Quality of Progress

In the famous story about the emperor's new clothes, or rather lack of them, only one little boy is willing to acknowledge that the "emperor is naked." Forty years on, the emperor, older and possibly wiser, is now fully dressed but has acquired a taste for borrowing and wearing his older cousins' and the court's fashion setters' (one an economist, the other a mathematician) ill-fitting clothes, which have not always been tailored to his size and needs. This small variation on the well-known story demonstrates one of the major quandaries that haunts FPA in proceeding toward better methods of verification: wholesale adoption of norms and standards of "good scientific practices" that were borrowed from other science disciplines. This results in relying on other sciences to serve as role models without investing enough thought in the relevance of these norms to the particular circumstances (problem types, available data types, nature of variables) found in international politics. To be sure, there have been some adjustments, but on the whole these imported standards of good scientific practices have acquired a difficult-to-challenge status and occasionally continue to obstruct necessary progress. Important reasons for the fallacies that will be identified in this essay can be traced to the stranglehold that these norms have had over the research culture in FPA (as well as over other domains of research in international politics). What is particularly difficult when dealing with these deleterious influences over knowledge development is that each of these norms makes sense on its own. They become an obstruction when they are taken too literally and to the extreme. The simultaneous application of several such norms results in a synergy of straitjacketing. Obviously a dose of these norms is a necessary condition for validity, but an overdose of the same measures is dangerous. The crux of this problem is that it is not so easy to determine how much is enough. In the absence of clear standards of sufficiency, there is a tendency to go to the extreme by applying a well-known fallacious heuristic: "If some is good a lot is much better."

What are these norms? I refer mostly to the norms of decontextualization and parsimony, precision, and the network of methods and rules that are derived from them. These have become part and parcel of the quest for "scientificism," a term that I use to describe the exaggerated concern with how scientific our research enterprise is along with defining "scientific" in narrow, strict terms that are applied inflexibly and without distinction. Initially these norms and their derivations represented necessary conditions for the emergence of good science in the physical and mathematical sciences. From there these methods penetrated and then came to dominate the discipline of economics. Consequently the success associated with their application made them vivid and cognitively available to be considered for emulation during the formative years of FPA, when international politics became sensitive to the need to transform itself into a more scientific field of research. Once adopted, they acquired a life of their own and became difficult to unlearn.

What we are facing is what social psychologists will recognize as an accumulation of a well-known set of cognitive biases.[10] The attention to and choice of norms of scientificity was driven by the salience and vividness of readily available examples of success (the availability bias). These have come to represent, and to be associated with, what is exclusively considered properly executed research (representativeness bias). Although it made sense at the time to use such norms as a starting and anchoring point, their effectiveness should have been reassessed with the passage of time and accumulation of experience. Yet the opposite has happened. As is common, the anchoring point acquired an immovable stability (the anchoring bias) that has stood in the way of reassessment and adjustment as generations of scholars have become socialized into this set of beliefs about good science. In fact, one could argue that these norms have evolved into institutions—that is, "shared concepts used by humans in repetitive situations organized by rules, norms and strategies"[11]— and have acquired the same rigidity and resistance to change that is so often associated with other institutions. In the following sections we explore and explicate how these general broad fallacies are expressed in specific inadequacies from the setting of the research agenda and research strategies to soft spots of methodological progress.

Anchored in the Past: The Costs of a Conservative Attention Span

A major weakness of FPA research has been excessive conservatism. It tends to remain focused on the traditional fields of diplomacy and security, where FPA has its roots. Conspicuously absent are a number of more recent but central research domains to which FPA could have and should have made a contribution. Most salient among these is the field of international political economy (IPE). With the increase of interdependence and globalization and the consequential importance of economic diplomacy, economic conflict, and economic cooperation, the application and expansion of theories and methods that have been the backbone of FPA research in the security field to the analysis of state foreign economic behavior could be logically expected. This, however, has not been the case. IPE remains the domain of largely structural explanations where the actors are states, transnational actors, organizations, and institutions. Surprisingly, it seems as if people—individuals or groups—do not play any role in economic decisions and processes, at least not a consequential one. To be sure the literature of IPE made a mellow but brief overture to incorporate the role of ideas and beliefs that should have provided a window of opportunity for a creative dialogue between these two fields. But the opportunity was never seized and faded away to the detriment of both FPA and IPE research. When reading in the IPE literature references to expectations, interests, preferences, beliefs, and change thereof, one keeps wondering who carries these cognitions. Do organizations have cognitions? Do institutions have beliefs? Where do they come from? Are they always exogenous or could they be endogenous? But these issues have never truly been a subject of concern, even when such issues were occasionally raised[12] only to be comfortably avoided and relegated again to blissful inattention.

A related but separate area of neglect is what has become an influential research area in the social sciences, that of institutionalism/neoinstitutionalism.[13] FPA could have contributed important insights to the literature by modifying the dominance of rational choice premises that underlay much of this literature.[14] FPA has much to say on issues that are at the center of the discussion on institutions, such as the consequences of limited access to information and constraints on optimal information processing. Similarly FPA can make a salient contribution to the analysis of transaction costs, especially on the costs of sharing information among multiple actors and coordinating the interests, objectives, and behaviors of actors in mixed games with a view toward reducing transaction costs. No less important can be unveiling the linkage between institutional failures and organizational, group, and individual frailties.[15]

A third issue barely addressed in spite of its increasing importance with the spread of democracy is the role of accountability and sociopolitical policy acceptability, as a concern shaping both the process and outcome of foreign policy decision making and decision implementation.

Fourth and no less puzzling is that in spite of the closeness of areas of interest, FPA and public policy have largely kept their distance from each other with few exceptions.[16] The literatures of both FPA and public policy reveal very little dialogue between these two research areas that could have fruitfully cross-fertilized each other's insight into the domestic and international policy environments.

Fifth, the combined effect of conservatism and complexity-aversion attitudes are at least in part responsible for the fact that FPA still lacks a theoretical framework that will allow us to move from the analysis of foreign policy as a two-level game (domestic and international) to a three-level game (domestic, international, supranational) and will account for the increasingly salient impacts of regionalization and globalization. More specifically, the emergence of the European Union (EU) as a major actor requires a theory of foreign policy analysis that looks at the three-way influences and interactions between the state's domestic arena, its international policy-making processes, and the role that the inputs of and interactions of the suprastate (the EU) institutions with individual national states have in shaping policy preferences, processes, and outcomes, as a consequence of the creeping devolution of authority from individual states to the EU.[17]

Sixth, systematic prescriptive efforts were relegated to a minor role and are often viewed with snobbish disdain in FPA in spite of the fact that one would expect foreign policy analysis to be deeply concerned with putting foreign policy to work effectively.[18] Questions of policy relevance continue to play a relatively marginal role in the big debates within FPA. Only in this impoverished policy-relevance context can it be understood why important issues of policy relevance—such as debiasing or the quality of governance, and even the seeming intuitively important criteria and assessments of when policymakers' judgments and the resulting policies are a success and when they are a failure[19]—have had a minimal role in theory construction.

But FPA has not only been marred by avoiding, neglecting, and actively ignoring important research subjects and being biased toward attention to the most traditional issue areas in international politics. There is also a host of problematic epistemological issues concerning how subjects and issue areas that were successful in attracting attention and were subject to extensive scholarly discussion have been approached and treated. This is elaborated in the next section.

Biases in Research Design and Strategies

Perhaps one of the most apparent epistemological deficiencies concerning the manner in which research has been conducted is what amounts for all practical purposes to decontextualization. It can take more than one form as will be clarified subsequently. But the crux of it is that research in foreign policy analysis, including foreign policy decision making, has tended to shy away from including context as integral to the research design and at best has incorporated only a very thin context. Serious attempts to incorporate systematically contextual variables in research design are sparse, because thick contextualization runs the risk of being treated as a violation of the tenets of what is considered "good, valid research"—parsimony. Theories and models are supposed to be generalizable across situations and to explain all or most contingencies, with as few variables as possible, thus being in fact too often context free. This is justified in the name of what has become one of the ultimate criteria for good hard-hitting research—that is, parsimony, a criterion borrowed from the practices of the hard sciences. This criterion in essence states that (1) explanations should be simplified and/or (2) the process of explanation should be economized. There is of course nothing wrong with these principles, except when they are taken too literally and applied with indistinguishing zeal, lacking in judgment and common sense, which should temper and regularize the application of the parsimony principle.[20] It is ironic of course that positivists, who were the strongest proponents of parsimony, neglected to apply their own standards of validity and failed to note that "again and again in the history of science what seemed to be hopelessly complex, before someone had a good theoretical idea, has turned out to be beautiful in its simplicity after that idea—and it is a necessary act of scientific humility to remember that again and again those ideas turned out to be wrong."[21]

The tendency toward decontextualization has, in my view, produced some important deleterious effects and biases in two central theoretical foci of FPA: the nature of the debate on rationality and the treatment of bounded rationality. The debate on rationality is one of the more persistent unresolved conflicts of view in FPA.[22] The disagreements have come to be framed in polarized terms that pit a view of human behavior as driven by rationally calculated motivations that conforms to the expected utility model against a view that behavior, even if intended to be rational, is driven by a range of cognitive and motivational constraints and biases that make rational choice impractical and an incorrect descriptive proposition. This debate is no longer productive as it is framed now. In fact, reality is much more complex than reflected by the debate. The same individuals, groups, and organizations may, within a single process of decision making, demonstrate different levels of (non)rationality, and this is even more true across time, issues, and separate decision opportunities. Practically no single individual, group, or organization is systematically and without fail rational or nonrational to the same extent all the time. It is, therefore, much more productive to perceive rationality in terms of a spectrum stretching between two poles, one of pure rationality and the other pure irrationality. In between there is a broad space that represents varying extents of nonrationality or bounded rationality (see figure 1).

The debate should thus focus on where and under what circumstances actors are likely to be closer to one pole or the other. Yet rephrasing the research questions in those terms implies contingency and complexity, which are a lot less convenient to deal with

Figure 1. Rationality as spectrum

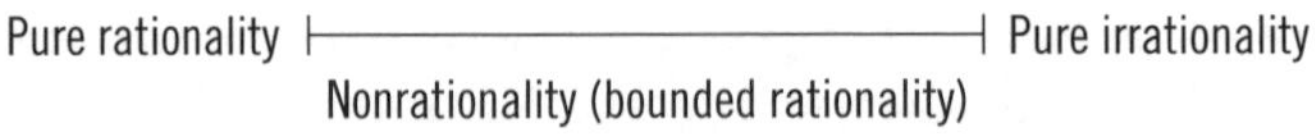

Pure rationality ├─────────────────────┤ Pure irrationality
Nonrationality (bounded rationality)

than a more simple, polarized, either-or type choice between rationality and bounded rationality.[23]

Another facet of this issue is the static form that bounded rationality research has acquired. Since Simon coined the term, its conceptualization has not evolved significantly.[24] Its simplicity seems to offer a riposte to the rivaling simple premises of rationality. Yet this has become an impediment to the development of a contingent theory of bounded rationality, which will recognize that bounded rationality is neither a unitary concept nor a unidimensional phenomenon. Bounded rationality represents a spectrum of decision-related behaviors that can take more than one form. Therefore, to take full advantage of this useful and productive concept, what was and is still needed is a typological specification of the definition of boundedness that will reflect the various ways and different extents of boundedness and the potential consequences from each boundedness type. I would argue that here too the absence of such a typology has resulted from complexity-avoidance. Bounded rationality was structured to be as simple and unambiguous as rationality. That was done irrespective of and without taking into account that the two were different "beasts" by definition. Rationality was a relatively clearly delimited and closed behavior type, while bounded rationality is an open-ended definition of behavior that can contain multiple forms of behavior all fitting the boundedness condition. Hence, rationality requires mostly a process of calculation, while bounded rationality largely involves a process of judgment.

That aside, a number of other cognitive and motivational biases are built into the parsimony imperative that result from cognitive constraints and shortcomings, to which scholars are as prone as other human beings. These biases have made context-free theorizing a tempting prospect, have become a difficult-to-shake-off habit, and have also taxed creativity and the process of scientific diversity.

Limitations on Memory, or Scholars as Intellectual Misers

It is a well-recognized fact that the human brain can handle only a limited information load, as so clearly indicated by the seminal study on "the magical number seven plus or minus two."[25] This is, of course, a powerful incentive for limiting the complexity of theorizing and explanations. By avoiding the complexity associated with context we have made a tacit decision that rather than expand our mental capabilities, we would narrow our insight and understanding. For all practical purposes we have turned our natural cognitive limits into a normative scientific merit. It is no wonder we are so obsessed with a search for a "do-it-all" paradigm that has few moving parts, and hence we have become attached to paradigms such as neorealism, rational choice theory, and their derivations that respond well to our biocognitive limitations. It should be noted that these paradigms have fewer than seven assumptions and seem to fit perfectly with available memory power.

The Aggregation and Sample Bias

Most methodologies that have a quantitative logic depend on sampling. The nature of information and its availability in many domains of foreign policy behavior does not provide readily available, sufficiently large samples of items or even allow for their artificial creation in an experimental context. Yet to be able to generalize we depend on a large enough sample size that (a) can be treated by applying one or more statistical methods and (b) has external validity. By allowing for context we might reduce the uniformity of sample populations and increase their diversity; consequently the sample has to be broken down into subsamples that may include such a small number of items that statistical treatment becomes irrelevant or impossible. Thus, incorporating context threatens in many cases to affect adversely the employment of quantitative methods that have come to play such an important role in theory building and especially in verification.

Multiple Causations and Causation Loops

The larger the number of relevant influences (variables) on the dependent variable, the more difficult and complex becomes the process of structuring the causal relationships among variables, and the more demanding is the tracing and mapping of causation directions. The larger the number of variables, the greater the chance for causation loops, which pose very serious problems of internal validity that act as impediments for the application of quantitative or quasi-quantitative research methods.

The Actor's Motive Bias

By eliminating context we are implicitly assuming that human behavior can be reduced to a relatively small number of standardized actions and reactions. In a way we apply to individual behavior a limited inventory of standard operating procedures that we assume to remain unaffected by differing contingencies. But what might be valid for organizational behavior is not necessarily correct about individuals. True, people prefer to be cognitive misers as long as is possible. But people are not, at least not all of them, inherently stupid to the point of systematically defying their self-interest in valid knowledge although veridicality is not their only motive.[26] They learn—sometimes sooner, sometimes later—that contingencies matter, that responses to problems that have some basic similarities but are also quite different have to be contingency-tailored, and that mindless, repetitive behavior may be ineffective and costly. In cases where accountability is important, it could serve as a powerful incentive for reflective rather than reflexive coping and response.[27] In other words, eventually people learn to become more context-sensitive. Therefore, theories about human behavior that are not context-sensitive miss an important, even critical, aspect of human motivation and behavior.

Slow Integration

The preceding points are some of the reasons why a critical task of theory-building—the process of integrating the multiple and diverse theoretical strands and pieces of FPA hypotheses and theories into a coherent whole that will cut across levels of analysis—has been subjected to the consequences of complexity aversion. One can compare the state of FPA research to a set of LEGO pieces that becomes really meaningful, although each piece has a separate existence, only when the pieces are assembled and by the way that they are put together. Each LEGO piece can be integrated in more than one way. Only by assembling them so that all the parts fit together to create a whole, meaningful structure is the task accomplished. This principle is even more the case with the building of knowledge structures. Instead, FPA reveals a clear preference, which is embedded in the incentive structure, for research that is narrowly, or even very narrowly, focused on a single or small number of hypotheses and variables that explain a fraction of a broader phenomenon. This is not to say that there have not been studies that emphasized the grand picture in taking a multilevel integrative approach to important theoretical and empirical questions of international politics.[28] But these are not the rule, and integrative studies were more often than not criticized for being nonparsimonious. These criticisms encouraged continued "fractionization," which remains the dominant feature of research.

Paradoxically, almost nobody denies the importance of integration, but at the same time there is a deeply ingrained reluctance among many to recognize and face trade-offs between theoretical integration and powerful prevailing methodological norms, and make the necessary choice between these norms and holistic theory-building by focusing on what is really important—the advancement of theory-building. This reluctance is not exceptional but part of a long-identified common bias: "Many people believe that their core values do not conflict and they need to be prodded, sometimes poked pretty hard into acknowledging that these values do conflict."[29] It is accompanied by an unstated assumption that somehow, someday these separate theoretical segments will come together and constitute a well-integrated theory that will be elegant, insightful, and of course parsimonious. How this is going to come about is rarely explained and specified.

Methodological Progress: How Real? How Much?

There is little doubt that any systematic review of the literature over time will reveal steady but major improvements and increased diversity in the methodologies used. These are reflected in better understanding of the conditions necessary for validity, in qualitative research as well as in quantitative research, and in the increased sophistication in methods of data processing and hypothesis-testing that include advanced statistical methods, formal modeling, dynamic game theory, experimental methods, and a plethora of other even more exotic methods. Those methodological advances have so heavily penetrated the way research is conducted and also our classrooms that they are considered indispensable to the training of younger generations of researchers. Most of these research tools have their origins in other disciplines where often the type of data available and data requirements are different from those of foreign policy–related data. Coming straight off the shelf of other research arenas, their fit with foreign policy data formats is not necessarily perfect. The use of these methods imposes premises that do not sit well with the realities of international politics (e.g., the nature of actors, their interests, their preferences, their motives, etc.). Consequently what is in many ways a truly admirable pace and scope of methodological progress has not come without leaving behind a trail of queries that have been either suppressed or inadequately answered. Rather than discuss particular methods in detail, I shall raise here three general conceptual issues concerning the quality and value of progress represented by methodological advancement in FPA. These apply to the valuation of numbers, precision, and the more general issue of the cost-effectiveness of methodological progress.

The search for meaningful theoretical simplicity has become increasingly a dominant imperative of theory-building and explanation, as the policy environment has continued to evolve since 1945 and has become more complex to comprehend and to attend to. The management of complexity was given a boost by the behavioral revolution of the 1960s. This revolution was accompanied by rigorous positivism and the rise to prominence of quantitative methods and formal modeling, which borrowed heavily from the harder disciplines in the social sciences (such as economics) and the natural sciences, and which seemed to put parsimony and effective management of complexity within reach.

As has been the case with other disciplines in the social sciences, the rise of behaviorism in the 1960s created a strong tendency toward identifying truth with numbers. The aphorism, "numbers don't lie," has gained currency in FPA. The increased sophistication of research methods and their mating with improved technology as a result of the computer revolution has made it a lot easier to generate, store, access, and process numbers and has made numbers-related methodological advancement a preferred target for growth.

Closely-associated with this impetus for progress was the precision imperative. This has been another feature of a persistent quest by the social scientists—the drive toward "scientificism" in line with the modality set by hard sciences and economics.[30] Precision took the form of attempting to bring the rigor of mathematical logic to arguments about state behavior in foreign policy, as well as attempting to describe international politics in an easy-to-define, grasp, and compare numerical format. But the enterprise was not without its difficulties. State behavior, at least not all important aspects of it, is not necessarily a natural candidate for treatment by these methods. A great deal of creativity was invested in tailoring these instruments to fit the subject matter of international politics. The results have not been equally convincing across all issue areas and research projects. The tailoring processes involved the imposition of highly-restrictive, difficult-to-justify assumptions that in some cases represented too much of a deviation from reality and in other cases required data transformation that raised serious validity questions. As a consequence these creative efforts resulted more than once in "precise imprecision." Both producers and consumers of this research product have to be aware of this and consider the question of whether the substitution of transparent imprecision (in the original raw data) for what are often hidden imprecisions (in the transformed data) is a worthwhile trade-off. It might be, but only if other features of the product compensate for it. Theodore Porter apparently has it right when he asserts that in "fields dominated by a relatively secure community, much of what we normally associate with the scientific mentality—such as an insistence on objectivity, on the written word, on rigorous quantification—is to a surprising degree missing. Scientific knowledge is most likely to display conspicuously the trappings of science in fields with insecure borders, communities with persistent boundary problems. That is, one has to look at a wider context for science to understand even the accepted forms of scientific production, the standards by which work is judged."[31]

A prominent illustration of the trust in numbers and related biases was the central role played by the concept and measurement of explained variance. Supposedly, uncertainties would be cleared away by theories that provide crisp answers based on a small number of relevant explanatory independent variables whose exact contributions to the explanation of variance in the dependent variable can be precisely calculated. Identifying a small number of critical variables that account for a large share of or, even better, most of the variance seemed at hand. This is indeed a desirable state of theorizing and verification, but only if one is confident about the process of transforming the raw data into a format that can be used in a meaningful measurable form without losing much of the actual meaning of the raw data, creating instead in fact an alternative data set, easier to use, but at the same time not an accurate representation that corresponds to the reality from which it was originally sampled. Yet in the worthy effort to establish a subdiscipline that has all the right scientific credentials, these issues of whether the data and variables are still really what they seem has become secondary and has been transcended by the grand objective of scientificism. Aside from the internal validity problem posed by quantitative data sets, what was central to this approach was the notion of the share and measurement of explained variance. It is essential to parsimony but misses the very realistic possibility that behavioral outputs would ultimately result from cumulative and interactive inputs, so that even a *small* increment of influence by a variable responsible only for a minor share of the variance could be the *deciding cause* for the particular output. In the absence of this small, even minute, influence, there would be no anticipated outcome no matter how important and extensive the weight of other variables is.

The prominence of behaviorism, and especially the powerful statistical and other methodological tools that it generated, have also been closely associated with the triumph of the logic of verification over the logic of discovery. The combination of easy-to-access databases and the availability of statistical methods and the computerized means to apply them at low cost has resulted in an advance of studies that conformed to verification standards of what was considered acceptable for publishing, even if the substantive contributions of too many of these studies were marginal or even questionable. In other words, research products increasingly reflected the fact that they could be easily produced by sitting in front of a computer with access to multiple databases and statistical software packages, rather than being a reflection of thoughtful or original research questions and creative conceptualization and theorizing. Consequently, political science in general, and FPA in particular, evidenced the proliferation of industrialized science at the expense of carefully crafted science. The bottom line is that the new technical opportunities for aggregate studies produced on the one hand heavily invested, exciting, and very important insights into state behavior.[32] But on the other hand, these same opportunities resulted occasionally in an incentive for creating substantial redundancies and an oversupply of scientific information of marginal value and even lesser utility. The excesses of this trend require that more attention and emphasis be given once more to the logic of discovery and the related "So what?" question in evaluating and publishing research products.

Similarly, for many years now formal modeling has seemed to hold the hope that it offers an epistemology that can combine theoretical richness and logical consistency, as well as precision and rigor.[33] But does the record justify and validate these expectations? It is highly debatable whether Robert Powell's statement that "formal models in international relations frequently are at least as rich causally as ordinary-language analyses" is a valid one.[34] There are structural limits on the extent to which complexity can be captured by formal models that cannot be easily overcome. In fact, earlier in the same paragraph, as well as elsewhere, Powell admits that "a model may be too simple in some absolute sense and one may hope to relax some restrictive assumptions as the modeling enterprise continues."[35] Unfortunately the last forty years of experience has given little credence to such hope because progress in that direction was slow and achievements less than anticipated. The modeling dialogue turned out to be a lot less productive than we could be led to believe. Indeed, it is too often true that "models are very spare . . . certainly too spare to explain any particular outcome in any degree of specificity,"[36] which raises salient questions about their suitability to generate useful foreign policy theories.[37]

Our argument does not claim that the cluster of approaches and methods generally described as formal theory has not made important contributions to FPA. But at the same time it takes the realistic view that formal modeling has delivered a lot less than it promised, and, extrapolating from the record so far, it remains an unlikely candidate to surprise us in the future with major breakthroughs. This is what makes the questions of cost-effectiveness so acute, especially when other competing but important and relevant work is practically ignored. To exemplify, Powell, in discussing the role of asymmetric information as a cause of war, points to the need to problematize where these asymmetries come from.[38] He defines it as an important task for the future. There is little indication in the book of awareness that this is not virgin ground and that an extensive, multidimensional, and rich body of literature in political psychology produced over the last thirty years has already successfully addressed these questions.[39] Herein is a potential impediment to progress, as defined earlier in the paper. When the stricture of a methodology, whatever its other merits,[40] does not allow for the incorporation and integration of important and relevant knowledge into the explanation and interpretation of the world, merely because it cannot be formulated in a particular manner required by formal modeling, not because it is untrue, then the methodology becomes an impediment to progress. In other words, the means determine the ends rather than the other way around. And I allow myself to be skeptical about whether in the future formal theory will be in a much better position to present a rich, convincing detailed analysis of these issues that will present competitive, different, and better answers than those already suggested by political psychology. This pessimistic view draws on the fact that after almost forty years, formal modeling's progress toward answering convincingly the type of important questions posed here is hardly astounding. To borrow the words of an old hand and chronicler of the Great Game in Central Asia: "I think, the Game really was a game with scores but limited substantive prizes."

This leads to my final point: scholars (even those who are adherents of the rational choice paradigm) seem to exclude scholarly work from the basic, rational, standard tests of value and utility they would consider necessary in practically every other domain of social activity requiring investment of resources—that is, a test of cost-effectiveness. There has not yet been a systematic "audit" comparing the research products that result from the application of more complex and more costly research methods with the products of less expensive research methods for quality or originality. We tend to assume that the costly methodologies pay off. It is time to consider criteria and auditing methods to evaluate the cost-effectiveness of methodological progress to find out whether what we are experiencing is actually significant progress or costly progress with relatively marginal returns on our investment. It is of course an irony that very often those who are the most committed believers in theoretical parsimony are also the most fervent practitioners of methodologies that are anything but parsimonious. We are so obsessed with methods that we do not stop and ask often enough and rigorously enough the "So what?" question regarding research findings. It would be wise not to fall prey to another instance of the representativeness bias by automatically associating highly-sophisticated, seemingly rigorous methods with a supposed substantive value-added to the knowledge product from the application of those methods.

Conclusions

Theory-building in the social sciences in general and in international politics in particular is the art of the possible. It also does not converge with the pure truth; at best it represents a practical truth. Evangelical scientificism and methodologism only stand in the way of creativity and are impediments to holistic theory-building, a stage that we are just beginning to reach and in which our fledgling efforts have resulted in some impressive and some less impressive results.

More specifically, several propositions flow from the arguments and observations in this paper. First, FPA requires a substantive adjustment and modernization of its research agenda to fit the changing nature of the policy environment and actors in the twenty-first century and to avoid becoming increasingly less relevant to the concerns of our times. Second, excessive concern with lack of parsimony is the result of the tyranny of methodology over common sense and relevance. In some way it reflects parroting of other disciplines and cross-disciplinary cloning rather than nuanced and thoughtful cross-disciplinary learning. Third, we are somewhat too permissive in our embrace of the premise of "multiple paths to knowledge." While in principle it is a correct and productive premise, it does not necessarily follow that all paths to knowledge are equally effective and have the same utility function. Furthermore, the different paths to knowledge may be incompatible.[41] Fourth, a unity of theory and praxis has to take into account the requirements of praxis and its diversity. This can be achieved only by attention to context and the building of contingent theories that reflect context-dependence. Context can appear in various roles or even multiple roles: that of cause, that of constraint, that of provider of meaning, and that of provider of differentiation and nuance. Fifth, we have started on the road to extending the reach and improving the quality of our research by looking outside the confines of the political science discipline, attempting to learn from other success stories. This has been the right thing to do. Yet, for reasons that go beyond the scope of this article, the study of international relations has been a field affected by fashions[42] mostly set in other disciplines concerning both what should be investigated and how research should be conducted. It is unfortunate that fashions have too often been adopted with a passion and sanctified by practice to the point that excludes the taking of a critical perspective to evaluate those fashions' contributions, their claims for originality, and the actual value added. Collective premature cognitive closure has made productive debates on the merits of one theory or method over another a ritual more than an actual process of learning. This is a reminder that effective learning, and hence progress, occasionally involves extensive unlearning or forgetting. There is still much that we need to learn, but FPA also carries excess baggage that we would be better off by dropping overboard, in spite of sunk costs. Finally, there is an urgent need for an innovative institutional incentive structure that will stimulate creativity rather than quench it by rewarding conservatism, conformism, and risk aversion, as is generally the case regarding the manner in which the discipline of political science awards and withholds the benefits of tenure, salary, and prestige.[43]

This paper should not be construed as an argument against more rigor, better methods, higher standards of scientific validity, and the employment of sophisticated formal methods and quantitative tools. But it is surely an argument for being practical and cautious about employing relevant standards of scientific validity and for not being carried away with the maxim, "If some is good a lot is better"—in order that we may avoid the pernicious consequences of seeing new technologies and methods that worked in other fields as panaceas for solving problems that are inherent to the unique attributes of our field of inquiry and are of a different breed. It is an argument that we should recognize the constraints that make FPA a subject more of scientific approximations than of scientific precision. But even more important, it is critical that we recognize the dichotomy between the logic of discovery and the logic of verification and understand that the two may converge, but that is not necessarily always the case. In those cases where the latter is true, it would be wiser and more productive to allow the logic of discovery to predominate over the logic of verification.

It might do us all good if in our quest for a scientific truth to which we are all passionately committed, we should keep in mind the following sagacious observation and advice: "Truth is both fragile and subtle.... science at its best is like a firm but gentle hand that holds a butterfly without crushing it."[44] It seems that in our fierce love for truth we occasionally embrace it so tightly that we crush it without even being aware of it, and then we feel righteous about it.

Having said all that, and although this paper takes a harsh critical view of the study of FPA, I conclude by reiterating the theme with which this paper opened and that has been repeated throughout the text. In spite of the many criticisms, perhaps not all acceptable to everybody, there is no doubt that when all is said and done a balanced evaluation will also take note of the immense amount of knowledge that has accumulated since the late 1950s. Not all of this knowledge is consensual, and there are ongoing debates and sharp disagreements between the dominant schools in the field. Encouraging debates and disagreements is the path away from stagnation and toward a lively and meaningful process of scientific growth and progress.

Notes

1. For example, C. Brown, *Understanding International Relations* (London: Macmillan, 1997), 79.
2. For useful reviews of many of the issue areas in FPA see C. F. Hermann, C. W. Kegley Jr., and J. N. Rosenau, eds., *New Directions in the Study*

of Foreign Policy (Boston: Allen and Unwin, 1987); M. Light, "Foreign Policy Analysis," in *Contemporary International Relations: A Guide to Theory,* ed. A. J. R. Groom and M. Light (London: Pinter, 1994), 93–108; L. Neack, A. K. J. Hey, and P. J. Haney, eds., *Foreign Policy Analysis: Continuity and Change in Its Second Generation* (Englewood Cliffs, N.J.: Prentice Hall, 1995). The literature referred to in the paper does not aspire to capture and reflect the full extent of the wealth of FPA literature. It is used to illustrate the main specific points made in the paper, with special emphasis on the more recent literature, rather than with the purpose of being all-inclusive.

3. Note, for example, the recent review of the state of political cognition research in which the author seems to be very pleasantly surprised by her findings, having started with very low expectations. K. M. McGraw, "Contributions of the Cognitive Approach to Political Psychology," *Political Psychology* 21, no. 4 (2000): 805–32.

4. For example, M. Holden, "The Competence of Political Science: Progress in Political Research Revisited," *American Political Science Review* 94, no. 1 (2000): 1–19.

5. For example, B. Bueno de Mesquita and J. D. Morrow, "Sorting through the Wealth of Notions," *International Security* 24, no. 2 (1999): 56–73; R. Powell, *In the Shadow of Power: States and Strategies in International Politics* (Princeton, N.J.: Princeton University Press, 1999).

6. H. A. Simon, *Models of Discovery* (Dordrecht, Holland: Reidel, 1977), xvi–xvii.

7. A clear but implicit dichotomy can be observed between journals that emphasize the logic of discovery and those that emphasize the logic of verification. A few illustrations will clarify this point: *International Organization* is clearly discovery-driven and has made this attribute an important aspect of its organizational culture, which has helped keep it on a consistent track in that sense for almost three decades in spite of regular changes of editors. In my view, this characteristic probably has made it the most consistently interesting and idea-rich journal in international studies. *The Journal of Conflict Resolution,* on the other hand, is verification-driven, while *Political Psychology* and *International Studies Quarterly* have an uneven record of volatility, tilting toward one side or the other depending on the composition of editorial teams and coincidence, but with a slight but obvious preference for criteria that emphasize the importance of verification. It should be noted that whatever a journal's main orientation, it does not exclude the other orientation but only gives it less prominence in editorial preferences.

8. M. G. Hermann, "When Leader Personality Will Affect Foreign Policy: Some Propositions," in *In Search of Global Patterns,* ed. J. N. Rosenau (New York: Free Press, 1976), 326–33; M. G. Hermann, "Personality and Foreign Policy Decision-Making: A Study of 53 Heads of Government," in *Foreign Policy Decision-Making: Perception, Cognition, and Artificial Intelligence,* ed. D. A. Sylvan and S. Chan (New York: Praeger, 1984), 58–80; M. H. Halperin, *Bureaucratic Politics and Foreign Policy* (Washington, D.C.: Brookings Institution, 1974); C. F. Hermann, ed., *In-*

ternational Crises (New York: Free Press, 1972); S. G. Walker, ed., *Role Theory and Foreign Policy Analysis* (Durham, N.C.: Duke University Press, 1987).

9. One example of overrating by decontextualization of seemingly convincing research findings is the case of the democratic peace hypothesis. On closer examination the generalized findings raised serious validity questions that have led to a much more restrictive and conditional view of the validity of the democratic peace hypothesis. See, for example, the review by Miriam Fendius-Elman, "The Never Ending Story: Democracy and Peace," *International Studies Review* 1, no. 3 (1999): 87–103.

10. D. Kahneman, P. Slovic, and A. Tversky, eds., *Judgment under Uncertainty: Heuristics and Biases* (Cambridge: Cambridge University Press, 1982); R. Nisbett and L. Ross, *Human Inference: Strategies and Shortcomings of Social Judgment* (Englewood Cliffs, N.J.: Prentice Hall, 1980); J. Reason, *Human Error* (Cambridge: Cambridge University Press, 1990); Y. Y. I. Vertzberger, *The World in Their Minds: Information Processing, Cognition, and Perception in Foreign Policy Decisionmaking* (Stanford, Calif.: Stanford University Press, 1990).

11. E. Ostrom, "Institutional Rational Choice: An Assessment of the Institutional Analysis and Development Framework," in *Theories of the Policy Process*, ed. P. A. Sabbatier (Boulder, Colo.: Westview, 1999), 37.

12. J. Goldstein and R. O. Keohane, eds., *Ideas and Foreign Policy: Beliefs, Institutions, and Political Change* (Ithaca, N.Y.: Cornell University Press, 1993); D. A. Lake and R. Powell, eds., *Strategic Choice and International Relations* (Princeton, N.J.: Princeton University Press, 1999).

13. For example, T. Eggertsson, *Economic Behavior and Institutions* (Cambridge: Cambridge University Press, 1990); E. G. Furubotn and R. Richter, *Institutions and Economic Theory: The Contribution of the New Institutional Economics* (Ann Arbor: University of Michigan Press, 1997); D. C. North, *Institutions, Institutional Change, and Economic Performance* (Cambridge: Cambridge University Press, 1990); B. G. Peters, *Institutional Theory in Political Science: The "New Institutionalism"* (London: Pinter, 1999); M. Rutherford, *Institutions in Economics: The Old and the New Institutionalism* (Cambridge: Cambridge University Press, 1996).

14. For example, L. L. Martin and B. A. Simmons, "Theories and Empirical Studies of International Institutions," *International Organization* 52, no. 4 (1998): 729–57.

15. For example, Y. Y. I. Vertzberger, *Risk Taking and Decisionmaking: Foreign Military Intervention Decisions* (Stanford, Calif.: Stanford University Press, 1998); D. Vaughan, "The Dark Side of Organizations: Mistake, Misconduct, and Disaster," in *Annual Review of Sociology*, vol. 25, ed. K. S. Cook and J. Hagan (Palo Alto, Calif.: Annual Reviews, 1999), 271–305.

16. For example, M. Bovens and P. 't Hart, *Understanding Policy Fiascoes* (New Brunswick, N.J.: Transaction, 1996); P. 't Hart, *Groupthink in Government: A Study of Small Groups and Policy Failures* (Amsterdam: Zwets and Zeitlinger, 1990).

17. A. Prakash and J. A. Hart, "Coping with Globalization: An Introduction," in *Coping with Globalization*, ed. A. Prakash and J. A. Hart (London: Routledge, 2000), 1–26; B. White, "The European Challenge to Foreign Policy Analysis," *European Journal of International Relations* 5 (1999): 37–66.
18. See A. L. George, *Bridging the Gap: Theory and Practice in Foreign Policy* (Washington, D.C.: United States Institute for Peace Press, 1993).
19. D. A. Baldwin, "Success and Failure in Foreign Policy," in *Annual Review of Political Science*, vol. 3, ed. N. W. Polsby (Palo Alto, Calif.: Annual Reviews, 2000), 167–82; D. L. Byman and M. C. Waxman, "Kosovo and the Great Air Power Debate," *International Security* 24, no. 4 (2000): 5–38; D. Larson and S. Renshon, *Good Judgment in Foreign Policy: Theory and Applications* (Lanham, Md.: Rowan and Littlefield, 2001); P. E. Tetlock, "Good Judgment in International Politics: Three Psychological Perspectives," *Political Psychology* 13, no. 3 (1992): 517–39.
20. It is worth noting that scholars rejecting theoretical complexity on the grounds of the lack of parsimony have not been in the least reluctant to accept technical (methodological) complexity. Perhaps they consider trading off theoretical simplicity at the cost of methodological complexity a justified transaction. From the same perspective those, like the author, less concerned with the costs of theoretical complexity perceive the costs of methodological complexity to be too high compared with the benefits from the gains of theoretical simplicity.
21. M. J. Levy, "Does It Matter If He's Naked? Bawled the Child," in *Contending Approaches to International Politics*, ed. K. Knorr and J. N. Rosenau (Princeton, N.J.: Princeton University Press, 1969), 89–90; also C. Beed and C. Beed, "Is the Case for Social Sciences Laws Strengthening?" *Journal for the Theory of Social Behaviour* 30, no. 2 (2000): 131–53; A. O. Hirschman, "Against Parsimony: Three Easy Ways of Complicating Some Categories of Economic Discourse," *Economics and Philosophy* 1, no. 1 (1985): 7–21; G. King, R. O. Keohane, and S. Verba, *Designing Social Inquiry: Scientific Inference in Qualitative Research* (Princeton, N.J.: Princeton University Press, 1994), 104–5; R. N. Lebow, "Beyond Parsimony: Rethinking Theories of Coercive Bargaining," *European Journal of International Relations* 4, no. 1 (1998): 31–66; C. Tilly, "To Explain Political Processes," *American Journal of Sociology* 100, no. 6 (1995): 1594–1610.
22. For some of the discussions and critical reviews of the promise and limits of the rationality paradigm see K. S. Cook and M. Levi, eds., *The Limits of Rationality* (Chicago: University of Chicago Press, 1990); J. D. Fearon, "Rationalist Explanations for War," *International Organization* 49, no. 3 (1995): 379–414; D. P. Green and I. Shapiro, *Pathologies of Rational Choice Theory: A Critique of Applications in Political Science* (New Haven, Conn.: Yale University Press, 1994); M. Kahler, "Rationality in International Relations," *International Organization* 52, no. 4 (1998): 919–41; S. Kelley, "The Promise and Limitations of Rational Choice Theory," *Critical Review* 9, no. 1–2 (1995): 95–106; R. E. Lane,

"What Rational Choice Explains," *Critical Review* 9, no. 1-2 (1995): 107-26; L. L. Martin, "The Contribution of Rational Choice: A Defense of Pluralism," *International Security* 24, no. 2 (1999): 74-83; Vertzberger, *Risk Taking and Decisionmaking*; S. M. Walt, "Rigor or Rigor Mortis? Rational Choice and Security Studies," *International Security* 23, no. 4 (1999): 5-48; and C. H. Zuckert, "On the Rationality of Rational Choice," *Political Psychology* 16, no. 1 (1995): 179-98.
23. For example, B. D. Jones, "Bounded Rationality," in *Annual Review of Political Science*, vol. 2, ed. N. W. Polsby (Palo Alto, Calif.: Annual Reviews, 1999), 297-321.
24. H. A. Simon, *Models of Man* (New York: Wiley, 1957).
25. G. A. Miller, "The Magical Number Seven, Plus or Minus Two: Some Limits on Our Capacity for Processing Information," *Psychological Review* 63, no. 2 (1956): 81-97.
26. Z. Kunda, "The Case for Motivated Reasoning," *Psychological Bulletin* 108, no. 3 (1990): 480-98.
27. P. E. Tetlock, "The Impact of Accountability on Judgment and Choice: Toward a Social Contingency Model," in *Advances in Experimental Social Psychology*, vol. 25, ed. M. P. Zana (San Diego: Academic Press, 1992), 331-76.
28. For example, A. Bennett, *Condemned to Repetition: The Rise, Fall, and Reprise of Soviet-Russian Military Intervention* (Cambridge: MIT Press, 1999); M. Brecher, *Crises in World Politics: Theory and Reality* (Oxford, England: Pergamon, 1993); R. N. Lebow, *Between Peace and War: The Nature of International Crisis* (Baltimore: Johns Hopkins University Press, 1981); C.A. Kupchan, *The Vulnerability of Empire* (Ithaca, N.Y.: Cornell University Press, 1994); R. N. Lebow and J. G. Stein, *We All Lost the Cold War* (Princeton, N.J.: Princeton University Press, 1994); Z. Maoz, *National Choices and International Processes* (Cambridge: Cambridge University Press, 1990); J. N. Rosenau, *Turbulence in World Politics: A Theory of Change and Continuity* (Princeton, N.J.: Princeton University Press, 1990); G. H. Snyder and P. Diesing, *Conflict among Nations: Bargaining, Decision-Making, and System Structure in International Crisis* (Princeton, N.J.: Princeton University Press, 1977); Vertzberger, *The World in Their Minds*; Vertzberger, *Risk Taking and Decisionmaking*.
29. P. E. Tetlock, "Coping with Trade-Offs: Psychological Constraints and Political Implications" (n.d., mimeographed), 45.
30. C. Argyris, *The Inner Contradictions of Rigorous Research* (New York: Academic Press, 1980); T. Mayer, *Truth versus Precision in Economics* (Aldershot, England: Elgar, 1993); T. M. Porter, *Trust in Numbers: The Pursuit of Objectivity in Science and Public Life* (Princeton, N.J.: Princeton University Press, 1995); M. N. Wise, ed., *The Values of Precision* (Princeton, N.J.: Princeton University Press, 1995).
31. Porter, *Trust in Numbers*, 230.
32. For example, M. Brecher and J. Wilkenfeld, *A Study of Crisis* (Ann Arbor: University of Michigan Press, 1997).
33. Bueno de Mesquita and Morrow, "Sorting through the Wealth of No-

tions"; R. B. Morton, *Methods and Models* (Cambridge: Cambridge University Press, 1999); Powell, *In the Shadow of Power*.
34. Powell, *In the Shadow of Power*, 37.
35. Ibid., 37 and concluding chapter.
36. Walt, "Rigor or Rigor Mortis?" 38. See also G. L. Munck, "Game Theory and Comparative Politics: New Perspectives, Old Concerns," *World Politics* 53, no. 2 (2001): 173–204.
37. C. Elman, "Why Not Realist Theories of Foreign-Policy Theory?" *Security Studies* 6, no. 1 (1996): 13–16.
38. Powell, *In the Shadow of Power*, 202–3.
39. The writings on the many different aspects of the forms, causes, and consequences of information asymmetries are too many to be cited in full; hence I shall cite just an illustrative sample: Brecher, *Crises in World Politics*; J. F. Burke and F. I. Greenstein, *How Presidents Test Reality: Decisions on Vietnam, 1954 and 1965* (New York: Russell Sage Foundation, 1989); A. L. George, *Presidential Decisionmaking in Foreign Policy: The Effective Use of Information and Advice* (Boulder, Colo.: Westview, 1980); O. R. Holsti, "Crisis Decision-Making," in *Behavior, Society, and Nuclear War*, vol. 1, ed. P. E. Tetlock, J. L. Husbands, R. Jervis, P. C. Stern, and C. Tilly (New York: Oxford University Press, 1989), 8–84; R. Jervis, *Perception and Misperception in International Politics* (Princeton, N.J.: Princeton University Press, 1976); D. W. Larson, *The Origins of Containment: A Psychological Exploration* (Princeton, N.J.: Princeton University Press, 1985); Lebow, *Between Peace and War*; J. S. Levy, "Misperception and the Causes of War," *World Politics* 38, no. 1 (1983): 76–99; J. S. Levy, "Learning and Foreign Policy: Sweeping a Conceptual Minefield," *International Organization* 48, no. 2 (1994): 279–312. J. A. Rosati, "The Power of Human Cognition in the Study of World Politics," *International Studies Review* 2, no. 3 (2000): 45–75; J. G. Stein and R. Tanter, *Rational Decision-Making: Israel's Security Choices, 1967* (Columbus: Ohio State University Press, 1980); D. A. Sylvan and S. J. Thorson, "Ontologies, Problem Representation, and the Cuban Missile Crisis," *Journal of Conflict Resolution* 36, no. 4 (1992): 709–32; P. 't Hart, E. K. Stern, and B. Sundelius, eds., *Beyond Groupthink: Political Group Dynamics and Foreign Policy-Making* (Ann Arbor: University of Michigan Press, 1997); Vertzberger, *The World in Their Minds*; S. G. Walker, "The Interface between Belief and Behavior: Henry Kissinger's Operational Code and the Vietnam War," *Journal of Conflict Resolution* 21, no. 1 (1977): 129–68.
40. E. M. S. Niou and P. C. Ordeshook, "Return of the Luddites," *International Security* 24, no. 2 (1999): 84–96.
41. On the question of incompatibility, see the dialogue between S. Smith, "Foreign Policy Theory and the New Europe," in *European Foreign Policy: The EC and Changing Perspectives in Europe*, ed. W. Carlsnaes and S. Smith (London: Sage, 1994), 1–20, and W. Carlsnaes, "In Lieu of a Conclusion: Compatibility and the Agent-Structure in Foreign Policy Analysis," in ibid., 274–87.
42. M. Brecher, "International Studies in the Twentieth Century and Be-

yond: Flawed Dichotomies, Synthesis, Cumulation," *International Studies Quarterly* 43, no. 2 (1999): 213–64.
43. Holden, "The Competence of Political Science," 15.
44. K. S. Bowers, "Situationism in Psychology: An Analysis and Critique," *Psychological Review* 80, no. 5 (1973): 333.

BELIEFS AND FOREIGN POLICY ANALYSIS IN THE NEW MILLENNIUM

Stephen G. Walker

Introduction

A main axis of intellectual tension in the area of foreign policy analysis over the past forty years is the issue of the importance of "beliefs"[1] in the explanation and prediction of foreign policy decisions and outcomes. The seminal decision-making approach to foreign policy articulated by Snyder, Bruck, and Sapin at midcentury was partly in reaction to a skewed emphasis by the realist tradition on external circumstances (e.g., the balance of power) and the omission of beliefs in explaining foreign policy decisions.[2] Snyder and his colleagues argued that this strategy of explanation came at the expense of neglecting the definition of the situation represented by the decision maker's beliefs about the external and internal setting for decision.

One of the consequences was to limit insights into the dynamics of international crises, an important area of foreign policy analysis during the cold war and crucial to realist concerns with the question of war and peace among the great powers in the international system. Subsequent research efforts by several scholars attempted to demonstrate the validity of the decision-making approach to international crises over the next several decades.[3] In spite of such efforts, a debate has occurred over whether beliefs are merely epiphenomena or important causal mechanisms in foreign policy analysis.

Are Beliefs Merely Epiphenomena?

As the subfield of foreign policy analysis evolved, the claims on behalf of the general approach and the focus on the decision maker's definition of the situation became increasingly qualified and diluted in several ways. To their credit, practitioners of the decision-making approach identified many of these limitations. Holsti concluded that beliefs were most likely to be influential in foreign policy decisions when the decision maker was faced with radical uncertainty, that is, situations that were ambiguous, nonroutine, novel, or unanticipated, prompting a reliance on old information in the form of preexisting beliefs rather than new information from the environment.[4]

George argued that even under those conditions beliefs were most directly and strongly related to the preferences of decision makers rather than to the actual behavior of states.[5] The impact on a state's behavior was likely to be diluted, as the impact of individual preferences was modified by other variables such as stimuli and conditions in the international environment and limitations on choice imposed by organizational or domestic circumstances.

More severe criticisms stemmed from the problems associated with aggregating from individual beliefs to collective decisions, which changes the decision-making unit in foreign policy analysis from the individual to larger entities such as small groups, bureaucratic organizations, special interest groups, or governmental institutions culminating in the state as the actor.[6] If the power to decide does not reside in the individual, then it becomes even more difficult to trace the microfoundations of decisions to beliefs. In accounts of state decision making at higher levels of aggregation, beliefs are reduced to epiphenomena, that is, merely doctrinal expressions of more fundamental bureaucratic interests, organizational structure, or institutional history.[7] They are important guides to action, but their contents are determined heavily by other antecedent variables, leaving little room for the autonomous impact of beliefs on behavior. While they are located close to the behavior to be explained, shared beliefs do not escape the "endogeneity trap."[8]

In sum, the cumulative effects of these trends in an increasing order of severity include the following self-criticisms and indictments by others of the impact and importance of beliefs on foreign policy and world politics: (1) beliefs are important and independent influences on foreign policy decisions only under a restricted range of conditions; (2) beliefs are just one variable within a larger complex of explanatory variables; (3) the impact of beliefs on foreign policy behavior tends to be indirect and general rather than direct and specific; (4) beliefs tend to be an intervening or dependent variable in foreign policy analyses rather than an independent variable; (5) beliefs are extraneous variables in foreign policy and world politics and best ignored except for the possible explanation of deviant cases when other explanations fail.

Are Beliefs Important Causal Mechanisms?

And yet "beliefs" of one kind or another still command a lot of scholarly attention and expenditure of intellectual resources. The transdiscipline of political psychology has emerged over the past twenty-five years with an international society, an annual meeting, a journal, and a summer institute that trains graduate students. Within the past decade a political psychology section has also been formed within the American Political Science Association. A preoccupation with the "agent-structure" problem and the recent "constructivist" turn in international relations theory has redirected international relations scholarship toward psychocultural phenomena as important causes of foreign policy behavior.[9]

During this revival, Goldstein and Keohane have suggested three types of causal powers associated with explanations of foreign policy and international politics that incorporate beliefs as mechanisms.[10] First, beliefs can perform as "worldviews" that inform the leader about the nature of the political universe and exert mapping effects.[11] That is, the leader infers from these beliefs who self and other are and what to do given this map of the social situation. Second, beliefs can also take the form of "principled beliefs" that exert ethical or normative power as steering effects on strategic decisions.[12] Third, beliefs may serve as "causal beliefs" about cause-and-effect relations in problem representation and have implications for action in the form of solution effects.[13]

It is possible to account for this resurgence partly by reference to the tenor of the times. With the unexpected end of the cold war, scholars became concerned with their inability to anticipate this development without incorporating the impact of changes in the beliefs of decision makers.[14] The vacuum that followed the end of the cold war was not simply a power vacuum with the demise of the USSR. There was also an intellectual vacuum, as both policymakers and scholars struggled to grasp the realities of the new world order. Without the precepts of a bipolar world in the post–cold war era to guide decisions, the impact of the beliefs of leaders in this uncertain environment was projected as likely to increase.[15]

The turn toward beliefs as causal mechanisms in one form or another may also be part of a wider reaction against rational choice theory that preceded the end of the cold war.[16] Postmodernists, constructivists, and political psychologists tend to share distaste for rational choice models of decisions, especially those that restrict the autonomous ability of agents to select goals for political action. The beliefs and identities of individuals are not easily subsumed under the interests and preferences of rational choice models within any of these schools of thought.[17] The arguments arrayed against rational choice models within the decision-making approach to foreign policy analysis range from rational choice theory's lack of descriptive power for how decisions are actually made to its inability to account for the actor's preferences or goals, which are often taken simply as givens in subjective utility and strategic models of rational choice.[18]

If one looks beyond the polemical exchanges to the research practices of scholars who employ some form of beliefs in their models, there is common ground shared by rational choice and other decision-making theorists. Beliefs are one explanation for "flawed" decisions, ones guided by misperceptions that make seemingly irrational choices to outside observers more "rational" once the flawed information on which they were based is taken into account.[19] Even foreign policy successes that appear to follow the ends/means maxims of rational choice may turn out to be the result of perceptions whose flaws cancel out one another.[20] More recent work by rational choice theorists also recognizes beliefs as important intervening variables between external circumstances and the foreign policy choices of decision makers.[21]

These examples suggest that the debate over rational choice is partly over "thin" versus "thick" models of rationality.[22] A thin model assumes that beliefs are relatively unimportant and that decision makers are highly influenced by circumstances. These external boundaries override the internal dispositions of leaders toward other courses of action. A thick model assumes that beliefs are relatively important and that decision makers have internal boundaries that limit the capacity for choice. These internal constraints may be either content-full or content-free biases, depending upon whether they refer to schemata or heuristics.[23] If beliefs are shared or simply recognized as representing the expectations of others, they may act as epistemic or cultural boundaries in much the same way that more idiosyncratic or internalized beliefs do but from an external location.[24]

A Strategy for Synthesis

The challenge facing theorists in the new millennium who begin with "beliefs" as the primordial concept in their approach to foreign policy analysis is to identify these internal and external boundaries of rational choice. Ironically, therefore, the best strategy may be to clarify and refine what it means to be "rational" even though the rational choice approach itself raises the hackles of political psychologists and others noted in the previous section. One example of this strategy is the introduction of prospect theory into foreign policy analysis.[25] A second example is to bring rational choice and cognitive models of decision making together in a common application.[26] A third example is to link psychological models of information processing with the insights of bounded rationality theorists operating out of other research traditions.[27]

More broadly, there are two general lines of inquiry associated with this strategy joined by a shared assumption and inspired by a common goal. A shared assumption is that beliefs are not merely boundaries but pivotal mechanisms for explaining choices and consequences in foreign policy and world politics.[28] A common goal is to demonstrate the various kinds of causal powers associated with beliefs that support this shared assumption. One line of inquiry is to focus on beliefs as microlevel mechanisms, while the other is to focus on beliefs as macrolevel mechanisms of choice.[29] This "two-lane" view of the research road ahead is consistent with a definition of political psychology as a branch of social psychology, which occupies an intellectual niche between the disciplines of psychology and sociology and has a focus on the links among individuals, social groups, and behavior at different levels of analysis.

Much of the work on foreign policy decision making over the past forty years has focused on beliefs primarily as microlevel, individual mechanisms rather than as macrolevel, social mechanisms. In the parlance of rational choice theorists, the emphasis has been on the "subjective" in subjective rational utility models rather than the "strategic" in strategic rationality models.[30] With the exception of some of the work on deterrence,[31] the focus in foreign policy analysis has been largely on the one-sided actions of states rather than the two-sided strategic interactions between them.[32]

An emphasis on strategic interactions in international relations theory outside a crisis context has been dominated by the realist and liberal schools who use instrumental rationality calculations about costs and benefits to inform their balance-of-power or institutional models.[33] The work of the constructivist school focuses on the creation of norms and institutions taken for granted by realists and liberals.[34] None of these three schools—realists, liberals, and constructivists—seems to think that individuals matter so much as social forces or interests in the formation of beliefs.

However, my sense is that individuals—particularly leaders—do matter in at least three ways: (1) the actions of leaders affect the formation, reinforcement, and alteration of shared beliefs and interests within a state; and (2) the beliefs of leaders in one state also affect the strategic interactions between states, (3) thereby having an impact on the beliefs and interests of leaders in other states. In other words, beliefs have steering effects on behavior and are subject to learning effects from stimuli in the form of cues from other leaders.[35]

A Research Agenda for Future Progress

One way to capture the dynamics of these three processes and the pivotal impact of beliefs is to analyze initiatives toward peace as well as toward war within the conventional model of an international crisis. This analytical move is consistent with a conceptualization of crises as turning points rather than simply confrontations,[36] while retaining the insights of the conventional crisis model as (a) involving a precipitant event, (b) prompting a series of moves by the protagonists, (c) reaching a turning point, and (d) ending with a "resolution" of a crisis in one of four outcomes—(1) settlement, (2) deadlock, or (3) domination by one side or (4) the other side.[37] In previous applications of the model, the transition from turning point to resolution may be peaceful or violent but usually follows the militarization of a conflict by the threat of force as the precipitating event.[38]

A reorientation of the model allows for the precipitating event to produce an initiative to de-escalate conflict or to escalate cooperation. Some examples include the announcement by Anwar Sadat that he would visit the Israeli Knesset to initiate a peace settlement with Israel regarding the Sinai Peninsula and the Gaza Strip, the initiative by Mikhail Gorbachev to reduce tensions between East and West in Europe, and Neville Chamberlain's adoption of the appeasement strategy in an attempt to reach a general settlement of issues between Great Britain and Nazi Germany. As these three cases indicate, respectively, the precipitating event may occur in the midst of a militarized dispute over a concrete issue, come during a protracted period of tension such as the cold war between the United States and the Soviet Union, or appear as a diplomatic initiative between states that have not yet become implacable antagonists.

This reconceptualization of the conventional crisis model expands the universe of cases for analysis in new and interesting ways. One can now view military initiatives and diplomatic initiatives within the same general analytical framework. Employing the same concepts and propositions for analyzing the dynamics that occur within this framework creates the opportunity to subsume and explain within the same theoretical context what appear superficially to be disparate processes. A cogent theoretical and empirical account of the successes and failures from such divergent initiatives as Gorbachev's "New Thinking" that led to the settlement of the cold war and Hitler's "*Ostpolitik*" that resulted in the escalation to world war requires a two-sided analysis. The respondent's perspective and behavior must also be incorporated.

A formal model that unites these processes is an expanded version of the international interaction game developed by Bueno de Mesquita and Lalman (see figure 1).[39] This game begins with a "move by nature"—that is, a precipitating event in the form of a stimulus from such environmental sources as decisions by third parties, a change in leadership, or a technological breakthrough. Singly or together, they prompt an initiative in the form of a demand (D) by one state toward another state, defined as a claim accompanied by a threat of force (F) in the event that the claim is not met. The target of the demand may choose not to make a counterdemand (~D), terminating the game (and the conflict) by acquiescence, or extend the game by issuing a counterdemand.

A counterdemand escalates the conflict to a *military* crisis defined as a confrontation in which the protagonists have exchanged threats to use military force. One of the parties in the conflict may choose force or not at this point, leading to a choice by the other. If the first does not choose force, then the other may either reciprocate, leading to negotiations, or choose force. If both sides choose force, the out-

Figure 1. The international interaction game. (From B. Bueno de Mesquita and D. Lalman, *War and Reason* [New Haven, Conn.: Yale University Press, 1992].)

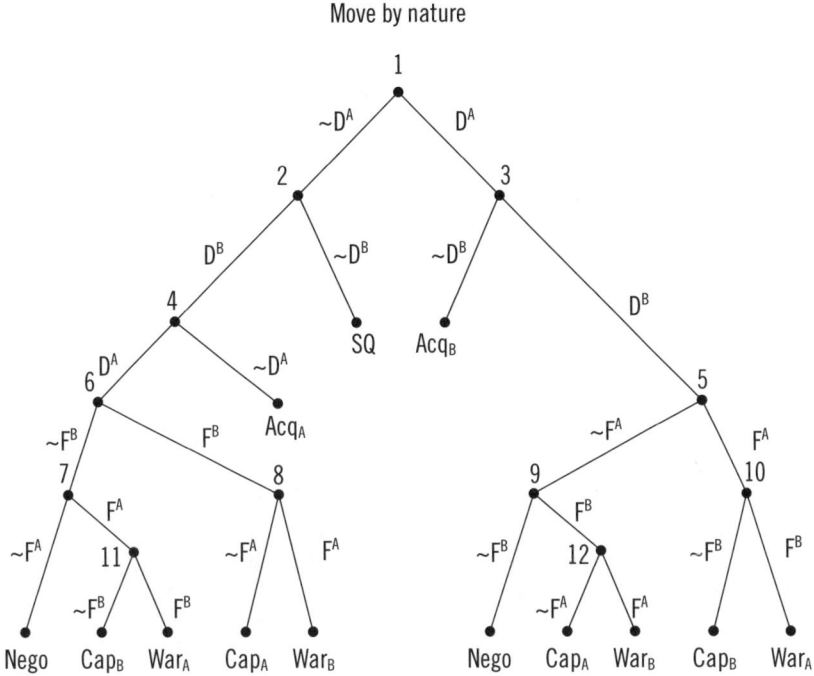

come of the conflict is war. If one chooses force while the other does not, then the conflict outcome is capitulation in favor of the state that chose force.[40]

The logic of this interaction game is fueled from the beginning by a threat to use force. Demands are the only *initiatives* fully specified in the game. A state's *responses* may be choices leading to acquiescence, capitulation, or negotiation, but the de-escalation process accompanying these choices is not modeled as an initiative. The interaction game begins either with a demand by state A or a demand by state B. If neither state initiates a demand, then the outcome is simply the status quo (SQ).

However, this one-sided view of state interactions is easily expanded in figure 2 to include cooperative initiatives following a move by nature. Either state A or state B initiates a proposal (P) defined as a claim accompanied by a promise to commit the re-

Figure 2. An expanded version of the international interaction game

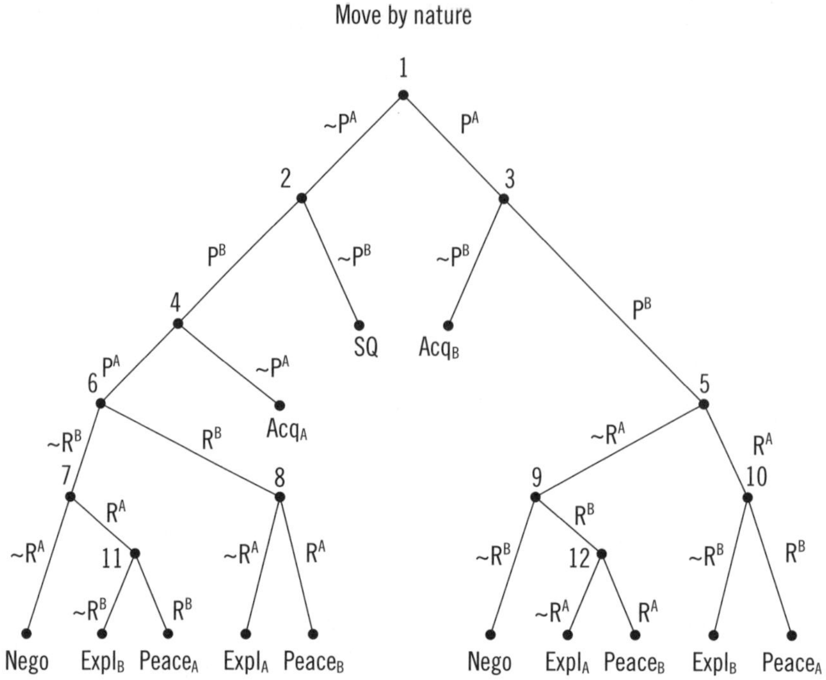

sources necessary to carry out the contents of the proposal. The target may choose not to respond with a counterproposal (~P), terminating the game with acquiescence, or extend the game by issuing a counterproposal.

A counterproposal escalates the interactions to a *diplomatic* crisis defined as a window of opportunity in which the protagonists have exchanged promises to use rewards. One of the parties may choose reward (R) or not (~R) at this point, leading to a choice by the other. If the first does not choose reward, then the other may reciprocate and continue negotiations, or choose reward. If both states choose reward, the outcome of their interactions is peace. If one chooses reward while the other does not, then the outcome is exploitation by the party that did not choose reward.

While the logic of the general interaction game is straightforward in its extended form as a decision tree, lacking in previous rational choice applications is a systematic examination and theoretical presentation of both the psychological processes and the strategic interaction processes that shape the course and fate of cooperative initiatives. Conversely, foreign policy analyses of the beliefs and psychological processes experienced by leaders initiating either cooperation or conflict are often one-sided accounts that do not focus heavily on the actual interactions between states, or they do not examine systematically the corresponding decision-making processes experienced by the other side. Even accounts of strategic interactions that explicitly recognize the theoretical importance of psychological processes often stop somewhat short of both measuring the beliefs of leaders and integrating these observations into their analyses.[41]

Conclusion

To sum up, an expanded focus on crises as turning points in international relations integrates threats of conflict and opportunities for cooperation, thereby synthesizing a focus on the respective explananda in the realist and liberal schools of international relations theory. Identifying beliefs as pivotal macromechanisms of bounded rationality within this framework brings the constructivist and rational choice schools into the analysis. Candidate theories with bounded rationality mechanisms include social identity theory and role theory at the macro level of analysis and prospect theory and cognitive consistency theory at the micro level.[42]

This approach also calls into question the criticisms of beliefs and the decision-making approach discussed earlier. Beliefs are not extraneous variables in foreign policy and world politics, which are best ignored unless they are needed to explain foreign policy fiascoes. They are pivotal variables with mapping, steering, and solution effects within a dynamic interactive causal model rather than being simply intervening or dependent variables in one-sided foreign policy analyses. The conceptualization of beliefs as important causal mechanisms rather than merely as structural boundaries enhances the possibility that their impact is likely to be more specific and direct instead of general and indirect. Beliefs are no longer just another variable within a larger complex of variables.

By combining a bidirectional, strategic approach with a two-level, psychological approach, the qualifications that beliefs are important and independent influences on foreign policy for only a narrow range of behavior or under a restricted range of conditions are also undercut. The restriction of explananda in cognitive models to a narrow range of behavior is relaxed by expanding the crisis framework to include both conflict and cooperation processes. Holsti's specified scope conditions, in which beliefs are relevant in a "weakly structured" situation characterized as ambiguous, nonroutine, novel, or otherwise unanticipated, are also expanded.[43] Under these conditions beliefs were postulated as microlevel mechanisms for shaping individual decisions. The converse of these conditions is a "strongly structured" situation where external constraints shape behavior. In these latter situations, however, there are also likely to be roles or social identities, which act as macrolevel mechanisms that constrain behavior and thereby expand the importance of beliefs as causal mechanisms.[44]

Notes

1. I put the word *beliefs* in quotation marks to indicate that I use it here generically to refer to the various conceptualizations for the products of cognition in the human mind—for example, schemata, attitudes, perceptions, images. Although the various research scholars that employ these different conceptualizations are arguably all part of the "cognitivist" research program in world politics, I also acknowledge that it is necessary and desirable to be more specific on the kind of "beliefs" employed when conducting a particular analysis. These cognitive constructs may also be shared with others, extending the scope of my usage to include the cultural beliefs of a group, society, or system of states. See P. E. Tetlock, "Social Psychology and World Politics," in *Handbook of Social Psychology*, ed. D. G. Gilbert, S. T. Fiske, and G. Lindzey (New York: McGraw-Hill, 1998), 869–912; J. Goldstein and R. O. Keohane, eds., *Ideas and Foreign Policy* (Ithaca, N.Y.: Cornell University Press, 1993); P. J. Katzenstein, ed., *The Culture of National Security* (New York: Columbia University Press, 1996); A. Wendt, *Social Theory of International Politics* (Cambridge: Cambridge University Press, 1999); V. M. Hudson and M. W. Sampson, eds., *Culture and Foreign Policy Analysis*, special issue of *Political Psychology* 20, no. 4 (1999).
2. R. C. Snyder, H. W. Bruck, and B. Sapin, eds., *Foreign Policy Decision-Making as an Approach to the Study of International Politics*, Foreign Policy Analysis Project Series, no. 3 (Princeton, N.J.: Princeton University Press, 1954).
3. For example, G. D. Paige, *The Korean Decision* (New York: Free Press, 1958); O. R. Holsti, R. A. Brody, and R. C. North, "Measuring Affect and Action in International Reaction Models," in *International Politics and Foreign Policy*, 2d ed., ed. J. N. Rosenau (New York: Free Press, 1969), 679–96; C. F. Hermann, "International Crisis as a Situational Variable," in ibid., 409–21; C. F. Hermann and L. P. Brady, "Alternative Models of International Crisis Behavior," in *International Crises*, ed. C. F. Hermann (New York: Free Press, 1972), 281–303; O. R. Holsti, *Crisis, Escalation, War* (Montreal: McGill-Queen's University Press, 1972); M.

Brecher, *Decisions in Israel's Foreign Policy* (London: Oxford University Press, 1974); G. H. Snyder and P. Diesing, *Conflict among Nations* (Princeton, N.J.: Princeton University Press, 1977); R. N. Lebow, *Between Peace and War* (Baltimore: Johns Hopkins University Press, 1981); M. Brecher, B. S. Steinberg, and J. G. Stein, "A Framework for Research on Foreign Policy Behavior," *Journal of Conflict Resolution* 13, no. 1 (1969): 75–101; M. Brecher and J. Wilkenfeld, *A Study of Crisis* (Ann Arbor: University of Michigan Press, 1997).
4. O. R. Holsti, "Foreign Policy Decisions Viewed Cognitively," in *The Structure of Decision*, ed. R. M. Axelrod (Princeton, N.J.: Princeton University Press, 1976), 18–54.
5. A. L. George, "The Causal Nexus between Cognitive Beliefs and Decision-Making Behavior," in *Psychological Models in International Politics*, ed. L. S. Falkowski (Boulder, Colo.: Westview, 1979), 95–124.
6. G. T. Allison, *Essence of Decision: Explaining the Cuban Missile Crisis* (Boston: Little, Brown, 1971); S. D. Krasner, *Defending the National Interest* (Princeton, N.J.: Princeton University Press, 1978).
7. S. Van Evera, "The Cult of the Offensive and the Origins of the First World War," *International Security* 9, no. 1 (1984): 58–108; D. D. Avant, "The Institutional Sources of Military Doctrine: Hegemons in Peripheral Wars," *International Studies Quarterly* 37, no. 4 (1993): 409–30; J. L. Snyder, *Myths of Empire* (Ithaca, N.Y.: Cornell University Press, 1991); Goldstein and Keohane, *Ideas and Foreign Policy*.
8. R. O. Keohane and L. L. Martin, "Institutional Theory as a Research Program," in *Progress in International Relations Theory: Metrics and Methods of Scientific Change*, ed. C. Elman and M. F. Elman (Cambridge: MIT Press, forthcoming).
9. A. Wendt, "The Agent-Structure Problem in International Relations," *International Organization* 41, no. 3 (1987): 335–70; A. Wendt, "Anarchy Is What States Make of It," *International Organization* 46, no. 2 (1992): 391–425; Wendt, *Social Theory of International Politics*; Katzenstein, *The Culture of National Security*.
10. Goldstein and Keohane, *Ideas and Foreign Policy*, 8–11.
11. See also A. L. George, "The 'Operational Code,'" *International Studies Quarterly* 13, no. 2 (1969): 190–222; George, "The Causal Nexus between Cognitive Beliefs and Decision-Making Behavior"; M. L. Cottam, *Foreign Policy Decision-Making: The Influence of Cognition* (Boulder, Colo.: Westview, 1986); K. L. Shimko, *Images and Arms Control* (Ann Arbor: University of Michigan Press, 1991).
12. See also M. N. Barnett, *Dialogues in Arab Politics* (New York: Columbia University Press, 1998); S. G. Walker, M. Schafer, and M. D. Young, "Systematic Procedures for Operational Code Analysis," *International Studies Quarterly* 45, no. 1 (1998): 175–190; S. G. Walker, M. Schafer, and M. D. Young, "Presidential Operational Codes and Foreign Policy Conflicts in the Post–Cold War World," *Journal of Conflict Resolution* 43, no. 5 (1999): 610–25.
13. See also D. A. Sylvan and J. F. Voss, eds., *Problem Representation in Foreign Policy Decision Making* (Cambridge: Cambridge University

Press, 1998); G. M. Bonham, M. J. Shapiro, and T. L. Trumble, "The October War," *International Studies Quarterly* 23, no. 1 (1979): 3–44; R. M. Axelrod, ed., *The Structure of Decision* (Princeton, N.J.: Princeton University Press, 1976).
14. Wendt, "Anarchy Is What States Make of It."
15. R. Jervis, "Leadership, Post–Cold War Politics, and Psychology," *Political Psychology* 15, no. 4 (1994): 769–78.
16. D. P. Green and I. Shapiro, *Pathologies of Rational Choice Theory* (New Haven, Conn.: Yale University Press, 1994).
17. R. K. Ashley, "The Poverty of Neorealism," *International Organization* 38, no. 2 (1984): 225–86; Wendt, *Social Theory of International Politics*; N. Geva and A. Mintz, eds., *Decision-Making on War and Peace* (Boulder, Colo.: Lynne Rienner, 1997).
18. *The Rational Deterrence Debate: A Symposium*, special issue of *World Politics* 41, no.2 (1989); Geva and Mintz, *Decision-Making on War and Peace*.
19. For example, R. Jervis, *Perception and Misperception in International Politics* (Princeton, N.J.: Princeton University Press, 1976); I. L. Janis, *Groupthink*, rev. ed. (Boston: Houghton Mifflin, 1982); D. A. Larson, *Origins of Containment: A Psychological Explanation* (Princeton, N.J.: Princeton University Press, 1985); Y. F. Khong, *Analogies at War* (Princeton, N.J.: Princeton University Press, 1992).
20. Y. I. Vertzberger, *The World in Their Minds* (Stanford, Calif.: Stanford University Press, 1990).
21. For example, B. Bueno de Mesquita and D. Lalman, *War and Reason* (New Haven, Conn.: Yale University Press, 1992); see also B. Bueno de Mesquita, *Principles of International Politics* (Washington, D.C.: Congressional Quarterly Press, 2000).
22. D. Little, *Varieties of Social Explanation* (Boulder, Colo.: Westview, 1991).
23. S. T. Fiske and S. E. Taylor, *Social Cognition*, 2d ed. (New York: McGraw-Hill, 1991). Whereas schemata are hypotheses about the environment, heuristics are the rules by which individuals test the hypotheses in a schema. By extension, heuristics may also be viewed as "content-free" schemata, that is, as rules functioning to organize incoming information even in the absence of person, self, role, or event schemata. See also Jervis, *Perception and Misperception in International Politics*; J. G. Stein, "Building Politics in Psychology," *Political Psychology* 9, no. 2 (1988): 245–72.
24. P. Haas, "Introduction: Epistemic Communities and International Policy Coordination," *International Organization* 46, no. 1 (1992): 1–35; Wendt, "Anarchy Is What States Make of It."
25. B. R. Farnham, ed., *Avoiding Losses/Taking Risks* (Ann Arbor: University of Michigan Press, 1994); J. S. Levy, "Prospect Theory, Rational Choice, and International Relations," *International Studies Quarterly* 41, no. 1 (1997): 87–112; R. McDermott, *Risk-Taking in International Politics* (Ann Arbor: University of Michigan Press, 1998).

26. R. K. Herrmann and M. P. Fischerkeller, "Beyond the Enemy Image and Spiral Model: Cognitive-Strategic Research after the Cold War," *International Organization* 49, no. 3 (1995): 415–50; Bueno de Mesquita and Lalman, *War and Reason*.
27. M. G. Hermann and C. F. Hermann, "Who Makes Foreign Policy Decisions and How?" *International Studies Quarterly* 33, no. 4 (1989): 361–88; A. Mintz, "The Decision to Attack Iraq," *Journal of Conflict Resolution* 37, no. 4 (1993): 595–618; B. R. Farnham, *Roosevelt and the Munich Crisis* (Princeton, N.J.: Princeton University Press, 1997).
28. P. Hedstrom and R. Swedberg, eds., *Social Mechanisms* (Cambridge: Cambridge University Press, 1998).
29. C. W. Kegley Jr., "Decision Regimes and the Comparative Study of Foreign Policy," in *New Directions in the Study of Foreign Policy*, ed. C. F. Hermann, C. W. Kegley Jr., and J. N. Rosenau (Boston: Allen and Unwin, 1987): 247–68; M. J. Shapiro, G. M. Bonham, and D. Heradsveit, "A Discursive Practices Approach to Collective Decision Making," *International Studies Quarterly* 32, no. 4 (1988): 397–419; Vertzberger, *The World in Their Minds*.
30. Little, *Varieties of Social Explanation*. The distinction between these types of rational choice models evokes echoes of a much deeper schism over methodological commitments regarding "inside-out" and "outside-in" explanations and interpretations of foreign policy and world politics. See J. D. Singer, "The Level-of-Analysis Problem in International Relations," in *The International System: Theoretical Essays*, ed. K. E. Knorr (Princeton, N.J.: Princeton University Press, 1961), 77–92; K. N. Waltz, *Theory of International Politics* (Reading, Mass.: Addison-Wesley, 1979); C. Elman, "Horses for Courses?" *Security Studies* 6, no. 1 (1996): 7–53; Wendt, "The Agent-Structure Problem in International Relations"; D. Dessler, "What's at Stake in the Agency-Structure Debate," *International Organization* 43, no. 3 (1989): 441–73; W. Carlsnaes, "The Agency-Structure Debate in Foreign Policy Analysis," *International Studies Quarterly* 36, no. 3 (1992): 245–70; R. L. Doty, "Aporia: A Critical Exploration of the Agent-Structure Problematique in International Relations Theory," *European Journal of International Relations* 3, no. 3 (1997): 365–92.
31. For example, A. L. George, D. K. Hall, and W. E. Simons, *Limits of Coercive Diplomacy* (Boston: Little, Brown, 1971); A. L. George and R. Smoke, *Deterrence in American Foreign Policy* (New York: Columbia University Press, 1974); R. N. Lebow and J. G. Stein, "Beyond Deterrence," *Journal of Social Issues* 43, no. 4 (1987): 5–71; R. N. Lebow and J. G. Stein, "Deterrence: The Elusive Dependent Variable," *World Politics* 42, no. 3 (1990): 336–69; P. K. Huth and B. M. Russett, "Testing Deterrence Theory," *World Politics* 42, no. 4 (1990): 466–501; R. J. Leng, *Interstate Crisis Behavior, 1815–1990* (New York: Cambridge University Press, 1993).
32. N. R. Richardson, "Dyadic Case Studies in the Comparative Study of Foreign Policy Behavior," in Hermann, Kegley Jr., and Rosenau, *New*

Directions in the Study of Foreign Policy, 161–77; J. Lepgold and A. C. Lamborn, "Locating Bridges: Connecting Research Agendas on Cognition and Strategic Choice," *International Studies Review* 3, no. 3 (2002): 3–30.

33. For example, R. Powell, *In the Shadow of Power* (Princeton, N.J.: Princeton University Press, 1999); R. L. Schweller, *Deadly Imbalances* (New York: Columbia University Press, 1998); R. O. Keohane, *After Hegemony* (Princeton, N.J.: Princeton University Press, 1984).
34. M. Finnemore and K. Sikkink, "International Norm Dynamics and Political Change," *International Organization* 4, no. 4 (1998): 887–918; Wendt, *Social Theory of International Politics*; Katzenstein, *The Culture of National Security*.
35. J. S. Levy, "Learning and Foreign Policy," *International Organization* 48, no. 2 (1994): 279–312.
36. J. A. Robinson, "Crisis: An Appraisal of Concepts and Theories," in Hermann, *International Crises*, 20–38; C. A. McClelland, "The Beginning, Duration, and Abatement of International Crises," in ibid., 83–108; M. Brecher, J. Wilkenfeld, and S. Moser, *Crises in the Twentieth Century* (New York: Pergamon, 1988).
37. Snyder and Diesing, *Conflict among Nations*; Bueno de Mesquita and Lalman, *War and Reason*; Leng, *Interstate Crisis Behavior, 1815–1990*.
38. Brecher, Wilkenfeld, and Moser (*Crises in the Twentieth Century*) are a partial exception to this generalization. They recognize the possibility of a crisis as a turning point in the transition from war to peace. However, they do not extend this logic and conceptualize it as applying to the escalation of cooperation as well as the de-escalation of conflict.
39. Bueno de Mesquita and Lalman, *War and Reason*.
40. Ibid., 30–35.
41. Attempts to close this gap in varying degrees include R. M. Axelrod, *The Evolution of Cooperation* (New York: Basic Books, 1984); J. S. Goldstein and J. R. Freeman, *Three-Way Street* (Chicago: University of Chicago Press, 1990); G. W. Breslauer and P. E. Tetlock, *Learning in U.S. and Soviet Foreign Policy* (Boulder, Colo.: Westview, 1991); Bueno de Mesquita and Lalman, *War and Reason*; Leng, *Interstate Crisis Behavior, 1815–1990*; Herrmann and Fischerkeller, "Beyond the Enemy Image and Spiral Model"; Lepgold and Lamborn, "Cognitive Processes and Strategic Choice"; R. J. Leng, *Bargaining and Learning in Recurring Crises* (Ann Arbor: University of Michigan Press, 2000); D. A. Larson, *Anatomy of Mistrust* (Ithaca, N.Y.: Cornell University Press, 2000).
42. J. Mercer, "Anarchy and Identity," *International Organization* 49 (1995): 229–52; S. Stryker and A. Statham, "Symbolic Interaction and Role Theory," in *Handbook of Social Psychology*, vol. 1, 3d ed., ed. G. Lindzey and E. Aronson (New York: Random House, 1985), 311–78; Wendt, *Social Theory of International Politics*; Farnham, *Avoiding Losses/Taking Risks*; C. Taber, "POLI: An Expert System Model of U.S. Foreign Policy Belief Systems," *American Political Science Review* 86, no. 4 (1992): 888–904; R. Little and S. Smith, *Belief Systems and International Relations* (New York: Blackwell, 1988); Walker, Schafer, and Young, "Systematic

Procedures for Operational Code Analysis"; Walker, Schafer, and Young, "Presidential Operational Codes and Foreign Policy Conflicts."
43. Holsti, "Foreign Policy Decisions Viewed Cognitively."
44. M. N. Barnett, "Institutions, Roles, and Disorder," *International Studies Quarterly* 37, no. 3 (1993): 271–96; Wendt, *Social Theory of International Politics.*

PUBLIC OPINION AND FOREIGN POLICY ANALYSIS

Where We Were, Are, and Should Strive to Be

Ole R. Holsti

This essay examines perspectives on public opinion and foreign policy, first during the formative years of the International Studies Association and, second, at the beginning of the new millennium. Because of limited space, the essay necessarily focuses on some main currents of theory and research at the expense of drawing subtle distinctions between various perspectives on the subject. The concluding section identifies some areas that should be near or at the top of our research agendas during the coming years.

Where We Were

When the International Studies Association was founded in 1958, the cold war was a dominant fact of international relations. To be sure, Stalin had died in 1953 and the next few years had witnessed the end of wars in Korea and Indochina, the Austrian State Treaty, and the Geneva summit conference, but the Soviet invasion of Hungary, the Berlin "deadline crisis," and the collapse of the Paris summit conference suggested that the period of détente in the mid-1950s was but a brief interlude rather than a major turning point in the cold war.

The dominant view of public opinion during that period can be stated succinctly. Ill-informed, emotion-driven, shortsighted, and self-absorbed publics constitute a major obstacle that threatens to prevent the United States and other Western democracies from playing a constructive role in an increasingly dangerous international system. This dolorous view of U.S. public opinion drew from and melded two quite different intellectual traditions, one European and the second American: classical realist political philosophy dating back to Thucydides, Machiavelli, and de Tocqueville, and the new "science" of public opinion polling that had emerged only during the decade prior to World War II.

The primary contributors to twentieth-century realism as a theory of international politics were Europeans, including British diplomat-historian E. H. Carr and German political theorist Hans J. Morgenthau. Despite some differences among realists, they shared a very jaundiced view of public opinion. Carr reserved some of his most vitriolic words for skewering Woodrow Wilson and other liberal statesmen who had attributed to the general public both the interest and wisdom to serve as an effective constraint on the war-making proclivities of leaders.

> Woodrow Wilson's "plain men throughout the world," the spokesmen of "the common purpose of enlightened mankind," had somehow transformed themselves into a disorderly mob emitting incoherent and unhelpful noises. It seemed undeniable that, in international affairs, public opinion was almost as often wrong-headed as it was impotent. . . . The breakdown of the post-War utopia is too overwhelming to be explained merely in terms of individual action or inaction. Its downfall involves the bankruptcy of the postulates [about public opinion] on which it is based.[1]

Although the intellectual roots of realism were largely European, it also flowered on campuses and elsewhere in postwar America. During the 1950s, diplomat-historian George F. Kennan and syndicated columnist Walter Lippmann, who had written two important books on public opinion during the 1920s, led the chorus of realist analysts who despaired of the ability of democracies to conduct effective foreign policies as long as publics, and their representatives in legislatures, had a significant voice in policy-making.[2] Writing in the middle of the decade, Lippmann was especially somber about the prospects for the democracies.

The unhappy truth is that the prevailing public opinion has been destructively wrong at the critical junctures. The people have impressed a critical veto upon the judgments of informed and responsible officials. . . . Mass opinion has acquired mounting power in this country. It has shown itself to be a dangerous master of decision when the stakes are life and death.[3]

The development of scientific polling was the second primary contributor to the dominant skeptical view of public opinion. Whereas the realist perspective drew heavily on a long European tradition, many of the initial advances in survey research were made by American pollsters such as George Gallup and social scientists in several disciplines. During World War II and the years immediately following that conflict, a good deal of research focused on various facets of a single question: Would the United States play an active role in the postwar world, or would it eschew a leadership role, turning most of its attention and energies inward, as it had done following World War I?

The pioneering students of public opinion on international issues—including but not limited to historian Thomas A. Bailey, sociologist Martin Kriesberg, and political scientists Gabriel A. Almond and James N. Rosenau—largely reinforced the skeptical perspectives of the realists.[4] Their analyses of survey data generated by Gallup and other major polling organizations led them to conclude not only that the American public is indifferent to and very poorly informed about world affairs but also that whatever opinions they have are so poorly rooted in any broader conceptions about international affairs that they are subject to wide, emotion-driven mood swings. According to Almond, "for persons responsible for the making of security policy these *mood* impacts of the mass public have a highly irrational effect. Often public opinion is apathetic when it should be concerned, and panicky when it should be calm."[5]

The proposition that public opinion lacks coherence and structure was reinforced by several pathbreaking studies of voters and the bases of their electoral decisions. In an essay drawing upon these voting studies, Philip Converse found that the political beliefs of the general public lack any "constraint" or underlying ideological consistency that might provide structure or coherence to political thinking and voting.[6] His analyses led him to conclude that mass political beliefs are best described as "non-attitudes."

The worst nightmares of those who feared that the public would force the United States to withdraw into a mindless isolationism did not, however, come to pass. United Nations membership, the Truman Doctrine, the Marshall Plan, NATO membership, and resistance to aggression in Korea, sometimes described as "the revolution in American foreign policy," would appear to have posed a puzzle for those most fearful of a powerful but feckless and isolationist public opinion. One answer seemed to emerge from a study of survey data by William Caspary.[7] He concluded that contrary to Almond and Lippmann, the public has in fact been quite "permissive" toward a wide range of international undertakings, including some—notably the Vietnam War, according to Caspary—that had a rather tenuous relationship to vital national interests.

A larger-scale study by Bernard Cohen, drawing heavily on interviews with foreign policy officials, came to a similar conclusion.[8] Finding the evidence of public constraints on foreign policy decision makers to be less than compelling, Cohen challenged diplomatic historians and foreign policy analysts to demonstrate rather than merely assert that public opinion in fact has any significant impact on policy; he even cast doubts on the conventional wisdom that public opinion establishes "limits" or boundaries beyond which any administration would venture only at its own electoral peril. Moreover, an important study of Congress indicated that the "electoral retribution" hypothesis was more valid for domestic than foreign policy issues; legislators had considerably greater leeway on the latter than the former.[9]

Thus, although the view of the public as apathetic, ill-informed, and incapable of holding coherent views on world affairs had not materially changed by the early 1970s, the more apocalyptic fears expressed by Almond, Lippmann, and other realists had been assuaged by the sense that, in fact, public opinion was at best a residual category in explaining foreign policy. Even analysts with doubts about the realist depiction of the state as a "unitary actor" turned their attention elsewhere within the domestic political arena—for example, legislatures, interest groups, organizational processes, bureaucratic politics, and the like. If the impact of public opinion on foreign policy ranges from little to none and from rarely to never, why devote much attention to it? Thus, public opinion had become something of a backwater in foreign policy analysis.

Where We Are

Just as World War II generated interest in and research about the nature of postwar public opinion, the Vietnam War served as the catalyst for reexamination of the prevailing view of public opinion as *volatile, lacking structure,* and largely *irrelevant* in the conduct of foreign affairs. As the costs of the war increased and the prospects for victory faded, the prescription espoused by Bailey, Almond, Kennan, Lippmann, and countless other realists—unshackle foreign policy decision makers from the dangerous grip of public opinion—came under increasing question. The decision makers responsible for American policy in Vietnam, derisively described by journalist David Halberstam as *The Best and the Brightest,* now seemed somewhat less than Olympian in their vision of the national interest.[10] Ironically, Hans Morgenthau was transformed from the towering theorist of realism to a public figure by his frequent speeches aimed at influencing the public against U.S. policy in Vietnam, and even Walter Lippmann came to see draft card burners as more enlightened on the war than President Johnson.

The Vietnam War also gave rise to a number of new survey projects on American foreign policy that attempted to go beyond some of the questions that had been the staples of existing polling organizations: internationalism versus isolationism, judgments of presidential performance, and levels of support for specific foreign policy undertakings. During the late 1960s the Verba-Stanford project probed deeply into opinions on the Vietnam War;[11] the Chicago Council on Foreign Relations initiated quadrennial surveys on many aspects of American foreign policy in 1974;[12] and two years later the Foreign Policy Leadership Project undertook the first of six surveys on the foreign and domestic policy views of opinion leaders.[13] As a result of these projects, as well as extensive analyses of growing survey archives generated by the Gallup Organization, the National Opinion Research Center, and many others, public opinion analysts have mounted serious challenges to the views that had prevailed three decades ago.

The previously cited study by Caspary was among the first to describe public opinion, at least through 1953, as stable rather than volatile.[14] A fuller and more systematic analysis of public opinion toward the wars in Korea and Vietnam posed another challenge to the thesis of irrational mood swings among the general public. Mueller found that public support for the American war effort in both conflicts eventually declined, but it did so in ways that seemed explicable and rational rather than random and mindless.[15] Increasing public opposition to U.S. participation in both conflicts followed a pattern that matched rising battle deaths, suggesting that the public used an understandable, if simple, rule of thumb to assess American policy.

The most comprehensive challenge to the thesis that public opinion is mindlessly volatile emerged from a series of studies by Benjamin Page and Robert Shapiro.[16] Using a database that included more than six thousand questions that had been posed by major polling organizations over a half century beginning in the mid-1930s, their analyses focused on the 20 percent of those that had been asked at least twice. Page and Shapiro found that public opinion in the aggregate is in fact characterized by a good deal of stability, no less on foreign policy than on domestic issues. Most important, when changes (defined as a difference of 6 or more percent from one survey to the next) took place, they appeared to be "reasonable, events-driven" reactions to the real world, even if the factual information upon which they were based was marginally adequate at best: "In particular, most abrupt foreign policy changes took place in connection with wars, confrontations, or crises in which major changes in the actions of the United States or other nations quite naturally affect preferences about what policies to pursue."[17] Similar conclusions about the importance of external events emerged from a study of the period spanning the Kennedy through the Reagan administrations.[18]

An interesting variant of the "rational public" thesis stipulates that public opinion serves as a counterweight against administration policies. Miroslav Nincic found public support for a conciliatory stance toward the Soviet Union during the hawkish Reagan administration while supporting more assertive policies when the more dovish Jimmy Carter was president.[19] Similar findings emerged from another study.[20] For at least the periods covered by Nincic and Mayer, these results not only challenged the thesis of volatility in public attitudes but turned that proposition on its head because the public was identified as a source of moderation and continuity rather than instability and unpredictability.

Philip Converse's chapter on the lack of coherence and structure in mass belief systems is a widely cited classic; it has also served as the springboard for a plethora of further methodological and empirical studies.[21] That literature is far too vast to summarize here. Although the more recent research has yet to achieve a consensus on all aspects of the question, there does appear to be some convergence on two points of relevance to foreign policy analysis. First, even though the general public is rather poorly informed about the factual aspects of international relations—if any study has seriously challenged that generalization, it has escaped my attention—attitudes about foreign affairs are in fact structured in moderately coherent ways. Indeed, low information and an ambiguous international environment may actually motivate rather than preclude having some attitude structure. For example, the concept of "cognitive miser" suggests that individuals may use a limited number of beliefs to make sense of a wide range of facts and events. Second, there is growing evidence that the single internationalist-to-isolationist dimension that dominated much of the early research is inadequate to categorize beliefs about international affairs.

An analysis of the first Chicago Council on Foreign Relations (CCFR) survey of elites and the general public used factor analysis and other statistical techniques to identify three distinct perspectives on international affairs: conservative internationalism, liberal internationalism, and noninternationalism.[22] An important further step on ways of describing foreign policy attitudes emerged from Eugene Wittkopf's secondary analyses of the four CCFR surveys conducted between 1974 and 1986.[23] His results identified "two faces of internationalism": militant internationalism (MI) and cooperative internationalism (CI). Dichotomizing and crossing these dimensions yields four foreign policy belief systems: *hard-liners* (support MI, oppose CI), *accommodationists* (oppose MI, support CI), *internationalists* (support both MI and CI), and *isolationists* (oppose both MI and CI). Strong support for the MI/CI scheme has also emerged from studies of opinion leaders, although they used different sampling designs and questions to construct the MI and CI scales.[24]

It is worth noting that the two dimensions of the MI/CI scheme correspond rather closely to the most venerable theoretical perspectives on international relations. Realist concepts such as security dilemma, relative capabilities, and a zero-sum view of conflict are also basic to the MI dimension. There are comparable similarities between the CI dimension and liberalism, including a view of security that encompasses more than geopolitical and military balances; the potential for institution building to reduce uncertainty and fears of perfidy, as well as information costs; the possibilities of improved international education and communications to ameliorate fears; and the positive-sum outcomes that may result from such activities as trade.

A further distinction between unilateralism and multilateralism as an important aspect of public opinion has also emerged from several studies.[25] Because many of the debates about post–cold war activities, including military interventions abroad, have revolved around the relative merits of "going it alone" versus "burden sharing," there is reason to believe that this distinction will become more rather than less important in describing public opinion.

A somewhat different way of describing the structure of attitudes on foreign affairs emerged from a study by Jon Hurwitz and Mark Peffley.[26] They proposed and tested a structure of foreign policy beliefs in which specific policy preferences are derived from broader postures—for example, militarism or isolationism—which are, in turn, constrained by a set of core values relating to international affairs. Thus, a few rather general beliefs, such as a "tough-minded" approach to international affairs, appear to have served as organizing devices that enable subjects to respond in a reasonably coherent manner to a wide range of issues, including defense spending, nuclear arms policy, policies toward the Soviet Union, and international trade.

Clearly, the research of the past several decades has yet to produce a consensus on many important questions about the coherence and substance of foreign policy beliefs among the general public. Nor does any of it suggest that the ill-informed publics of yesteryear have been transformed into knowledgeable and sophisticated analysts of international affairs. Nevertheless, it is also clear that the earlier consensus depicting public attitudes as lacking any real coherence has been challenged from many quarters, only a few of which have been touched upon here. A good deal of credible evidence suggests that members of the general public use various rules of thumb, not necessarily confined to the traditional internationalist or isolationist blueprints, for organizing their political thinking. These rules of thumb may often appear to be somewhat simplistic, but it should be borne in mind that even top-ranking decision makers have been known to use such simplifying adages as "the lessons of Munich," "the domino theory," and "the lessons of Vietnam" to help them diagnose and cope with the complexities of international affairs.

Among the most important questions about public opinion are these: To what extent, on what kinds of issues, under what circumstances, and in what types of political systems, if any, does it have an impact on public policy? If it does have an influence, what are the means by which public attitudes become known so that they can have an impact on decision makers? As these are also the most difficult questions to answer, it is not surprising that we have many analyses describing the state of, or trends in, public opinion and far fewer compelling studies tracing out its impact on the foreign policy process.

There is quite a bit of anecdotal evidence that many presidents have followed Theodore Roosevelt in thinking of the White House as a bully pulpit from which to convey diagnoses of world affairs and to drum up support for preferred policies. Despite the advantages that presidents enjoy in this respect, they have also differed in the degree of success that they have enjoyed. Although President Reagan, "the great communicator," was unable to build a groundswell of public approval for his efforts to intervene in the civil wars in El Salvador and Nicaragua, his less verbally gifted successor, George Bush, generally gained strong support for his foreign policies. At least one noted public opinion analyst has asserted that the Vietnam War marked a major watershed because the public is no longer willing to accept the proposition that "the president knows best,"[27] and some subsequent studies have provided supporting evidence for that proposition.[28]

The more difficult question concerns public influence on policymakers. Again there is anecdotal evidence of presidential concern about the state of public opinion. Franklin Roosevelt seemed fascinated by the possibilities of polling the public, and he secretly commissioned Hadley Cantril to provide him with regular reports on such questions as likely public attitudes toward America's appropriate international role after the guns of World War II had stopped firing. In contrast, his successor, Harry S. Truman, publicly expressed disdain for pollsters and the value of evidence that they might provide—including the confident prognoses by Gallup and other pollsters that Thomas Dewey would win the 1948 presidential election by a landslide. In more recent administrations, polling has become institutionalized. For example, the Reagan White House privately commissioned at least 184 surveys, an average of almost two per month.[29]

We have relatively few "insider" accounts from opinion analysts who served policymakers, but those that exist suggest that the general public is not viewed merely as an essentially shapeless lump that can readily be molded by public relations activities or a compliant media to meet the immediate policy needs.[30] According to Beal and Hinckley, "opinion polls are at the core of presidential decision making."[31] There is also evidence, however, that recent presidents have become less responsive to public preferences; polling data have often been used to develop strategies for leading or manipulating the public rather than as guidance on policy decisions.[32]

In addition to anecdotal evidence, three methodologies have been employed to assess the public-policymaker relationship: quantitative-correlational analyses, intensive case studies, and interview-based research. Although the evidence has not given rise to a consensus, a significant part of it has raised questions about the universal validity of the proposition that foreign policy–makers and processes are impervious to public influences.

The conventional wisdom that voting behavior is grounded in domestic rather than international issues—in Bill Clinton's phrase, "It's the economy, stupid"—was challenged by Aldrich, Sullivan, and Borgida in a systematic study of presidential campaigns between 1952 and 1984.[33] Their analyses revealed that in five of the nine elections (1952, 1964, 1972, 1980, and 1984) foreign policy issues had "large effects." Other studies of voting behavior have shown the importance of retrospective evaluations of performance, including the conduct of foreign policy, on voter choice, especially when the incumbent is a candidate.[34]

Two additional quantitative studies have measured the congruence between changes in public opinion and a broad range of policies over extended periods. The first, an analysis of public opinion and policy outcomes spanning the years 1960 to 1974, revealed that in almost two-thirds of 222 cases, policy outcomes corresponded to public preferences. The consistency was especially high (92 percent) on foreign policy issues.[35] The second study of the opinion-policy relationship covered an even longer period (1935 to 1979), which included 357 significant changes of public preferences.[36] The results also revealed a high degree of congruence between opinions and foreign policy (62 percent); the figure for domestic policy was only slightly higher (70 percent).

These findings are impressive, but even the best correlational study cannot wholly dispel all doubts about causality; the possibilities for erroneous interpretation of even impressive correlation coefficients are well known, especially when there is reason to wonder whether a simple, one-directional model of influence is sufficient to capture the complexities of the foreign policy–making process. One of the authors of these studies[37] has acknowledged that "not even time-series analysis can provide a magic bullet that will kill all the demons of causal ambiguity." The problem of causality, as V. O. Key pointed out, is this: "If one is to know what opinions government heed, one must know the inner thoughts of presidents, congressmen, and other officials."[38] For this reason, intensive case studies using archival research, elite interviews, or a combination of both are invaluable to supplement quantitative-correlational research.

Not surprisingly, existing case studies have yielded somewhat mixed results. For example, Doris Graber found in an analysis of four cases during the Adams, Jefferson, Madison, and Monroe administrations that in each instance public opinion was "an important factor in decision making, but by no means the most important single factor."[39] In contrast, in a study encompassing the quarter century of the McKinley, Roosevelt, Taft, and Wilson presidencies, Hildebrand revealed that if public opinion even entered into executive decisions, it was only after policy decisions had already been made.[40]

Some recent case studies suggest that the impact of public opinion varies according to the type of issue, the stage in the policy process, the decision context, and policymakers' beliefs about and sensitivity to public opinion. Thomas Graham analyzed the impact of public opinion on four arms control issues—international control of atomic energy, the Limited Test Ban Treaty, the SALT I/ABM Treaties, and SALT II—spanning seven American administrations from presidents Truman through Carter.[41] He distinguished between four stages in the policy process: getting the issue on the agenda, negotiations, ratification, and implementation. Although public opinion had an important impact in all four cases, it also varied according to the stage in the policy process. Public opinion had a direct impact on getting the issue on the agenda and on ratification of the agreements, but only an indirect effect on negotiations and implementation.

Archival research on four defense and foreign policy episodes during the Eisenhower administration confirmed that distinctions between stages in the policy process as well as the decision context are important for understanding the ways in which public opinion may affect the policy process.[42] Graham's cases included four decision contexts: *crisis* (the 1954 Formosa Straits confrontation with China), *reflexive* (the French defeat at Dien Bien Phu), *innovative* (response to the Soviet launch of the Sputnik space satellite), and *deliberative* (the "New Look" defense policy). The impact of public opinion varied across the four cases.

Lawrence Jacobs and Robert Shapiro have undertaken the most ambitious analysis of the impact of public opinion in their study of the relationship between private presidential polling and presidential behavior in administrations since that of John Kennedy.[43] In addition to archival research, they have interviewed top White House personnel as well as those engaged in conducting the surveys. By combining analyses of survey data, archival evidence, and interviews, their research design represents a major step toward providing a more detailed and nuanced answer to the questions posed at the beginning of this section.

This description of the current state of theory and research on public opinion and foreign policy is necessarily cursory rather than comprehensive; it blurs rather than highlights some distinctions and controversies, and it largely overlooks methodological issues except at the very broadest level. It has attempted to convey the sea change in thinking about public opinion and foreign policy during the period since the founding of the International Studies Association. While there appears to have been considerable theoretical, empirical, and methodological progress during that time, there are still major steps that should appear on the agenda for future research.

Where We Should Strive to Be

According to one hypothesis, the end of the cold war, the declining salience of foreign policy for much of the public, and the complexity of post–cold war issues will combine to reduce the impact of public opinion, thereby giving policymakers greater latitude in making decisions.[44] An alternative line of reasoning suggests that the influence of public opinion in the conduct of foreign affairs may well increase during the post–cold war era. The case against public opinion is that effective diplomacy requires at least three features, none of which is enhanced by more active public participation: secrecy, speed, and flexibility; these are also most likely to be essential in times of war, crisis, and confrontation. Although security concerns remain vital, the top tiers of post–cold war foreign policy agendas are also likely to include issues on which publics and their representatives are likely to hold strong views and regarding which the thesis that "the president [or prime minister, chancellor, etc.] knows best" may seem less compelling than during World War II or the cold war. Many of these "intermestic" issues also cut across conventional international-domestic boundaries. They include trade, refugees and immigration, the international environment, and intrastate religious, ethnic, racial, and nationalist conflicts in which one or more parties may call for assistance or intervention from abroad. Both of these hypotheses may be valid, depending on the administration, issue, and circumstances, but whatever the case, it makes sense to consider ways of improving our understanding of public opinion and its relationship to foreign policy.

As noted earlier, the *opinion-policy link* is less well-developed than other areas of inquiry. Although there have been important studies of this type in recent years, some questions that merit further consideration include these:

Upon what indicators of public sentiments, if any, did leaders rely?

Did leaders use information about public preferences primarily in order to align policies with them, or in order to develop strategies for influencing or manipulating the public?

Did policymakers rule out certain courses of action because of a belief that a lack of public support would reduce or eliminate the prospects of success?

Did policymakers decide upon certain foreign policy undertakings, even if the chances of success were deemed very slight, because of a belief that the public demanded some action?

How, if at all, did expectations of future public reactions affect the appraisal of policy options by policymakers?

How, if at all, did calculations about the electoral or other domestic political consequences of certain decisions restrain or motivate policymakers?

Were the timing of foreign policy decisions and the choice of means to carry out an undertaking influenced by beliefs about what the public would or would not accept, would or would not demand?

How accurately did policymakers gauge public sentiments? In cases of policymakers "misreading the public,"[45] what were the reasons for the miscalculation? Did motivated or unmotivated biases enter into misreading public preferences?

Cross-National Studies

Cross-national studies constitute a second major area for further research. The role of public opinion in foreign policy is often a central issue in the flourishing contemporary debates about the "democratic peace" theory—the proposition that democracies do not go to war against each other. Even among democracies, the nature and impact of public opinion may vary across countries and political systems. Moreover, the expansion of democracies during the past decade has created opportunities for research on a much wider range of issues than could have been contemplated during the cold war in Eastern Europe, the republics of the former Soviet Union, Latin America, and elsewhere. Such opportunities are even becoming available in China.

Standard Questions

Standard questions are also a high priority. There is ample evidence that the wording of questions and the context in which they are posed can significantly affect responses. Even minor variations in questions about a single issue, asked at the same time, can yield quite different responses. Consequently, drawing inferences from responses to a single question can be hazardous, but one can do so with greater confidence if identically worded questions appear regularly in surveys conducted over an extended period. Unfortunately, relatively few questions about foreign and defense policy have been posed with the same frequency or regularity as, for example, those asking about presidential performance in the United States. Even a question about the merits of an active U.S. role in the world, first used in several surveys during World War II, was asked only once during the 1960s. One of the many important contributions of the seven Chicago Council on Foreign Relations surveys since 1974 is that there has been a carryover of some key questions from survey to survey, providing opportunities for assessing trends. Richard Sobel has proposed a list of thirty questions for polling on foreign policy crises, but progress toward developing a list of standard questions has lagged.[46] Cross-national research will present some special challenges in this respect because it cannot be assumed that simple word-for-word translations of questions from one language and culture will necessarily convey the same meaning elsewhere.

Conclusion

Has research on public opinion and foreign policy fulfilled the hopes of the late 1950s? The question does not seem germane because at that time the subject did not seem especially interesting and thus hopes were not very high. The fears that a misguided public would prevent wiser leaders from pursuing policies needed to protect and promote vital national interests, while also avoiding a nuclear war, had begun to recede, at least in part because of the sense that public opinion was not all that important in coping with the crucial issues of the day. The next four decades witnessed significant challenges to the previous views, although a new consensus has yet to be achieved on many significant questions about the nature, structure, and impact of public opinion. No doubt the lack of consensus is one reason that the subject remains a vibrant area of inquiry.

Today the general public is less frequently described in the frightening terms that dominated thinking during the 1950s. One of the classic studies of recent years is entitled "The Rational Public," and another has coined the term "low information rationality" to describe the manner by which the public deals with a complex world.[47] Moreover, opportunities for gaining information about the world have never been greater. Cheap international travel, dramatically rising graduation rates from secondary schools and universities, and new information technologies that even dedicated science fiction fans of the 1950s could hardly have imagined have contributed to these opportunities. Indeed, a distinguished political scientist, a former president of the International Studies Association, and onetime skeptic about the role that the public could play in foreign affairs, has written that the electronic information revolution has provided general publics with the information and analytical skills necessary to become vital players in global affairs.[48]

Nevertheless, there are also reasons for disquiet. The possibility that increasing survey data will merely be used by leaders to manipulate the public has already been mentioned. A closely related concern is the persistent poverty of international knowledge. Many studies reveal that levels of information about foreign affairs among publics in the industrial world remain abysmally low, most notably in the United States. One disturbing example illustrates the point. Gallup surveys commissioned by the National Geographic Society in 1948 and 1988 revealed that basic geographic knowledge—for example, identification of the largest country in the world, or location of Great Britain on a map—has actually declined during the forty-year interval. Considering that geography has virtually dropped out of school curricula and that many universities no longer house geography departments, perhaps those troubling results are not especially surprising. Only 10 percent of Americans could identify any of the nations involved in post–cold war expansion of NATO, and no doubt even some of those would not have been able to locate Hungary, Poland, and the Czech Republic on a map. In those circumstances, could there have been a principled debate in the United States on adding new members to NATO?

There are many reasons to applaud the more benign and realistic view of the general public that has emerged from several decades of research, but it is hardly a time for complacency, especially among educators. At what point does "low information rationality" become "no information irrationality"? Perhaps preventing the former from becoming the latter should be the most important item on our agenda concerning public opinion and foreign policy.

Notes

1. Edward Hallett Carr, *The Twenty Years' Crisis, 1919–1939: An Introduction to the Study of International Relations* (London: Macmillan, 1939), 50–51, 53.
2. George F. Kennan, *American Diplomacy, 1900–1950* (New York: Mentor Books, 1951); Walter Lippmann, *Essays in the Public Philosophy* (Boston: Little, Brown, 1955).
3. Lippmann, *Essays in the Public Philosophy*, 20.
4. Thomas A. Bailey, *The Man in the Street: The Impact of American Public Opinion on Foreign Policy* (New York: Macmillan, 1948); Martin Kriesberg, "Dark Areas of Ignorance," in *Public Opinion and Foreign Policy*, ed. Lester Markel (New York: Harper, 1949); Gabriel A. Almond, *The American People and Foreign Policy* (New York: Harcourt, Brace, 1950; reprint, with a new introduction, New York: Praeger, 1960); James N. Rosenau, *Public Opinion and Foreign Policy: An Operational Formulation* (New York: Random House, 1961).
5. Gabriel Almond, "Public Opinion and National Security," *Public Opinion Quarterly* 21, no. 2 (1956): 371–78.
6. Philip Converse, "The Nature of Belief Systems in Mass Publics," in *Ideology and Discontent*, ed. David E. Apter (New York: Free Press, 1964), 206–61.
7. William R. Caspary, "The 'Mood Theory': A Study of Public Opinion and Foreign Policy," *American Political Science Review* 64, no. 2 (1970): 536–47.
8. Bernard C. Cohen, *The Public's Impact on Foreign Policy* (Boston: Little, Brown, 1973).
9. Warren E. Miller and Donald E. Stokes, "Constituency Influence in Congress," *American Political Science Review* 57, no. 1 (1963): 45–56.
10. David Halberstam, *The Best and the Brightest* (New York: Random House, 1972).
11. Sidney Verba et al., "Public Opinion and the War in Vietnam," *American Political Science Review* 61, no. 2 (1967): 317–33.

12. John E. Rielly, ed., *American Public Opinion and U.S. Foreign Policy, 1975* (Chicago: Chicago Council on Foreign Relations, 1975). Also similarly titled monographs in 1979, 1983, 1987, 1991, 1995, and 1999. A report on the 2002 CCFR survey will be available in late 2002.
13. Ole R. Holsti and James N. Rosenau, *American Leadership in World Affairs: Vietnam and the Breakdown of Consensus* (London: Allen and Unwin, 1984).
14. Caspary, "The 'Mood Theory.'"
15. John E. Mueller, *War, Presidents, and Public Opinion* (New York: Wiley, 1973).
16. Benjamin I. Page and Robert Y. Shapiro, *The Rational Public: Fifty Years of Trends in Americans' Policy Preferences* (Chicago: University of Chicago Press, 1992); Benjamin I. Page and Robert Y. Shapiro, "Changes in Americans' Policy Preferences, 1935–1979," *Public Opinion Quarterly* 46 (1982): 24–42.
17. Page and Shapiro, "Changes in Americans' Policy Preferences, 1935–1979," 34.
18. William G. Mayer, *The Changing American Mind: How and Why American Public Opinion Changed between 1960 and 1988* (Ann Arbor: University of Michigan Press, 1992).
19. Miroslav Nincic, "The United States, the Soviet Union, and the Politics of Opposites," *World Politics* 40, no. 4 (1988): 452–75; Miroslav Nincic, *Democracy and Foreign Policy: The Fallacy of Political Realism* (New York: Columbia University Press, 1992).
20. Mayer, *The Changing American Mind.*
21. Converse, "The Nature of Belief Systems in Mass Publics."
22. Michael Mandelbaum and William Schneider, "The New Internationalism," in *Eagle Entangled: U.S. Foreign Policy in a Complex World,* ed. Kenneth A. Oye, Robert J. Lieber, and Donald Rothchild (New York: Longman, 1979), 40–63.
23. Eugene R. Wittkopf, *Faces of Internationalism: Public Opinion and American Foreign Policy* (Durham, N.C.: Duke University Press, 1990).
24. Ole R. Holsti and James N. Rosenau, "The Structure of Foreign Policy Attitudes among American Leaders," *Journal of Politics* 52 (February 1990): 94–125; Ole R. Holsti and James N. Rosenau, "The Structure of Foreign Policy Beliefs among American Opinion Leaders—After the Cold War," *Millennium* 22 (summer 1993): 235–78.
25. Eugene R. Wittkopf, "On the Foreign Policy Beliefs of the American People: A Critique and Some Evidence," *International Studies Quarterly* 30, no. 4 (1986): 425–45; Ronald H. Hinckley, "Public Attitudes toward Key Foreign Policy Events," *Journal of Conflict Resolution* 32, no. 2 (1988): 295–318; William O. Chittick, Keith R. Billingsley, and Rick Travis, "A Three-Dimensional Model of American Foreign Policy Beliefs," *International Studies Quarterly* 39, no. 3 (1995): 313–31; Bruce M. Russett, *Controlling the Sword: The Democratic Governance of National Security* (Cambridge: Harvard University Press, 1990).
26. Jon Hurwitz and Mark Peffley, "How Are Foreign Policy Attitudes Structured? A Hierarchical Model," *American Political Science Review* 81, no. 4 (1987): 1099–1120.

27. Daniel Yankelovich, "Farewell to 'the President Knows Best,'" *Foreign Affairs* 57, special issue (1979): 670–93.
28. Michael Clough, "Grass-Roots Policymaking," *Foreign Affairs* 73 (January–February 1994): 2–7; Maxine Isaacs, "The Independent American Public: The Relationship between Elite and Mass Opinions on American Foreign Policy in the Mass Communication Age" (Ph.D. diss., School of Public Affairs, University of Maryland, 1994).
29. Robert Y. Shapiro and Lawrence R. Jacobs, "Public Opinion, Foreign Policy, and Democracy" (paper prepared for the Conference on Polls, Policy, and the Future of American Democracy, Northwestern University, Evanston, Ill., May 13, 2000).
30. Hadley Cantril, *The Human Dimension: Experiences in Policy Research* (New Brunswick, N.J.: Rutgers University Press, 1967); Ronald H. Hinckley, *People, Polls, and Policy-Makers: American Public Opinion and National Security* (New York: Lexington Books, 1992).
31. Richard S. Beal and Ronald H. Hinckley, "Presidential Decision Making and Opinion Polls," *Annals of the American Academy of Social and Political Science* 472 (March 1984): 72–84.
32. Lawrence R. Jacobs and Robert Y. Shapiro, *Politicians Don't Pander: Political Manipulation and the Loss of Democratic Responsiveness* (Chicago: University of Chicago Press, 1999); Shapiro and Jacobs, "Public Opinion, Foreign Policy, and Democracy."
33. John H. Aldrich, John L. Sullivan, and Eugene Borgida, "Foreign Affairs and Issue Voting: Do Presidential Candidates 'Waltz before a Blind Audience'?" *American Political Science Review* 83, no. 1 (1989): 123–41.
34. Morris P. Fiorina, *Retrospective Voting in American National Elections* (New Haven, Conn.: Yale University Press, 1981); Paul Abramson, John H. Aldrich, and John Rohde, *Change and Continuity in the 1988 Election* (Washington, D.C.: Congressional Quarterly Press, 1990).
35. Alan D. Monroe, "Consistency between Public Preferences and National Policy Decisions," *American Politics Quarterly* 7, no. 1 (1979): 3–19.
36. Benjamin I. Page and Robert Y. Shapiro, "Effects of Public Opinion on Policy," *American Political Science Review* 77, no. 1 (1983): 175–90.
37. Benjamin I. Page, "Democratic Responsiveness? Untangling the Links between Public Opinion and Policy," *PS: Political Science and Politics* 27 (March 1994): 17–21.
38. V. O. Key Jr., *Public Opinion and American Democracy* (New York: Knopf, 1961), 14.
39. Doris A. Graber, *Public Opinion, the President, and Foreign Policy: Four Case Studies from the Formative Years* (New York: Holt, Rinehart and Winston, 1968), 318.
40. Robert C. Hildebrand, *Power and the People: Executive Management of Public Opinion in Foreign Affairs, 1897–1921* (Chapel Hill: University of North Carolina Press, 1981).
41. Thomas W. Graham, "The Politics of Failure: Strategic Nuclear Arms Control, Public Opinion, and Domestic Politics in the United States—1945–1980" (Ph.D. diss., Political Science Department, MIT, 1989).

42. Douglas C. Foyle, *Counting the Public In* (New York: Columbia University Press, 1999).
43. Lawrence R. Jacobs and Robert Y. Shapiro, "The Rise of Presidential Polling: The Nixon White House in Historical Perspective," *Public Opinion Quarterly* 59, no. 2 (1995): 163–95; Jacobs and Shapiro, *Politicians Don't Pander.*
44. Shapiro and Jacobs, "Public Opinion, Foreign Policy, and Democracy"; James M. Lindsay, "The New Apathy: How an Uninterested Public Is Reshaping Foreign Policy," *Foreign Affairs* 79 (September–October 2000): 2–8.
45. Steven Kull and I. M. Destler, *Misreading the Public: The Myth of a New Isolationism* (Washington, D.C.: Brookings Institution Press, 1999).
46. Richard Sobel, "Polling in Foreign Policy Crises: Ascertaining the Questions to Ask" (unpublished manuscript, Princeton University, 1995).
47. Page and Shapiro, *The Rational Public;* Samuel L. Popkin, *The Reasoning Voter* (Chicago: University of Chicago Press, 1991).
48. James N. Rosenau, *Turbulence in World Politics: A Theory of Change and Continuity* (Princeton, N.J.: Princeton University Press, 1990).

SIMULATION AND EXPERIMENTATION IN FOREIGN POLICY ANALYSIS

Some Personal Observations on Problems and Prospects

Jonathan Wilkenfeld

While many in the field of foreign policy analysis associate me most closely with the systematic study of foreign policy behavior in general, and conflict and crisis decision making in particular—most notably, the International Crisis Behavior (ICB) Project[1]—I have chosen to highlight a somewhat different direction that my recent research has taken. During the past two decades, almost as a sideline, I have been heavily involved in the conceptualization and development of simulation approaches to the teaching of international politics and foreign policy. The network-based, distributed foreign policy simulations offered by the International Communications and Negotia-

---

While I take full responsibility for the contents of this paper, a number of people have made very significant contributions to my thinking on these issues over the past several years. The most important are my collaborators in simulation and experimental environments. Key ICONS collaborators have been Betsy Kielman, Brigid Starkey, Mark Boyer, Joyce Kaufman, Doreen Bass, Patty Landis, Judith Torney-Purta, Harold Guetzkow, Beth Blake, David Crookall, Robert Noel, Barry Hughes, Leopoldo Schapira, and Richard Brecht. In the experimental phase of my work, I owe much to Sarit Kraus, Tara Santmire, Joe Oppenheimer, Kim Holley, J. Joseph Hewitt, Michael Harris, Toni Santmire, Phillip Schrodt, Charles Taber, Alex Mintz, Nehemia Geva, Michael Lebrun, and Kristian Gleditsch. The Conflict and Negotiation (CAN) Research Group at the University of Maryland—David Andersen, Victor Assal, Christopher Frain, Amy Pate, David Quinn, Tara Santmire, and Kathleen Young—has provided able assistance in both empirical and experimental data collection and analysis. Over the years, this work has been generously supported by the National Science Foundation (currently under grants SES9905575 and IIS9820657), the U.S. Institute of Peace (under grants SG-35-95 and SG-52-00), the U.S. Department of Education (Title VI and FIPSE), IBM, and Sun Microsystems.

tions Simulations (ICONS) Project, centered at the University of Maryland, now reach about sixty university classrooms each academic year, and ICONS exercises have been run in more than thirty-five countries since their inception in 1982. More recently, ICONS has worked with high school teachers and curriculum experts, and the high school version is employed in about 150 high schools each year. In addition to the University of Maryland, there are now ICONS centers at the University of Connecticut and Whittier College in California, as well as in Israel.[2]

But even that is not what I really want to focus on here. My work in foreign policy analysis during the last decade has increasingly involved the use of experimental approaches to the study of foreign policy decision making. It is my adventures, and in many cases misadventures, in this new realm that I want to focus on in this paper. I begin with some background on experimentation in political science in general, and in international politics in particular. This will be followed by the story of how I got involved with this approach in the first place. Finally, in order to examine what experimentation can and cannot do for us, I present a research design and some preliminary data in which both cross-national and experimental approaches are used to extend our knowledge on one particular phenomenon in international politics, the process of mediation in international disputes.

Experimental Design in Political Science

While experimentation remains outside the mainstream of international relations, and of political science in general, efforts have been made in recent years to bolster the acceptance of experiment-based research designs within the field. Kinder and Palfrey offer a treatise on why experimentation should be integrated into political science as a way to "supplement, not replace, traditional empirical methods."[3] What is it that experiments offer political scientists? Experimentation allows researchers to isolate a crucial independent variable by providing the means to control extraneous factors, and it allows analysts to look at the effect of that variable by comparing the results of those who were exposed to the variable with the results of an unexposed control group.[4] Experimentation provides researchers a precise view of a certain phenomenon, a certain relationship. It is this quality that makes experimentation valuable: it is the most reliable means of examining and understanding the nature of a causal relationship, of demonstrating the internal validity of a theory in political science.[5]

Experiment-based research provides insights into relationships that are difficult, if not impossible, to observe in any other way. Snyder argues that the insights and depth of understanding that experimentation can uniquely provide make it an important heuristic tool in the "discovery phase of science-building."[6] Because the results of experiments can enlighten analysts' understanding of *how* and *why* a relationship exists and functions, this type of research allows for the refinement of general or preliminary theories in a way distinct from examinations of large-N (quantitative) or small-N (qualitative) empirical data.[7] Without the empirical data that generate initial hypotheses and theories, there is no starting point for experimental research. But experimental research allows for the continued evolution and the "better articulation" of existing theories.[8]

Some political scientists have come to appreciate the potential benefits of experimentation and have applied it to their research. Bositis records that while only nine articles using experimental research designs appeared in major political science journals between 1924 and 1950, 104 such articles appeared from 1980 to 1989 alone.[9] McGraw, too, sees experimentation as a methodology "on the rise" in political science, especially in the areas of public opinion, collective action, public policy, and—relevant to our study—decision making.[10]

Among a few scholars, though, efforts have long been made to incorporate experiments into the core realm of international relations research. In 1970, the International Political Science Association convened a special roundtable conference to examine experimentation and event simulation as a means to build and test international relations theories. The conference generated a series of essays documenting experiment-based efforts to refine and enhance theories of international relations.[11] This conference was, itself, a follow-up to a vast experiment launched by Guetzkow in the late 1950s and early 1960s.[12] His Inter-Nation Simulation set a precedent—all too often forgotten by scholars of international relations—for how experimentation can be used to inform and improve international relations. For instance, the project generated results that illuminated understandings of how perceptions affect interstate relations. Given the technological advances made since Guetzkow's undertaking, we can only expect an increase in what we are able to learn from international relations–focused experiments today.

The Conflict and Negotiation (CAN) Research Group

About twelve years ago, I began a lengthy collaboration with Sarit Kraus, a computer scientist specializing in distributed artificial intelligence. (I had barely heard of artificial intelligence in general at that point.) Kraus had been working on developing an automated agent capable of participating with other automated agents or with human players in the Diplomacy board game. With a strong interest in modeling the negotiation process from a bargaining and game-theoretic perspective, she was directed to me by her associates in the University of Maryland Institute for Advanced Computer Studies, some of whom had heard of my work on ICONS. It was apparent from the beginning that although we had very different training, we had a joint interest in better understanding how humans (in my case) and machines (in Kraus's case) negotiated in difficult (crisis) situations in order to reach mutually-beneficial agreements. Whereas my objective was to understand the conditions under which negotiations ended without the resort to violence, Kraus's objective was to understand how intelligent agents (machines) could be endowed with negotiation skills such that they could share scarce resources (tools like printers, Internet access, etc.) or cooperate to perform tasks. In both cases, negotiations are employed in situations where time is critical to some or all parties, resources are scarce, and tasks may require cooperative behavior. We wanted to minimize the amount of time spent on negotiation and maximize the likelihood of reaching mutually-beneficial outcomes.[13]

Sustained by significant support since 1992 from the National Science Foundation, the U.S. Institute of Peace, and Sun Microsystems, and with a research team consisting of professors and graduate students at the University of Maryland, the Hebrew University, and Bar Ilan University, we have produced a significant body of work on the dual fronts of automated agents and international negotiation. Our areas of expertise include negotiation and decision theory in social science in general and political science in particular, cognitive schema theory within psychology, and intelligent systems and distributed artificial intelligence in computer science. Our experimental work has been characterized by several features that tend to set it apart from other experimental work in foreign policy analysis.[14] First, we have focused exclusively on behavior in crisis, with a particular emphasis on the effects shortness of time and a high level of threat have on crisis dynamics and outcomes.[15] Second, our subjects had access to an elaborate decision support system (DSS), which, when properly used, could provide information on the utilities associated with various outcomes and hence enhance the subjects' ability to maximize expected utility, even under conditions of incomplete information.[16] Third, all communications among the participants have taken place in controlled network environments, allowing for detailed analysis of the types of tools they consulted as well as the content and form of their interactions during the negotiation. Together, we hoped these features would help provide a rich environment in which experiments could be run and their results assessed.[17]

Summary of CAN Research Work to Date

At the core of our experimental work to this point is the development of a strategic model of negotiation with an accompanying DSS based on three different scenarios: a hostage crisis (involving an Indian plane hijacked by Sikh separatists and forced to land in Pakistan),[18] a fishing dispute (based on the Canada-Spain dispute of 1995),[19] and the Ecuador-Peru Border Dispute of 1981 (see following).[20] Five broad sets of research issues were addressed in our previous work.

The Impact of the Use of DSSs on the Utility-Maximizing Behavior of Crisis Negotiators

Experimental research led to the following conclusions: (a) average utility scores were higher for DSS users than for nonusers, and agreements were reached more frequently by DSS than by non-DSS users; and (b) in simulations that ended in agreement as opposed to opting out, the player most closely associated with the mediator role tended to send approximately the same number of messages to the other two players.[21]

The Impact of the Dynamics of Crisis Negotiations on Their Outcomes

Experimental research led to the following conclusions: (a) DSS-supported negotiators are most strongly motivated by utility maximization, while non–DSS-supported negotiators tended to be motivated by a desire to uphold principles; (b) DSS-supported negotiators are more successful than non–DSS-supported negotiators in achieving high utility outcomes; (c) the existence of a DSS-supported negotiator among the adversaries is likely to result in higher overall utility scores than when no such negotiator is present; and (d) crisis negotiations in which one of the parties has access to a DSS are more likely to end in agreement than are non–DSS-supported negotiations.[22]

The Relationship between the Level of Cognitive Complexity of Crisis Negotiators and the Outcomes of Crisis Negotiations

Experimental research led to the following conclusions: (a) negotiators at higher levels of cognitive complexity developed greater proficiency with the DSS; and (b) negotiators did not show an overall relationship between cognitive complexity and crisis outcome, either in terms of the achievement of higher utility scores or in terms of a greater tendency to reach agreement.[23]

The Impact of the Mix of Cognitive Complexity Levels among Crisis Negotiators on the Outcome of the Crisis

Experimental research led to the following conclusions: (a) the more homogeneous the cognitive levels of the negotiators, the more likely they were to reach agreement; and (b) the more homogeneous the cognitive levels of the negotiators, the more quickly they reached agreement.[24]

The Impact of the Mix of Cognitive Complexity Levels among Crisis Negotiators and Crisis Mediators on the Outcome of the Crisis

A set of experiments involving a two-party fishing dispute led to the following preliminary finding: agreements were reached with greatest frequency when the cognitive complexity level of the mediator was higher than that of the disputants.[25]

Merging Empirical and Experimental Approaches: Searching for More Robust Explanations

Thus far, this paper has focused exclusively on recent contributions made by experimental work to our understanding of international phenomena: utility-maximizing behavior in crisis negotiation, levels of cognitive complexity and the process of negotiation, and most recently, cognitive complexity and receptivity to mediation. While this research has led to better understanding of experimentation, it has taken place with relatively limited reference to larger research questions in international politics and foreign policy. The main point of this paper is to demonstrate how a merged research design can take advantage of data derived from both large-N empirical studies and studies based on experimental methods to extend the range of questions we can ask (and presumably answer) about the dynamics of international politics. For this purpose, ongoing research at the University of Maryland on mediation in international crises provides the backdrop for discussion. Data recently collected on the role of mediation in international crises for the International Crisis Behavior Project will be juxtaposed with experimental work on mediation in international crises.

Mediation in International Crises

The United Nations defines mediation as "a method of peaceful settlement of an international dispute where a third party intervenes to reconcile the claims of the contending parties and to advance his own proposals aimed at a mutually-acceptable compromise solution."[26] Mediation generally occurs and is most relevant when the conflicting parties have reached a stalemate in fighting or in the negotiation process, or in both, and the parties usually accept mediation when they feel that a mediator's presence will facilitate an agreement that is more favorable than can be achieved via dyadic negotiations.[27] The list of potential mediators is quite extensive: a single state (small-, medium-, or large-sized powers), a group of states, an international governmental organization, a regional governmental organization, a private transnational organization, a private individual, or a mixture of any of these. A number of scholars, including Bercovitch, Princen, Young, Susskind and Babbitt, and Rubin discuss the characteristics of the parties and the disputes themselves that are likely to enhance the success of mediation.[28]

While there is no general consensus, the literature on mediation seems to have converged on three basic roles that mediators can play in a negotiation, and most authors agree that the roles change as the mediator and disputants "gain information and skill."[29] First is the mediator as communicator or facilitator,[30] serving as a channel of communications between two parties when a stalemate has been reached or when communications have broken down and face-to-face negotiations are not possible. This type of mediation is also referred to as third-party consultation,[31] good offices, or process facilitation.[32] The second role defined by Touval and Zartman is mediator as formulator. Here the mediator provides a substantive contribution to the negotiations in order to assist the conflicting parties in conceiving of a way to resolve their dispute when the parties reach a rigid impasse in the negotiation process. Hopmann suggests that this role is particularly effective when the parties' emotions are running high, and he highlights certain processes that the mediator as formulator may use to propose solutions: asking the parties to brainstorm, suggesting that issues be fractionated or linked together, inventing new solutions, and so forth. The third and final role that Touval and Zartman discuss is that of the mediator as manipulator. In addition to formulating solutions, this type of mediator uses its domestic, regional, or international position and its leverage—"resources of power, influence, and persuasion"—to "manipulate the parties into agreement."[33] The mediator as manipulator becomes a party to the solution, if not the dispute itself,[34] and often needs to augment the appeal of its solution by using carrot-and-stick measures (adding and subtracting benefits to and from the proposed solution).[35] Hopmann indicates that only a powerful mediator can play this role, and he cites two modes of mediator involvement as manipulator: influencing the direction of the negotiation process by raising the costs of disagreement and the rewards for agreement; manipulating the international environment to push the parties toward agreement.

Burton, Carnevale and Pegnetter, Fisher, Keashly and Fisher, and Kelman argue that the mediator as facilitator/communicator is the most effective role, while Bercovitch, Bercovitch and Houston, and Touval and Zartman feel that the mediator in a formulator and manipulator role will be most effective because of the amount of leverage that such a mediator possesses.[36] Princen notes that while it is often necessary to employ directive strategies to bring about an agreement between parties, the use of threats so closely associated with the directive/manipulative role can damage the "atmosphere of good will, trust, and joint problem solving" between the parties, which, if exacerbated enough, can break down negotiations.[37]

In the preliminary analysis presented here, two sets of questions pertaining to mediation are explored using the International Crisis Behavior data set on 412 international crises between 1918 and 1994: (1) under what circumstances is mediation most likely to occur? and (2) what types of outcomes are most closely associated with mediation? From the experimental perspective, the question to be explored is how different types of mediation, as opposed to no mediation, affect the utility-maximizing behavior of negotiators, the pace of crisis abatement, and the satisfaction with mediation. Let us turn first to the empirical findings based on ICB.[38]

Empirical Findings on Mediation in International Crises

First, some descriptive findings regarding mediation in twentieth-century international crises.[39] We should note at the outset that 29 percent of all international crises between 1918 and 1994 exhibited some form of mediation.

Threat. If we classify crises by level of threat perceived by the crisis actors, it turns out that mediation occurs at the highest rate in crises characterized by territorial threat.

Polarity. Instances of mediation appear to be increasing. The data show the following trend for frequency of mediation: multipolarity (1918–39) 27 percent; World War II (1939–45) 9 percent; bipolarity (1945–62) 20 percent; polycentrism (1963–89) 34 percent; and post–cold war unipolarity (1989–94) 62 percent.

System level. Mediation occurred with the following frequency at various system levels: subsystem 35 percent; mainly subsystem 23 percent; mainly dominant system 14 percent; and dominant system 8 percent.

Ethnic origins of crisis. Mediation occurred as follows: secessionist crises 34 percent; irredentist crises 51 percent; nonethnic crises 22 percent.

Geographic proximity. The pattern of mediation occurrences was as follows: contiguous actors 34 percent; near-neighbors 22 percent; distant actors 14 percent.

The second set of questions has to do with the types of crisis outcomes most closely associated with mediation in the twentieth century. As was the case above, we are concerned only with whether or not mediation occurred, leaving questions concerning type of mediation and type of mediator to a later paper.

Mediation and content of outcome. In those cases in which mediation occurred, outcomes involving ambiguous terminations— where one or more parties experienced compromise or stalemate— were prevalent in 60 percent of the cases. Conversely, when mediation did not occur, the majority of cases, 54 percent, showed definitive outcomes—involving a mix of victory and defeat.

Mediation and form of outcome. Crises in which mediation occurred were more likely to terminate in agreement—formal, semiformal, tacit—than were nonmediated crises—63 percent versus 27 percent. Conversely, most nonmediated crises terminated through unilateral acts—52 percent compared with only 18 percent for mediated crises.

Mediation and extent of satisfaction with outcome. Mediated crises produced more satisfying outcomes for the actors involved—41 percent of mediated crises showed all or most parties satisfied with the outcome, compared with only 25 percent for the nonmediated crises.

Mediation and escalation or reduction of tensions. While we find a trend toward long-term tension-reduction among mediated crises—60 percent versus 50 percent for nonmediated crises—the results are not statistically significant.

Clearly, then, mediation makes a difference. With mediation, outcomes are more likely to involve compromise, agreements are more likely to be reached, the parties are more likely to be satisfied, and there appears to be a tendency toward reduction of tensions over time.

Experimental Findings on Mediation in International Crises

The empirical findings derived from ICB provide us with a general picture of the effects that mediation—writ large—has on crisis and crisis negotiations. But these data cannot provide the full story of how mediation affects crisis processes and outcomes, nor do they reveal either the dynamics of interaction between the crisis actors and the mediator or the effects of different styles of mediation. An experimental research design, though, can build upon these general empirical findings and allow us to pursue more extended research questions.

The experimental environment in which mediation in international crisis was studied consists of a generalized decision support system for individual decision makers, a crisis scenario, and a communications system for both negotiators and mediators.[40] For purposes of these very preliminary experiments, a scenario loosely based on the Ecuador-Peru Border Dispute of 1981 was chosen. This case, part of an ongoing protracted conflict between 1935 and 1994 (ultimately terminating in 1998), which produced a total of four international crises,[41] involved a historical instance of successful mediation by the Organization of American States, which called upon the United States, Argentina, Brazil, and Chile to intervene. Four possible outcomes were built into the simulated negotiation: territorial division, cease-fire, arbitration, and status quo. In part, we sought to establish the reliability of our experimental environment through our ability to replicate in broad general terms the outcome of this historical case.

The original research design called for three groups of subjects drawn from a population of political science majors at the University of Maryland currently taking courses in aspects of international politics. Pairs of students were to take on the roles of Ecuador and Peru under three different circumstances: no mediation, mediator as facilitator, and mediator as manipulator.[42] Ultimately, only fifteen simulations were run, and we dropped the no-mediation control groups. While the small N and the lack of a control group severely limit our ability to generalize from these preliminary results, the findings do point in some interesting directions that are consistent with our main point: that experimental designs are able to address questions that we have difficulty getting at in more conventional empirical designs. Some highlights of these preliminary experimental results follow.

Mediation and expected utility. Among simulations that ended in agreement, mediator as manipulator produced mean utility point outcomes that were 20 percent higher for Ecuador—the weaker of the two actors in this crisis—and 9 percent higher for Peru, as compared with the outcomes for mediator as facilitator. However, mediator as facilitator produced mean utility point differences between the two parties that were 29 percent lower than for mediator as manipulator. That is, mediation as facilitation seemed to produce outcomes characterized by greater mutual benefit.

Mediation and pace of crisis abatement. Among all outcomes, simulations with mediator as manipulator terminated in 34 percent less time than simulations with mediator as facilitator. However, among the simulations that terminated in agreement between Ecuador and Peru, termination time was 11 percent shorter for facilitative than for manipulative mediation. The perceptions of participants in the simulation mirror these empirical results. One hundred percent of the respondents who worked with the mediator as manipulator believed that the mediator sped up the pace of crisis abatement. Results for the mediator as facilitator were more ambiguous: 40 percent believed that the mediator sped up the negotiation process; another 40 percent believed that the mediator actually slowed the abatement process down; while 20 percent believed that the mediator had no effect on the pace.

Expectations for mediation. Prior to the simulation, 58 percent of subjects anticipated that the involvement of a mediator in the negotiations would make it easier or much easier to achieve a desired outcome. Following the simulation, 67 percent of respondents who had been subject to mediator as manipulator continued to believe that the mediator made crisis abatement easier. A noticeable change occurred among those who were subject to mediator as facilitator: within that group, only 20 percent of respondents believed that the mediator had made it easier to reach an outcome, while 40 percent believed that the mediator had actually made it more difficult.

Satisfaction with outcome. No significant relationship was found between how satisfied a negotiator was with the outcome of the simulation and the type of mediator involved in the negotiation. Among those who worked with the mediator as manipulator, 67 percent achieved an outcome they considered to be satisfactory or very satisfactory, while 60 percent of those who worked with the mediator as facilitator found the outcome of their negotiation to be satisfactory. Interestingly, all of the respondents who indicated that the outcome for their country was unsatisfactory also indicated that mediator involvement made the negotiations more difficult.

Satisfaction with mediation. "The grass is always greener on the other side": of those involved in the mediator-as-facilitator negotiations, 60 percent noted that they would have preferred the mediator to have been more forceful or much more forceful. No respondents wished that this type of mediator had been less forceful. On the other hand, 100 percent of respondents from the mediator-as-manipulator simulations reported that they wished the mediator had been less, or much less, forceful. Even those who achieved an outcome they considered to be satisfactory believed this mediator played too forceful a role.

In sum, mediator as manipulator produced higher utility outcomes for both parties, while mediator as facilitator produced greater mutual benefit (smaller gap between the utility values for the two parties). Mediator as manipulator generally resulted in shorter elapsed time to outcome in general, but mediator as facilitator produced shorter elapsed time to agreements. Most negotiators who experienced mediator as manipulator believed that mediation made it easier to reach a desired outcome, while only a small portion of negotiators who experienced mediator as facilitator felt that mediation had helped reach a desired outcome. However, all parties were dissatisfied with mediation: most of those who experienced facilitation would have preferred a *more* forceful mediator, while all subjects who experienced manipulation expressed a desire for *less* forceful mediation. Finally, there were no discernible differences in satisfaction with the outcome resulting from the two forms of mediation.

Prospects and Limitations for Experimental/Simulation Work in Foreign Policy Analysis

At one time or another, we have all bemoaned the fact that foreign policy analysis is plagued by a combination of relatively small Ns and relatively large numbers of variables potentially contributing to the foreign policy decision-making process. On the surface, experimental work can successfully address both of these issues. With a more or less unlimited supply of willing undergraduates as subjects, our N is virtually limitless. By carefully constructing our simulation models and controlling our experimental environments, we can limit the number of variables we have to consider in any given experimental run. If this is the case, why are there not more eager scholars flocking to the simulation laboratories, and why are those of us who are there having so much trouble?

First, I would argue that the transition from simulation environment, whose primary application in political science is for instruction and training, to the experimental laboratory is not a simple one. First and foremost, most of us lack any real training in experimental design (how many graduate programs in political science offer courses in this area?). What to the experimental psychologist seems natural requires of the political scientist a very real investment of time and energy, and a lot of trial and error. Thus, even with the prospects of great advancements in knowledge seemingly at our fingertips, too few of us venture into the unknown terrain of the experimental laboratory.

Moreover, once in the lab, we are faced with a host of other seemingly-insurmountable obstacles. Consider our subjects: typically college freshmen (a few months out of high school) or, if we're lucky, upperclassmen. Cluttering their brains on any particular day are the aftermath of the previous evening's indiscretions and plans for tonight, swarming hormones, extreme hunger, thirst, and a strong need for a cigarette (if not worse), not to mention their at best neutral positions—if not downright hostility—toward having to participate in the experiment in the first place. Combine that with their relatively uninformed position on the nature of the international system in general, and foreign policy decision making in particular, and you are lucky if you can get anything that resembles replicable results.[43] That is not to say that real-world decision makers don't have extraneous things on their minds, but at least we know that some of their attention is focused on policy issues.

Even if these two problems could somehow be neutralized, the issue of the simulation itself remains. We know from the simulation literature that a model should be detailed enough to represent the important aspects of the reality it is meant to represent but not so detailed as to overwhelm the participant with information (even though we know that that is exactly what happens to real-world decision makers, particularly in crisis). This turns out to be an extremely difficult undertaking. In our own case, we have some evidence to suggest that in our previous round of experiments involving a model of a fishing dispute roughly resembling the dispute between Canada and Spain in 1995, we not only packed the model with excessive detail but then superimposed an elaborate mediation process, and the results showed that the subjects were not coping and were therefore making decisions based on only partial use of the decision support tools they had available to them. If you add to all this the expense and time involved in the design and execution of a series of experiments, it is not surprising that relatively few political scientists venture into this domain.

Given this rather bleak picture, where do I see simulation and experimental design fitting into the array of approaches now dominating the field of foreign policy analysis? At the level of political psychology, there are simply some characteristics of decision makers and decision making that we are never going to be able to study systematically with anything approaching a large enough N to allow for careful statistical work. It is here, under controlled laboratory environments, that we can begin to make progress in understanding how decision makers cope with and process information in crisis versus noncrisis environments, how third parties can affect the course of and outcomes to contentious situations, how actor attributes such as power (of various sorts) affect their negotiation strategies and behavior, and the circumstances under which violent strategies are chosen. While nothing can substitute for the data we can glean from in-depth case studies, the experimental environment—

when properly specified—can help us fill in the gaps in our knowledge and ultimately allow us to generalize beyond a limited experimental environment.

But to do this right, we must begin to properly train the next generation of experimental foreign policy analysis scholars. This is not everyone's cup of tea, nor should it be. Nevertheless, it does offer an important alternative to the cross-national and case study approaches that dominate the field of foreign policy analysis today. But we lack the experimental infrastructure, the culture of the laboratory, and perhaps most important, the channels by which experimental results can become important sources of information as we seek to better understand the behavior of political decision makers. And it is critical that we be able to demonstrate more convincingly that results obtained in experimental environments can help us better understand the behavior of real decision makers in critical situations. Much work remains to be done on this front.

Notes

1. M. Brecher and J. Wilkenfeld, *A Study of Crisis*, paperback with CD-ROM ed. (Ann Arbor: University of Michigan Press, 2000).
2. B. Starkey, M. Boyer, and J. Wilkenfeld, *Negotiating a Complex World: An Introduction to International Negotiation* (Boulder, Colo.: Rowan and Littlefield, 1999); see also http://www.icons.umd.edu.
3. D. Kinder and T. Palfrey, "On Behalf of an Experimental Political Science," in *Experimental Foundations of Political Science*, ed. D. Kinder and T. Palfrey (Ann Arbor: University of Michigan Press, 1993), 1.
4. D. T. Campbell and J. C. Stanley, *Experimental and Quasi-Experimental Designs for Research* (Chicago: Rand McNally, 1963).
5. J. A. Laponce, "Experimenting: A Two-Person Game between Man and Nature," in *Experimentation and Simulation in Political Science*, ed. J. A. Laponce and P. Smoker (Toronto: University of Toronto Press, 1972), 3–15; D. A. Bositis, *Research Designs for Political Science: Contrivance and Demonstration in Theory and Practice* (Carbondale: Southern Illinois University Press, 1990); K. McGraw, "Political Methodology: Research Design and Experimental Methods," in *A New Handbook of Political Science*, ed. R. E. Goodin and H. D. Klingemann (New York: Oxford University Press, 1993), 769–86.
6. R. C. Snyder, "Some Perspectives on the Use of Experimental Techniques in the Study of International Relations," in *Simulations in International Relations*, ed. H. Guetzkow et al. (Englewood Cliffs, N.J.: Prentice Hall, 1963), 7.
7. R. A. Brody, "The Study of International Politics *qua* Science: The Emphasis on Methods and Techniques," in *Contending Approaches to International Politics*, ed. K. Knorr and J. N. Rosenau (Princeton, N.J.:

Princeton University Press, 1969), 110–28; Kinder and Palfrey, "On Behalf of an Experimental Political Science."
8. A. Franklin, *Experiment, Right or Wrong* (New York: Cambridge University Press, 1996).
9. Bositis, *Research Designs for Political Science*, 65.
10. McGraw, "Political Methodology."
11. Laponce and Smoker, *Experimentation and Simulation in Political Science*.
12. H. Guetzkow et al., *Simulations in International Relations*.
13. S. Kraus, J. Wilkenfeld, and G. Zlotkin, "Multiagent Negotiation under Time Constraints," *Journal of Artificial Intelligence* 75 (1995): 297–345; J. Wilkenfeld, S. Kraus, K. Holley, and M. Harris, "GENIE: A Decision Support System for Crisis Negotiations," *Decision Support Systems* 14 (1995): 369–91.
14. See N. Geva and J. Mayhar, "The Cognitive Calculus of Decisions on the Use of Force" (paper presented at the annual meeting of the American Political Science Association, Washington, D.C., August 28–31, 1997); A. Mintz, N. Geva, S. Redd, and A. Carnes, "The Effect of Dynamic and Static Choice Sets on Political Decision Making," *American Political Science Review* 91, no. 3 (1997): 553–66; P. Tetlock and A. Belkin, eds., *Counterfactual Thought Experiments in World Politics: Logical, Methodological, and Psychological Perspectives* (Princeton, N.J.: Princeton University Press, 1996).
15. For a more formal definition of crisis, see Brecher and Wilkenfeld, *A Study of Crisis*.
16. For a discussion of decision support systems in general and their application to negotiation in particular, see Wilkenfeld et al., "GENIE: A Decision Support System for Crisis Negotiations."
17. A secondary, though no less important, interest was the creation of a controlled environment in which negotiators could be trained for work in conflict management and resolution.
18. See Kraus, Wilkenfeld, and Zlotkin, "Multiagent Negotiation under Time Constraints"; J. Wilkenfeld, S. Kraus, and K. Holley, "The Use of Decision Support Systems in Crisis Negotiations," in *Encyclopedia of Library and Information Science*, ed. A. Kent (New York: Dekker, 1999).
19. J. Wilkenfeld, S. Kraus, Tara Santmire, and C. Frain, "The Role of Mediation in Conflict Management: Conditions for Successful Resolution" (paper presented at the annual meeting of the International Studies Association, Washington, D.C., February 16–20, 1999); J. Wilkenfeld, S. Kraus, Tara Santmire, and C. Frain, "The Role of Mediation in Conflict Management: Conditions for Successful Resolution," in *Methodology in International Relations*, ed. Z. Maoz et al. (forthcoming).
20. For details on our experimental procedures, see Tara Santmire, J. Wilkenfeld, S. Kraus, K. Holley, Toni Santmire, and K. Gleditsch, "The Impact of Cognitive Diversity on Crisis Negotiations," *Political Psychology* 19, no. 4 (1998): 721–48.
21. K. Holley and J. Wilkenfeld, "The Use of Decision Support Systems in International Education" (paper presented at the annual meeting of the

International Studies Association, Washington, D.C., March 28–April 1, 1994); S. Kraus, J. Wilkenfeld, M. Harris, and E. Blake, "The Hostage Crisis Simulation," *Simulation and Gaming* 23 (1992): 398–416.
22. Wilkenfeld et al., "GENIE: A Decision Support System for Crisis Negotiation."
23. J. Wilkenfeld, S. Kraus, Tara Santmire, K. Holley, and Toni Santmire, "Cognitive Structure and Crisis Decision Making" (paper presented at the annual meeting of the International Studies Association, San Diego, April 16–20, 1996).
24. Santmire et al., "The Impact of Cognitive Diversity on Crisis Negotiations."
25. Wilkenfeld et al., "The Role of Mediation in Conflict Management."
26. United Nations, *Handbook on the Peaceful Settlement of Disputes between States* (New York: United Nations, 1992), 40.
27. S. Touval and I. W. Zartman, "Introduction: Mediation in Theory," in *International Mediation in Theory and Practice*, ed. S. Touval and I. W. Zartman (Boulder, Colo.: Westview, 1984), 7–17; P. T. Hopmann, *The Negotiation Process and the Resolution of International Conflicts* (Columbia: University of South Carolina Press, 1996); I. W. Zartman and S. Touval, "International Mediation in the Post–Cold War Era," in *Managing Global Chaos: Sources of and Responses to International Conflict*, ed. C. A. Crocker and F. O. Hampson, with P. Aall (Washington, D.C.: U.S. Institute of Peace Press, 1996), 445–61.
28. J. Bercovitch, "International Mediation: A Study of the Incidence, Strategies, and Conditions of Successful Outcomes," *Cooperation and Conflict* 21, no. 3 (1986): 155–68; J. Bercovitch, "Mediation in International Conflict: An Overview of Theory, a Review of Practice," in *Peacemaking in International Conflict: Methods and Techniques*, ed. I. W. Zartman and J. L. Rasmussen (Washington, D.C.: U.S. Institute of Peace Press, 1997), 125–53; T. Princen, *Intermediaries in International Conflict* (Princeton, N.J.: Princeton University Press, 1992); O. R. Young, *The Intermediaries: Third Parties in International Crises* (Princeton, N.J.: Princeton University Press, 1967); L. Susskind and E. Babbit, "Overcoming the Obstacles to Effective Mediation of International Disputes," in *Mediation in International Relations*, ed. J. Bercovitch and J. Z. Rubin (New York: St. Martin's Press, 1992), 30–51; J. Z. Rubin, "Conclusion: International Mediation in Context," in ibid., 249–72.
29. Princen, *Intermediaries in International Conflict*, 65.
30. Touval and Zartman, introduction to Touval and Zartman, *International Mediation in Theory and Practice*; J. W. Burton, *Global Conflict: The Domestic Sources of International Crisis* (Brighton, England: Wheatsheaf Books, 1984); Hopmann, *The Negotiation Process and the Resolution of International Conflicts*.
31. L. Keashly and R. J. Fisher, "A Contingency Perspective on Conflict Interventions: Theoretical and Practical Considerations," in *Resolving International Conflicts: The Theory and Practice of Mediation*, ed. J. Bercovitch (Boulder, Colo.: Lynne Rienner, 1996), 235–61; H. C. Kelman, "Informal Mediation by the Scholar/Practitioner," in Bercovitch and Rubin, *Mediation in International Relations*, 64–96.

32. Hopmann, *The Negotiation Process and the Resolution of International Conflicts.*
33. Touval and Zartman, introduction, 12.
34. Hopmann qualifies the notion of the manipulative mediator being a party to the dispute by stating that this mediator "almost" assumes the role of a disputant in the negotiation process. Hopmann, *The Negotiation Process and the Resolution of International Conflicts.*
35. Touval and Zartman, introduction; Zartman and Touval, "International Mediation in the Post–Cold War Era," in Crocker and Hampson, *Managing Global Chaos.*
36. J. W. Burton, *Conflict and Communication: The Use of Controlled Communication in International Relations* (New York: Free Press, 1969); P. J. Carnevale and R. Pegnetter, "The Selection of Mediation Tactics in Public Sector Disputes: A Contingency Analysis," *Journal of Social Issues* 41, no. 2 (1985): 65–81; R. J. Fisher, "Third Party Consultation: A Method for the Study and Resolution of Conflict," *Journal of Conflict Resolution* 16, no. 1 (1972): 67–94; R. J. Fisher and L. Keashly, "Distinguishing Third-Party Interventions in Intergroup Conflict: Consultation Is Not Mediation," *Negotiation Journal* 4, no. 4 (1988): 381–93; Kelman, "Informal Mediation by the Scholar/Practitioner"; Bercovitch, "International Mediation"; J. Bercovitch and A. Houston, "The Study of International Mediation: Theoretical Issues and Empirical Evidence," in Bercovitch, *Resolving International Conflicts,* 11–35; and Touval and Zartman, introduction.
37. Princen, *Intermediaries in International Conflict,* 58.
38. Since the International Crisis Behavior data sets did not originally contain variables focusing explicitly on mediation, coding was undertaken in 2000 on five new variables pertaining to mediation: whether or not mediation took place, who served as mediator, impact of mediation on type of outcome, impact of mediation on pace of abatement, and timing of mediation. Coding was performed by Amy Fields and Heather McQueeney, under the supervision of David Quinn. It should be noted that this coding was based on information contained in the ICB crisis summaries (Brecher and Wilkenfeld, *A Study of Crisis*). All of the following conditions had to be present for the case to be considered one of mediation:

    - A third party intervenes in a new or ongoing negotiation process.
    - Mediator is not a direct party to crisis.
    - Mediator's results are nonbinding. Crisis actors determine the outcome of the crisis. The mediator does not have decision-making power.
    - Mediation is a nonviolent form of intervention.
    - Mediator's presence is voluntary; that is, mediator can leave the negotiations.
    - Mediation begins once a stalemate between the adversaries has been reached.

39. For the sake of brevity, detailed statistical findings will not be presented in this paper.

40. The experimental environment is described more fully in Santmire et al., "The Impact of Cognitive Diversity on Crisis Negotiations"; Wilkenfeld et al., "GENIE: A Decision Support System for Crisis Negotiations"; J. Wilkenfeld, K. Young, V. Assal, and D. Quinn, "Mediating International Crises in the 20th Century" (paper presented at the International Studies Association convention, Hong Kong, July 26–28, 2001).
41. For a discussion of these crises in detail, see Brecher and Wilkenfeld, *A Study of Crisis.* The scenario and decision support systems, developed by Kathleen Young, David Quinn, and Chris Frain, are available from the author upon request. A more extended discussion of this research project appears in Wilkenfeld, Young, Assal, and Quinn, "Mediating International Crises in the 20th Century."
42. Due to limitations on the number of subjects available at this stage of our research, the role of "mediator as formulator" was not examined in this research design.
43. I am reminded of one of the very first works I became familiar with in simulation, a study by Hermann and Hermann that used the Inter-Nation Simulation (INS) to attempt to replicate the conditions leading to the outbreak of World War I. They checked for seemingly everything, yet curiously they couldn't get war to break out. As it turned out, a student playing one of the key roles was an avowed pacifist and simply wouldn't go to war under any circumstances. C. F. Hermann and M. G. Hermann, "An Attempt to Simulate the Outbreak of World War I," *American Political Science Review* 61, no. 2 (1967): 406–16.

INTERNATIONAL SECURITY, PEACE, AND WAR

SECURITY THEORY
Six Paradigms Searching for Security
Edward A. Kolodziej

This survey of security theory is divided into two parts. The first defines security as a political concept and phenomenon. This discussion provides a point of departure for reviewing prevailing security theories. The second, and longest, section briefly examines and evaluates the claims of six competing research programs concerned directly or indirectly with security. These include realism, neorealism, economic liberalism, liberal institutionalism, behaviorism, and constructivism. These research programs can be distinguished on the basis of their ontological, epistemological, methodological, and evidentiary assumptions about actors and their behavior. Given space constraints, the discussion will identify only the principal differences between these research paradigms and their implications for security theory.

To forge links between this theoretical discussion and hard facts, I assess the capacity of each paradigm to explain the implosion of the Soviet Union and the end of the cold war. The enormous shifts in power that these changes in world politics represent are, arguably, a plausible, if provisional, test of these research programs and their relevance to security theory. No attempt will be made to exhaustively critique each school of thought, a task well beyond the scope of this evaluation. This overview argues that in greater or lesser measure, each has something worthwhile to contribute to our understanding of these tectonic changes in the structure and processes of global politics. This optimism challenges the pessimism adopted by many scholars. They severely criticize these research paradigms for their failure to explain, much less to predict, the collapse of the Soviet system and the postwar bipolarity.[1] Conversely, this evaluation resists the temptation of some analysts who insist that their approach, however beset now, will eventually be validated in the post–cold war era, if enough time is allotted for their predictions to be realized.[2]

Based on this survey, four conclusions are drawn about the state of security theory today. First, there exists no one paradigm capable of explaining the security behavior of relevant actors. Second, there exists no one methodology capable of providing a definitive theory of actor behavior. Third, there exists no one policy prescription available to actors to solve their security dilemmas.[3] Fourth, and following from these generalizations, there is no agreement across these research programs about which actors in world politics have decisive influence and impact on security. Competing actors, aside from the state, include all forms of economic association—notably multinational corporations—the rise, enlargement, and increasing pervasiveness of global capitalist markets conceived as a political and socioeconomic institution; the expansion in the number, scope, and power of transnational actors; and the growing significance of individuals and small groups and national and international public opinion. While the state remains central to most security research programs, the many competitors identified by these research programs seriously limit the development of a comprehensive theory of security in an increasingly globalized world.

In contrast to much conventional wisdom, concerned about the proliferation of security theories and their contesting claims,[4] the overall conclusion to be drawn from this brief survey is that depending on the research or policy problem posed, these paradigms provide useful, if not fully satisfactory, theoretical tools to pursue important questions bearing on the use, threat, control, and elimination of force relevant in explaining the outcomes of increasingly interdependent exchanges of the world's populations and states.

As Imre Lakatos suggests, the present pluralism and the competition of these research programs are very likely the best we can do for now until a comprehensive theory of security can be developed that either surmounts these specialized perspectives or incorporates them into a common framework of analysis.[5] None of the research programs outlined in this essay can be conclusively tested in the sense of being confirmed or rejected on the strength of a single event or chain of events, like the end of the cold war. As William Wohlfort suggests, "Strictly speaking, no particular finding about the Cold War's end will suffice to 'falsify' an entire research program.... For a single series of events to constitute a critical test of a theory, it must not only be inconsistent with the theory but be unambiguously ruled out by it."[6] Conversely, a theory of international relations or security that has little or nothing to say about the enormous political changes ushered in by the implosion of the Soviet Union and the collapse of global bipolarity would be hard pressed to retain its credibility and viability as a research program.

What Would Security Look Like If You Bumped into It in a Dark Room?

There are few more contested terms or concepts than "security." For many it is associated with the preservation of the state and the nation-state system. For others, security is primarily concerned with the physical security of individuals in civil society and their reliance on the state to arbitrate their differences and to defend them against foreign aggression. These Hobbesian notions have since been enlarged by those who would include economic welfare and the material well-being of populations as central security concerns. As economic development, industrialization, and modernization relentlessly progress around the globe, security for many observers is transformed into threats to the global environment or commons, evidenced by widespread pollution of the earth's air, water, and arable land and the rising problem of global warming.[7] Still others conceive security to be a fundamentally psychological phenomenon. Whatever causes anxiety or angst to the individual or social psyche—say the threat of nuclear war or terrorism—becomes a central security issue.

It is readily apparent that if security were understood to extend to so broad a range of human experience, it would soon lose much of its defining power. Security would have no clear, objective referent to discipline-systematic study. Security would simply change with the eye of the beholder. These contrasting and conflicting definitions of security seriously hamper the development of a theory of security. If the actors and the domains of investigation as well as the behavior of the actors within each domain change according to the interests, values, and perceptions of the observer, then no general theory of security is likely possible. The fear of many analysts that security as a term will be so broadly defined that it will be useless as a basis for describing, explaining, and predicting actor behavior would appear to be justified.[8] Security would explain too much and too little.

To provide some consistency and coherence to this analysis, this discussion, as a first move, invokes a traditional understanding of security, dating to the Melian Dialogue and to the Hobbesian conceptualization of security. The Melian Dialogue posed the issue of security in terms of power, principally material power and coercive threats.[9] Hobbes generalized this condition of conflict between societies by rooting the problem of security in the very makeup (i.e., ontology) of individuals. Their infinite and conflicting preferences and their unswerving will to get their way in their exchanges with homologues created a social condition of permanent and perpetual conflict. Since getting one's way was a function of power, all preferences could be standardized. If politics is simply a struggle for power and not a search for the ideal polity, as classical Greek and Christian thought conceived the problem of politics, a science of politics and of political behavior is possible. The precondition for such a science was the survival or security of the actors engaged in this ceaseless struggle. From a Hobbesian perspective, the political phenomenon of security arises whenever and wherever an exchange between actors occurs in which the desired outcome from the transaction is to be resolved by force or the threat of force. Even Hobbes's provisional solution of the Leviathan or the modern state, possessed of awesome power to resolve conflicts between actors, is problematic. However greater the capacity for survival and security of the state may be compared with that of actors, its existence and its interests are no less subject to human preferences and to the countervailing power of actors opposed to its authority, power, and policies.[10]

This understanding of security has the virtue of being generalized across all transactions of individuals and their humanly constructed agents. From all such exchanges the properties of force and threats of violence are abstracted from the preferences in which they are embedded. A theory of security can be isolated for examination from the more daunting task of assessing the human worth of the contesting values in play. This permits the analyst to develop a pure theory—or Weberian ideal—of security. Hobbes, who was arguably the first to conceptualize this condition of force as a permanent, underlying determinant of human exchanges, drew the conclusion that humans were perpetually at war of all against all. Unless arrested by mutual consent (impossible by what was real about humans) or by some awesome power (the Leviathan), life would be "solitary, poore, nasty, brutish, and short."[11] Carl von Clausewitz simply projected this individual condition to the relations of states.[12] Pure war between states was conceived as the "ideal" or pure endgame toward which armed conflict was directed. Real war, the historical representation of the pure case, typically fell short of its "ideal" endpoint. Either a host of "frictions" prevented the rivals from eliminating each other or, and the more likely and generalized explanation, their political aims fell short of pure war for its own sake.

This understanding of security and the tendency of violent or force-incipient exchanges to move toward a pure case or Weberian "ideal" provide theorists with a potentially definable set of transactions around which a theory of security might be developed. However, as some theorists argue (notably economic and institutionalist liberals and constructivists), the Hobbesian assumption of perpetual conflict between egoistic actors or between states is not necessarily an insurmountable ontological limitation. This claim widens the theoretical lens to include not only the determinants of those conditions and incentives inducing actors to threaten and use violence but also those factors and forces prompting actors to eschew coercion in resolving their differences. Security theory must then embrace not only all those transactions that are *within* the domain of violence or threats associated with a transaction—the position of realists and neorealists and some liberal institutionalists—but also those transactions and power determinants that limit violence and force. A theory of security would entail potentially empirically-verifying observations about the incentive structures and processes of actor decisions and actions, inducing them to resolve their exchanges by peaceful or violent means. Security theory as a subfield of international relations theory would be principally concerned with explaining both peace *and* war, since one could not be understood in the absence of the other. At the risk of simplification, security theory may begin with Hobbes, but it must end with Kant and the possibility of perpetual peace if it is to be comprehensive and coherent.[13]

A final introductory clarification is also necessary. A theory of security is not a theory of strategy. The latter, however worthwhile, is a narrowly-conceived understanding of security. It focuses principally on the important and practical question of what ways are likely to be cost-effective in compelling an adversary by force or threats to accede to one's will. There is much to be said for this conceptualization of security when opponents appear to be clearly engaged in threatening their rivals to get their way as World Wars I and II and the cold war suggest. Hitlers, Stalins, or Maos are not willed away by wishes. However, it would be a mistake to identify a theory of security with a theory about strategies of security, narrowed to only those transactions between actors in which the actors seek advantage by reference to countervailing, reflexive force. To equate this form of analysis with a theory of security risks trapping the analyst in a vicious circle. This move isolates security theory from the broader and ultimately-determining considerations associated with international relations theory. Such conceptual isolation is healthy neither for the broader field of international relations theory nor for strategic theory. Both need to inform the other if either is to be validated.[14] At a practical policy level, closure may be premature; actors may well be misled to believe that strategies to resolve differences with rivals are ruled out by the assumptions made by the strategist, whether advising peace or war. At a theoretical level, both conflict and cooperation in human exchanges have to be included in any theory of security if the behavior, interests, aims, and values of actors are to be adequately explained.

Explaining the End of the Cold War: The Clash of Paradigms

Realism and Neorealism

Realism has a long and venerable history. Its roots can be traced to Thucydides's account of the Peloponnesian War. While realist theorists differ across a spectrum of assumptions about actor behavior, they converge on the notion that power, notably material power and principally violence, is the final arbiter of differences between actors. Power is central to a theory of security; it is the driving force behind actor behavior in international relations. At a state level, realists stress that the claim of states to sovereignty and to a monopoly of legitimate violence in settling disputes at home and in defending the state and its population abroad privileges security over all other competing values. States implicated in the quest for power mutually confront a security dilemma from which none can escape. That dilemma can be relaxed, but it cannot be surmounted, as long as states dispose ultimate military power under conditions of anarchy. The state has no choice but to pursue power as an overriding imperative. Failure to do so imperils its existence and its dependent populations.

Whereas classical realism works principally at the unit or state level,[15] neorealism focuses narrowly at the system level. It stipulates the system of states as a causal force operating on all of the units of the system. Units are constrained by the anarchy of this structure. That constraint is materially defined by the distribution of capabilities, most prominently military force, across the system. In this self-help system of functionally-undifferentiated units, states are driven by a security imperative; they are obliged to concentrate their resources in ceaseless efforts to improve their position within the system and their relative power with respect to competitors. All exchanges between states, even those that appear benign such as trade or investments,[16] are matters of high politics if the material power of each state is changed by these transactions.

Anarchical systems may be multipolar or bipolar. With respect to the cold war, Kenneth Waltz argued that bipolar systems were inherently more stable than multipolar systems. The overwhelming material power of the United States and the Soviet Union allegedly decreased uncertainty about the power implications of shifting alliances, since the power of the alliance leader was less dependent on allies than under a multipolar system. Superpower calculations about their relative power vis-à-vis their rival were, arguably, less prone to error. Alliances were also supposedly more stable; the superpowers relied less on their partners to balance their adversary than would have been the case in a multipolar system. They also possessed sufficient capabilities to keep their allies from defecting, and if defections nevertheless arose, they counted for less in the balance.[17]

Realism and neorealism provided what appeared to be a compelling explanation for the superpower struggle and the long peace after World War II. Classical realism placed the superpower struggle in a historical context traceable to centuries of competition between the European states for hegemony over Europe and, through their empires, over the world. The United States and the Soviet Union were depicted as simply the latest in a succession of contender powers for world domination. Their contrasting domestic regimes, economic systems, and ideologies, however significant to explain their behavior along noncoercive axes of exchange, were subordinated to what were portrayed as the objective conditions of power characterizing their armed competition. Peace depended on a superpower equilibrium, tilting often precariously on a delicate balance of nuclear terror.

Neorealists reached the same conclusion about the long peace as their realist colleagues. Where they differed was their contrasting explanations of state behavior. Whereas realists understood conflict between states as arising from the dyadic power relations of the states, neorealists identified the system itself as the principal source of conflict, characterized by the decentralized distribution of violent capabilities, viz, anarchy. They claimed to have identified a scientific principle of conflict, independent of its historical representation either in the European state system or in the cold war or in any other historical system. Units within a decentralized system—states today—that failed to address anarchy as an imperative of their survival would be penalized by other states and selected out in the evolutionary struggle for relative power and position. The historical and shifting explanatory power of classical realism was purportedly placed on an ahistorical conceptual foundation.

Critics have been unsparing in their attacks on realism and neorealism.[18] These research programs are dismissed by many theorists for their failure to explain, or even to anticipate, the peaceful end of the cold war, the abrupt breakup of the Soviet Union, or the rise of an ascendant Western coalition of liberal, market democratic states. Neither would have predicted the collapse of the Soviet state into its constituent republics as long as the coercive arms of the state—the military, the police, and supportive civil bureaucracies—were intact and functioning. Under realist-neorealist assumptions, neither the state nor its leadership could be expected to permit the dissolution of the state. Nor was the relinquishment of the Soviet sphere of influence, principally in Eastern Europe, supposedly consistent with realist theory.

Conversely, the Western coalition was able to surmount the security dilemma in constructing a security community premised on peaceful change. The economic and technological success of the West, resting on democratic regimes and market rules, prompted the economic and political reforms launched by the Gorbachev government. These are explained more by reference to internal or domestic pressures for enhanced economic performance (perestroika) and openness (glasnost and democratization) than by external power shortfalls vis-à-vis the United States and its allies.[19] These unit-level adaptations appear particularly telling for neorealism, which implicitly rejects unit-level changes as a decisive determinant of system change.

Realist partisans have retorted to these criticisms. Given their more flexible and plastic understanding of power, realists have fought back to reclaim the theoretical high ground. They argue that the real and widening disparities between economic and technological capabilities of the West and East and, accordingly, the rising military superiority of the United States compelled internal Soviet reform at home and retrenchment abroad. Rather than a repudiation of realist assumptions, these shifts in Soviet policy and behavior purportedly vindicated realist expectations. For realists, in contrast to their neorealist allies, the perception by Soviet leaders of this growing imbalance in power and their response to this gap as well as to domestic pressures for improved economic growth and performance are compatible with realist theory. The détente sought by the Gorbachev regime with the West reflected Soviet weakness. It was a logical adjustment to Western power. Détente promised to slow the arms race, narrow the East-West military gap, shift scarce resources from military to economic priorities, and bolster the Soviet Union's long-term competitive position by attracting Western capital and technology. If the West temporarily succeeded in relaxing the security dilemma in their relations as they allied to meet the Soviet challenge, realists still expected (and some Soviets, too) that balancing against the ascendant power—the United States—would commence again. By positing an indeterminate future in which the incentives of states to seek relative gains would persist, the claims of realists and especially neorealists are precluded from being subject to conclusive invalidation.[20]

Economic Liberalism

Classical and neoclassical liberal economic theory moves from a state-as-unit or systemic level of analysis to the choices of individual consumers and producers. Liberal economic theory bases its theory of behavior on individuals rather than on states or systemic structures. Many, including some liberal economic theorists, may well argue that liberal theory has little or nothing to say about security. That would be a mistake for several reasons. First, liberals have always stressed the peaceful effects of commerce and economic exchange if individuals are free to register their choices in global markets. Dating at least from the nineteenth century, with the rise of the Manchester School and British adoption of free-trade policies, liberals have insisted that increasing economic interdependence and the costs of dissolution of these mutually-beneficial transactions—ever expanding, deepening, and thickening—made wars less likely, even impossible to contemplate by state leaders or their populations. This expectation and the bolstering evidence of the increasing economic interdependence of the European states and peoples on the eve of World War I persuaded Norman Angell and liberal theorists to reject the possibility of a general war.[21]

Even the wholesale carnage of World War I did not dissuade liberals from identifying military bureaucracies and states, putatively moved by atavistic or national passions, as the primary sources of war rather than free markets and economic pursuits. Joseph Schumpeter's response to Lenin's theory of imperialism pivoted on Schumpeter's contention that those engaged in commerce preferred peace to war to advance their interests.[22] Resonances of these lines of analysis persist in several, seemingly discrete, areas. There are those who, following Angell, restate the costs of a general war as the principal obstacle to its eruption, even if nuclear weapons had not been invented.[23] There are also those who contend that the Atlantic security community and specifically the European Union, nested within that community, can be explained partially, but critically, by the widening and deepening of economic interdependence that all but precludes a resort to force by any state to ensure its security and welfare interests.[24]

There are more profound, theoretical reasons undergirding liberal theory than these historical and empirical referents, however compelling their surface persuasion. The pure or ideal model of "economic man" animating liberal theory is an economic maximizer. The pursuit of wealth and welfare dictates the efficient allocation of human and material resources over time. The model of perfect competition predicts the long-term tendency of individuals and other economic units, notably firms, to maximize economic gains by relying on the signaling of relative prices for goods and services and the factors of production in increasingly globalized markets. Alternative economic institutions, particularly command economies dependent on bureaucratic and state ownership of the means of production, are inherently incapable of responding—efficiently, effectively, and innovatively[25]—to the ceaseless and rising demands of individuals and nations for "more now."[26] The form and subjectively-determined properties of these economic demands could only be known by the individuals possessing them. Only free markets, unfettered in theory by the coercive constraints of states, bureaucrats, or monopolists, are capable of registering these subjective demands objectively to orient the allocation of inherently scarce resources in maximizing wealth for the greatest number. Much the same way that neorealists argued that states were selected out by the evolutionary struggle for power if they did not maximize their relative position, so liberal economists argued that alternative economic systems to free markets would be selected out of the evolutionary process. They were incapable of solving the knowledge problem posed by the assumed subjective value of individuals, ever striving for material well-being.[27] Economic man would always prefer more than less economic gain. Only free markets could satisfactorily address these informational and valuational problems through market pricing.

Liberal theory has much to say about the forces pressing on Soviet decision makers in opting for economic and political reform, however disastrous it proved for their particular personal positions. It helps to explain, too, Communist Chinese market reforms since 1979 and the determination of the Beijing regime to become integrated into Western-dominated global markets even at the risk of losing Communist party political control of the Chinese mainland. What market theory is unable to explain is the coercive determination of property and contractural rights. These inherent elements of a theory of order fall outside the scope of liberal economic theory. Hence, neoclassical economic theory has no theory of power. Power is assumed away by stipulating free choice in a perfect market under conditions of full information to guide the choice of actor strategies to maximize their material welfare. Populations are reduced to individual, uncoerced buyers and sellers expressing their subjective values by registering their preferences through relative prices in potentially homogeneous and integrated world markets. Institutional economic theory has attempted to partially fill this void in neoclassical liberal theory, but to the satisfaction neither of many liberal economic theorists nor, and much more so, their realist critics.[28] Left begging in liberal economic theory is why the Soviet Union collapsed into its constituent national republics and why many of these remain unstable as a consequence of continuing ethnic, religious, and national strife. Nor has the Russian Federation been able to install free markets as many liberal economists expected because it has yet to define the property and contractual rights needed to make Russian markets work.

If the world now claps with one hand in applauding the ascendancy of markets as the provisional solution to global welfare, markets still produce inequalities of wealth. Those drawing on Marxist theory insist that these inequalities remain the principal sources of conflict in the world society. Non-Marxists argue, too, that the state must be brought back into economic theory. It is rapidly emerging as the principal mechanism to address both the problem of income inequality between the North and South and between individuals and groups within states of the developed North.[29] The state is also expected to produce order and to redistribute wealth through taxation and borrowing to meet collective goods claims for education, infrastructure, environmental protection, or health and material assistance to the lame, the halt, the young, the infirm, and the old.[30] The pricing mechanisms of the market may well be useful in attacking some of these problems, evidenced by the Kyoto Protocol and its application of cost and market rules to control greenhouse emissions, but the sanctioning of those practices remains keyed to state cooperation and their enforcement capacity. American refusal to ratify the protocol underscores the subordination of market mechanisms to political power and national priorities achieved more by feat than playing by market rules. Market theory per se has little to say about these environmental concerns and the value placed by individuals, groups, and states on ways to address them. These shortcomings of liberal theory and market practices may be insufficient to resurrect currently discredited Marxist predictions of coming capitalist crisis and war, but they do suggest that liberal thought is unable to account for continued political conflict within national civil societies and between states.[31]

Liberal Institutionalism

Liberal institutionalism draws on the preceding theories rather than advancing an alternative theory of behavior. It adopts the realist and economic liberal beginning point of the rational egoist maximizer, whether applied to the individual actor or the state.[32] If institutionalists have difficulty explaining the end of the Soviet state, they have less difficulty explaining progressive superpower cooperation. Drawing both on microeconomic theory and game theory, Thomas Schelling laid the theoretical foundation to explain cooperation between armed rivals. They had a mutual interest in avoiding unwanted wars, of limiting the human and material losses of hostilities, and of bringing such conflicts to a swift close on terms congenial to their preferred, if differentially defined, interests. They might not surmount their rivalry, but they had powerful incentives to cooperate on arms control and disarmament policies for mutual if differing advantage.[33]

Robert Axelrod's groundbreaking *The Evolution of Cooperation* broadened the evidentiary basis of Schelling's insights and deepened his analysis of why egoists could be expected to cooperate.[34] Based on the results of a simulation study, Axelrod contended that tournament results revealed that egoists could learn through repeated exchanges to cooperate to limit the costs of defection and to maximize the gains of cooperation. A simple tit-for-tat strategy proved to be the winning strategy. It proved to be "nice, provocable, forgiving and clear"[35] to the players; it signaled each that all of the players could mutually gain from cooperation rather than attempting to improve their positions by defecting. The incentive to cooperate was increased further if players were certain that their exchanges and their mutual dependency would continue. According to Axelrod, the "shadow of the future" constrained them from cheating since defection would be countered by mutual defection and loss. Once cooperation as a strategy gained ground among egoists, its gains became apparent. First through evolutionary trial and error and progressively through accelerated learning, cooperation could be installed and institutionalized.

Liberal institutionalists built on Axelrod's theoretical insight to reinforce their claim that institutions, arising from the repeated exchanges of egoists, could both constrain their behavior and foster opportunities for cooperation. The security dilemma could be relaxed by the collective, absolute benefits produced by institutions and shared rules, norms, and principles of behavior. Institutions introduced greater transparency to actor motivation and behavior. Actors could increasingly rely on their partners to adapt to and comply with institutional rules. Greater predictability ipso facto decreased uncertainty and reduced the incentive of actors to hedge or compensate for possible defection by taking out insurance in the form of arms races and expansionist policies. These moves would presumably encourage a spiral of defections to the mutual disadvantage of all parties.

To increased transparency, decreased uncertainty, and greater predictability were added the progressively lowered transaction costs of cooperation. Building on the economic theory of the firm and social cost theory, liberal institutionalists pointed to the incentive of decreased transaction costs that institutions afforded their adherents.[36] If firms and multinational corporations could be partially explained by their supposed greater efficiency in cutting market transaction costs, so also could international organizations and new and powerful transnational actors, with their own aims and interests and agendas, explain what appeared to be the growing cooperation of states.[37]

The realist picture of incessant state conflict and the pursuit of relative gains in power and position was replaced by the notion of complex interdependence. By focusing on absolute rather than relative gains, egoists had incentive to cooperate across interdependent domains of interaction. Moreover, complex interdependence produced multiple international actors—corporations, intergovernmental and nongovernmental organizations, and individuals. They worked through multiple channels to bypass or to constrain state behavior. Their agendas for action were no less complex. The growing number of actors and their overlapping and conflicting agendas blurred the traditional distinction between high and low politics. Nonsecurity problems necessarily rose in importance on the list of state priorities as zero-sum security concerns declined in importance. The growing number of problems posed by interdependence were progressively less amenable to unilateral appeals to force and threat than before. In this expanding setting of increasing, deepening, and thickening interdependence, the role of military force, however much still useful, was being downgraded by other preferred and more relevant noncoercive policy instruments.[38]

If institutionalist theory is unable to explain the end of the cold war and the breakup of the Soviet Union if national and ethnic factors are included in the equation, institutionalists are able to include observations within their research programs about the behavior of the state and international actors ignored or slighted by realist and neorealist theorists. The benefits of détente pursued by Gorbachev and his reformers could be accommodated by liberal institutionalist expectations. The multilateralization of security interests through arms control agreements, such as the elimination of intermediate-range ballistic missiles between the Soviet Union and the United States, could be harmonized, if not fully explained, by reference to institutionalist notions of cooperation. Similarly, domestically-driven economic reforms and the determination of command economies to adapt to the superior decision-making properties of free markets are easily incorporated into institutionalist thinking. Even the role of ideas and values could be assigned marginal explanatory power, as an intervening variable in orienting actor behavior, to reequilibrate the preponderant weight assigned by realists and liberal economists to exogenous, material factors as determinants of actor behavior.[39] Liberal institutionalists do a better job than their competitors in describing actor behavior. Parsimony is sacrificed to complexity and, consequently, explanations and predictions based on the liberal institutionalist paradigm are less coherent and more problematic.

Hard facts and observation are preconditions for assessing the validity of a theory. By insisting on the complexity of international exchanges, the influence of transnational actors, and the constraints of international institutions, institutionalists play a very useful role in theory development. The richer descriptions they provide of international actor behavior guard against too early closure by suppressing observations of actor behavior at odds with a security theory's explanations and predictions. It also problematizes reliance on convenient ceteris paribus assumptions to avoid unsettling contradictory empirical observations. This conceptual defense mechanism may save theories to fight another day, but at the expense of addressing empirical data that contests the explanatory and predictive power of the theory.

Behaviorism

Behaviorism is not a theory of security. Rather, it is a collective noun embracing a wide range of research programs that address security issues, most notably war. These research programs are loosely associated with each other by their commitment to a set of shared methodological approaches to the study of security and international relations. Questions of ontology and epistemology, central to realist or constructivist paradigms, respectively, are subordinated to prevailing methodological and evidentiary rules associated with quantitative measures of actor behavior. Mathematical and statistical measures and objectively-discernible and potentially-replicable evidence are used to test propositions about actor behavior. Whereas classical realism, whether viewed from a Hobbesian individual or state perspective, makes assumptions about the actors' makeup, most researchers practicing a scientific approach to explaining actor behavior and, specifically, to behavior having a security content are neutral with respect to the composition of the state, that is, whether states are inherently or essentially disposed to cooperation and conflict. Instead, these researchers attempt to measure the behavior of actors under different but clearly specified conditions to establish correlations between observed behavior and these conditions.[40] These theorists reduce the cold war to a data point.[41] The same methodological and evidentiary rules are applied to all applicable cases of interest to the researcher. The cold war and the implosion of the Soviet Union do not count for more or less than other relevant data or cases assembled by the researcher to test a proposition posed by the research design. The ideographic approach of historians or many realist theorists is eschewed, however rich and textured their detailed descriptions of conflict and war. Actor behavior is subject to empirical verification across time and space in terms of the expected behavior of the actor(s) under examination, measured typically at statistically-significant levels of occurrence.

It is difficult to generalize across the vast and growing scholarly output associated with behavioral research programs. If researchers concerned with explaining war are representative of those focused on security studies, it would appear appropriate to adopt Manus Midlarsky's characterization of the variety and richness of these theoretical perspectives as "the search for *theories* of *wars*" rather than for a unified theory applicable to all cases of armed conflict.[42] Midlarsky divides his useful overview of war studies into systemic, nation-state dyadic, and state-centered theories of war. Each category embraces a wide number of studies appropriate to the level of analysis and the actor—typically the state—under scrutiny.

At a systemic level, the debate among behaviorists is between those who contend that either a multipolar or a bipolar system is more stable, that is, less prone to armed hostilities and war. Rather than deduce whether one or the other is more war-prone, the approach favored by Waltz,[43] behaviorists attempt to identify all relevant cases in which differently configured multipolar systems, including the limiting bipolar model, can be identified and categorized to test their respective dispositions to induce actors to use force and threats and to resort to war. War is also operationalized by universally applied counting rules. It is typically defined as a hostile exchange between states resulting in a specific level of deaths and casualties. This standardizes war statistically and ostensibly frees the war event from historical circumstances not directly pertinent to the model or statistical test being applied. Such a science of international relations and, by extension, of security purports to go beyond what J. David Singer terms "the selective recall of historical anecdotes or, worse yet, . . . folkloristic hunches about how individuals allegedly behave. . . ."[44] Systems might assume a hierarchic structure or a decentralized system of units of approximately equal material power or some kind of ordering principle between these extremes. To date, systemic research studies of war proneness have scarcely been conclusive. However much behavioral researchers may share a common methodology and positivist assumptions about valid and reproducible data, they continue to differ over how they measure their specified variables, over the space and time and domains of actor behavior, and over the statistical models applied to often noncomparable data sets.

These differences are no more acutely apparent than the choices made by researchers of what level of analysis of actor behavior they wish to measure and test. In contrast to systemic theorists, many behaviorists prefer to focus at a unit or state level of analysis. This does not preclude the incorporation of systemic research results into their depictions of actor behavior. These are assumed to be taken into account in the calculations made by the actors in their transactions. Borrowing directly from microeconomic expected utility theory, these theorists substitute the pursuit of power and its relevance to war as the utility to be maximized rather than the economic liberal stipulation of material wealth or welfare. States as rational actors are expected to estimate the probability of achieving their objectives in light of the structure of the international system and, most relevantly, of the countervailing power likely to be arrayed against them by other states. Decision makers are expected to always choose the strategy most likely to yield "the highest expected utility."[45] The utility of that strategy is demonstrated over time by how it performs. The predictions of actor behavior depend supposedly on objective determination, and not on the analyst having to guess or interpret the ideational values or psychological makeup of the actor or its capacity to process information about the real world. The strength and weakness of expected utility theory is that it is almost flawless in its postprediction capacity since whatever results arise from strategic action are confirmed by these winning strategies.

Still other researchers prefer to go below the state or unitary actor level of analysis to explain or predict war. Much attention has been devoted in the past decade to the proposition that democracies do not fight each other. This Kantian expectation, resurrected by Michael Doyle,[46] has been bolstered by a proliferation of empirical studies that, despite their individual reservations, converge on this proposition. Three principal causes are assigned as explanation for this pattern of behavior. First, democratic ideology values cooperation and consensus over force and threats in making collective choices. Second, democratic institutions mutually restrain the struggle for power internal to the state. Legislative, executive, and judicial branches balance each other. These checks and balances are assumed to be projected in the exchanges of democratic polities since they are presumably socialized to accept limits on their power. Finally, pluralistic politics and frequently changing coalitions and alliances preclude a zero-sum game in which contestants are permanently put at a disadvantage or are excluded from participating in the making and application of rules for the society. Ideology, institutions, and pluralistic politics create an open society where decisions are more transparent and where other states, most notably other democracies, are able to identify those responsible for what decisions a state makes and the constraints under which those choices are being made.[47]

All of these behavioral approaches reconceptualize actor behavior in terms of those methods and rules of evidence that can meet empirical and replicable tests. For behaviorists, unless cases or data can be reduced to universally-applied methods and rules of evidence, testable generalizations across observations are precluded. From this research viewpoint, the cold war and the implosion of the Soviet Union are instances of a larger set of actor actions and reactions relevant to a pattern of behavior of interest to the researcher. The conceptualizations of actors as participants in a conflict of global proportions are subordinated to these methodological protocols and standardized rules for collecting, organizing, and measuring data appropriate to the propositions to be validated or rejected.

Behaviorists expect not only that persistent work will identify propositions that hold over time and space but also that such knowledge will accumulate to form a body of testable, scientific knowledge about actor behavior. Few among the most ardent partisans of behaviorism would argue that the expectation of accumulated knowledge has been realized or that it will be achieved any time soon.[48] This shortcoming, accentuated by failure of a behavioral approach to anticipate the end of the bipolar system and the ascendancy of Western liberal market democracies, exposes behavioral approaches to the criticism of relevance and salience. The research designs of interest to the analyst are privileged over those of the actors engaged in a deadly struggle and over what these actors believe they need to know about the political conditions and constraints under which they act to succeed. However much simplification and research controls are necessary for a science of security to progress, this proposition-testing approach opens behaviorists to charges of having no theory to guide their research programs. Realist and constructivist critics reject the idea that this approach can produce a general theory of actor behavior of international relations or security. For neorealists, like Waltz, no list of propositions can sum up to a theory of state behavior. Rules and principles of behavior can well be identified, but they are to be understood as derivatives of a general condition of power and its distribution across units under conditions of anarchy.[49]

Similarly, the correlation between democracies and nonwar can well be observed and the properties of democracies, as noted earlier, can be cited as the causes for peace. But this association of democratic properties with nonwar is a correlation, not a theory explaining either why democracies allegedly do not fight or why a world society of democratic regimes would necessarily be peaceful in resolving differences. Constructivists argue that, whether explaining war or peace, a behavioral approach—no less than realists and neorealists—assumes as given what is to be demonstrated. This is true whether the focus is on why populations prefer democratic regimes over alternatives or on why states have arisen as central actors in world politics. Security as a value ostensibly lies in how the identities of social actors are constructed. From the perspective of this constructivist critique, international relations is fundamentally not about the material conditions of power under which actors behave but about the ideational and normative determinants of these actors and the meaning, significance, and value they attach to these material conditions, partially or fully as extensions of their identities. These ideational determinants are reflected in the culture, religion, and language of the actors. They infuse meaning into what most other theorists assume are the material and exogenous determinants of actor behavior.

Constructivism

Constructivism, like behavioral research programs, represents a broad array of theorists and scholars rather than a coherent school of thought. Constructivists challenge the narrow scope of the actors and factors associated with the rival paradigms sketched above. This challenge assumes two forms. The first is based on epistemological, methodological, and evidentiary grounds. Constructivists stipulate a "cultural-institutional environment" that shapes and shoves actor behavior.[50] The norms attributable to actors by constructivist researchers are argued to have causal effect. Rejected is the assumption of realists and neorealists that reduces these justifications to rationalizations of coercive power and material capabilities. Nor do constructivists accept the notion of neoliberal scholarship that the norms arising from international regimes and institutions are purely functional and instrumental, principally intervening variables in the exchanges of egoistic actors and subject to the shared, if differentially-enjoyed, utilities that institutions provide. Both material and rational instrumental reductionism are asserted to be inconclusive in explaining state behavior or the state's conception of its interests, most prominently those bearing on its survival and security. As three prominent theorists explain: "it makes little sense to separate power and culture as distinct phenomena or causes: material power and coercion often derive their power from culture. . . . The issue is what accounts for power, not whether power is present."[51]

The second line of constructivist attack is more fundamental and rests on ontological grounds. Most of the researchers already discussed assume the state and its interests as given. State interests, whether in pursuit of relative (realists/neorealists) or absolute (economic and institutionalist liberals) gains, are exogenously determined. Constructivists problematize both the state and its interests. Stress is placed on the formation of actor identities. Background cultural-institutional norms are alleged to define the identity of an actor or state. That identity then defines the interests of the state-actor. These interests are not uniform over time and space, nor is the state necessarily unitary. Why is the United States indifferent, for example, to the possession of nuclear weapons by France or Great Britain, both with substantial nuclear striking power, but feels threatened by the possibility that Iraq or North Korea might possess even one nuclear weapon? Why do the states of NATO form a Deutschian security community, dedicated to the peaceful resolution of conflicts even after the targeted rival, the Soviet Union and its satellites, has passed from the scene?[52] Thomas Risse-Kappen argues that the democratic norms of these states defined these states as sharing a collective identity and interest in the peaceful resolution of differences.[53] States may exist under conditions of anarchy, but

"Anarchy Is What States Make Out of It," as Alexander Wendt asserts.[54] The cultural-institutional environment, essentially nonmaterial and ideational in composition, can purportedly reconstitute and transform the identities of states, the interests they believe important, and what forms of power they employ in pursuit of these interests.

Constructivists may be divided into two broad groups. "Light" constructivists concede the force of material factors in driving actor behavior. They do not reject outright the assumptions of other research paradigms. Rather, they insist on ideational factors, too, to explain outcomes in world politics.[55] Case studies and process-tracing studies are relied upon to offset the rationalist-deductive and large-N statistical studies underwriting behavioral research or the ad hoc presumptions of realist and neorealist theory.[56]

"Heavy" constructivists, on the other hand, go further. The material conditions within which actor exchanges are embedded are radically subordinated in their causal effect to the meaning and value attributed by actors to these factors, whether military capabilities or economic and technological resources. The identities constructed by actors determine their interests, policies toward each other, and behavior. This subjective conception of social identities and the endogenous determination of actor interests that it implies all but cuts off heavy constructivists from mainstream social science and its attempt to describe, explain, and predict actor behavior. *Erklären,* or explanation, is totally sacrificed to *Verstehen,* or the subjective understanding of the components of actor makeup, thought, and action. This position risks burning all conceptual bridges to prevailing and competing social science research programs. Adopting a postmodernist position, more philosophical than social scientific, heavy constructivists assert the primacy of norms as power and the derivation of these informing and controlling norms as a product of the discourse and discursive practices of actors.[57] No tree falls unless it is heard by human ears; humans *are* the measure of what they see and value.

Constructivists of different persuasions and levels of commitment offer a range of explanations for the end of bipolarity and the self-destruction of the Soviet Union as a state. Some focus on the cognitive reformulation of the external environment by key elite decision makers, specifically Soviet premier Mikhail Gorbachev. They suggest that the political learning of the Soviet leader and his partisans induced a fundamental change in their understanding of the military power arrayed against the Soviet state (détente over unremitting conflict), the technological and economic determinants of sustained growth (perestroika), and the popular supports for exterior and interior reform programs (glasnost and democratization).[58] Ideas count as critical intervening variables that direct the strategic choices of decision makers in adapting to their material environment or in their attempts to impose their preferences on other actors and the power structures within which they act. Still others focus on structural constraints, like the reassertion of nationalism and the delegitimation of the Communist regime throughout Eastern Europe and within the Soviet Union itself, to explain the collapse of the Soviet empire.[59]

Constructivism and its adherents are strong on identifying hard facts at odds with the assumptions and findings of other security paradigms. These researchers are less helpful in providing a coherent theory either of international relations or of security. Case studies provide rich, thick, and textured interpretations of actor behavior that would appear to highlight and validate the causal force of identities, the impact of identity on interests, and background and fundamentally subjective cultural-environmental structure or ideas, values, and norms in directing actor thought, decisions, and actions. However, these studies are not easily replicable in the same sense that large data sets can presumably be assembled in like manner, if all researchers use the same rules for categorization and counting relevant to the collection process and to the proposition being tested.

Nor can the findings of a case or several cases be generalized over a large number of cases or actor decisions. Constructivism has no clear theory of agency in the way that rational actor or realist or liberal economic theory possesses. The former can assume that actors engaged in surviving and in pursuing their security interests will always prefer more power or gain than less or, if a liberal institutionalist, more absolute power and gain than less. Similarly rational economic decision makers always prefer more material goods than less. They are aided in this pursuit by markets that provide them with relative prices to allocate scarce resources either as suppliers or consumers of goods and services. Constructivists do not have a fixed point from which to develop their research designs and findings. They do not posit a maximizing utility interest that orients actor behavior and dictates strategies and choices. The notion of utility itself is a property of identity and the interests flowing from identity.

These criticisms aside, the value of constructivist contributions should not be underestimated or dismissed. The constructivist research program has widened the scope of theoretical and empirical research and underscored the discrepant outcomes of actor behavior that need to be reconciled with the countervailing research assumptions and paradigms of other approaches. Constructivists reintroduce history into the study of international relations. They problematize power, interests, identities, and ultimately the state itself. As Peter J. Katzenstein concludes, "The historical evidence compels us to relinquish the notion of states with unproblematic identities."[60]

Conclusion

So where does the *tour d'horizon* leave us? On the one hand, we might despair over this disarray of paradigms and competing research programs. Clearly, there is no one approach, one methodology, or one set of policy prescriptions at the disposition of actors to solve their varied, overlapping, and conflicting security problems. Indeed, the very notion of what actors are is critical for the study of security, and the forces shaping their behavior remain open questions. This brief overview reveals these shortcomings of prevailing security theory and research.

On the other hand, and following Lakatos, pluralism serves us better than we might believe—or wish. Depending on the security question to be addressed, each of these paradigms, in greater or lesser measure, has something potentially worthwhile to say about the behavior of relevant actors. They can, arguably, assist actors in understanding their security problems and in solving them. In retrospect, it would appear that a realist and neorealist perspective had relevance during the interwar period and even thereafter as the cold war unfolded insofar as the interests of the Western liberal market democracies and their survival were concerned. What, for example, does liberal institutionalism or liberal economic theory have to say about genocide in Rwanda or ethnic cleansing in the former Yugoslavia or racial and religious civil war in Sudan or continuing Middle East hostilities between Arabs and Jews?

Conversely, as the logic and power of market mechanisms and democratization have grown apace around the globe, formerly persuasive realist and neorealist paradigms have lost force. The creation of a security community in the northern hemisphere between the liberal democracies would appear to have relaxed if not definitively surmounted the security dilemma besetting nation-states and the nation-state system. These trends in the globalization of market and democratic behavior, and the exogenous and endogenous factors explaining actor choices that their decisions and actions imply, must still be reconciled with the continuing force of national, ethnic, and religious identities at odds with expected actor behavior. The notion of the sovereign, unitary state within a self-help system, however attractive as a logical construct, is progressively less persuasive and impressive if the domestic veil is lifted to reveal how state policy is made. It is increasingly less persuasive when the welfare demands of populations everywhere for "more now," for larger and sturdier social safety nets, or for a greater say in constructing their security arrangements are taken into account in describing and explaining state behavior. Nor do these democratizing forces—economic and political—appear to be fully explicable solely by reference to the exchanges of isolated, egoistic actors.

There is no golden age, as some would argue,[61] to which analysts can repair when security theory and actor practice were seemingly in harmony. Nor is such a golden age clearly discernible on the horizon today. Yet never, too, have security studies been more healthy and potentially more relevant to the differing and contesting needs of a proliferation of major actors in world politics.

Notes

1. See Pierre Allan and Kjell Goldmann, eds., *The End of the Cold War: Evaluating Theories of International Relations* (Dordrecht, Netherlands: Nijhoff, 1992); John Lewis Gaddis, "International Relations Theory and the End of the Cold War," *International Security* 17 (1992–93): 5–58; Charles W. Kegley Jr., ed., *Controversies in International Relations Theory: Realism and the Neoliberal Challenge* (New York: St. Martin's, 1995); Richard Ned Lebow and Thomas Risse-Kappen, eds., *International Relations Theory and the End of the Cold War* (New York: Columbia University Press, 1995).
2. See John J. Mearsheimer, "Back to the Future: Instability in Europe after the Cold War," *International Security* 15 (1990): 5–57; John J. Mearsheimer, "The False Promise of International Institutions," *International Security* 19 (1994): 5–49; Stephen M. Walt, "The Renaissance of Security Studies," *International Studies Quarterly* 35, no. 2 (1991): 211–39; Kenneth N. Waltz, "The Emerging Structure of International Politics," *International Security* 18 (1993): 44–79.
3. These points are developed at greater length in Edward A. Kolodziej, "Security Studies for the Next Millennium: Quo Vadis?" in *Critical Reflec-*

tions on Security and Change, ed. Stuart Croft and Terry Terriff (London: Cass, 2000), 18–38.
4. See Lawrence Freedman, "International Security: Changing Targets," *Foreign Policy* 110 (spring 1998): 53ff.
5. Imre Lakatos, "Falsification and the Methodology of Scientific Research Programmes," in *Criticism and the Growth of Knowledge,* ed. Imre Lakatos and Alan Musgrave (Cambridge: Cambridge University Press, 1970), 91–195.
6. William C. Wohlforth, "Realism and the End of the Cold War," *International Security* 19, no. 3 (1994–95): 95.
7. See the symposium in *Arms Control* for these divergent perspectives. Stuart Croft, ed., *Symposium on Security Studies,* special issue of *Arms Control* 13 (1992).
8. Freedman, "International Security."
9. Thucydides, *The Peloponnesian War* (New York: Modern Library, 1951), 330–37.
10. Hedley Bull, *The Anarchical Society: A Study of Order in World Politics* (London: Macmillan, 1977).
11. Thomas Hobbes, *Leviathan* (New York: Dutton, 1950), 104; see also Dennis H. Wrong, *The Problem of Order: What Unites and Divides Society* (Cambridge: Harvard University Press, 1994).
12. Carl von Clausewitz, *On War* (Princeton, N.J.: Princeton University Press, 1976).
13. Immanuel Kant, "Perpetual Peace: A Philosophical Essay," in *The Theory of International Relations,* ed. M. G. Forsyth et al. (New York: E.P. Dutton and Company, Inc., 1950), 200–44.
14. David A. Baldwin, "Security Studies and the End of the Cold War," *World Politics* 48, no. 1 (1995): 117–41. The distinction between a theory of security and strategy is central to the debate over what is security studies. See Edward A. Kolodziej, "Renaissance in Security Studies: Caveat Lector!" *International Studies Quarterly* 36, no. 4 (1992): 421–28; and Walt, "The Renaissance of Security Studies." For a recent restatement of the centrality of strategy over security theory, see Colin S. Gray, *Modern Strategy* (Oxford: Oxford University Press, 1999).
15. The leading statement of the traditional realist argument is, of course, Hans Morgenthau, *Politics among Nations: The Struggle for Power and Peace* (New York: Knopf, 1948).
16. Robert Gilpin, *The Political Economy of International Relations* (Princeton, N.J.: Princeton University Press, 1987); Joseph M. Grieco, *Cooperation among Nations* (Ithaca, N.Y.: Cornell University Press, 1990).
17. Kenneth N. Waltz, *Theory of International Politics* (Reading, Mass.: Addison-Wesley, 1979). For a contrasting view see Karl W. Deutsch and J. David Singer, "Multipolar Power Systems and International Stability," *World Politics* 16, no. 1 (1964): 390–406.
18. For a review of these criticisms and a thoughtful defense of realism, see Wohlforth, "Realism and the End of the Cold War"; William C. Wohlforth, ed., *Witnesses to the End of the Cold War* (Baltimore: Johns Hop-

kins University Press, 1996); William C. Wohlforth, "Reality Check: Revising Theories of International Politics in Response to the End of the Cold War," *World Politics* 50, no. 4 (1998): 650–80.
19. Marshall I. Goldman, *What Went Wrong with Perestroika* (New York: Norton, 1991).
20. Mearsheimer, "Back to the Future"; Waltz, "The Emerging Structure of International Politics."
21. Norman Angell, *The Great Illusion* (London: Heinemann, 1909).
22. Joseph Schumpeter, *Imperialism* (New York: Meridian, 1955).
23. John Mueller, *Retreat from Doomsday* (New York: Basic Books, 1989).
24. John Gerard Ruggie, "International Regimes, Transactions, and Change: Embedded Liberalism in the Postwar Economic Order," *International Organization* 36, no. 2 (1982): 379–415; John Gerard Ruggie, ed., *Multilateralism Matters: The Theory and Practice of an Institutional Form* (New York: Columbia University Press, 1993).
25. János Kornai, *The Socialist System: The Political Economy of Communism* (Princeton, N.J.: Princeton University Press, 1992).
26. Adam Smith, *The Wealth of Nations* (Oxford, England: Clarendon, 1976).
27. Friedrich von Hayek, *Individual Freedom and Economic Order* (Chicago: University of Chicago Press, 1948); Friedrich von Hayek, *The Fatal Conceit: The Errors of Socialism* (London: Routledge, 1988).
28. Robert Gilpin, *War and Change in World Politics* (Cambridge: Cambridge University Press, 1981); Gilpin, *The Political Economy of International Relations*; Douglass C. North, *Institutions, Institutional Change, and Economic Performance* (Cambridge: Cambridge University Press, 1990).
29. Lester Thurow, *The Future of Capitalism* (New York: Morrow, 1996).
30. Peter Evans, Dietrich Rueschemeyer, and Theda Skocpol, eds., *Bringing the State Back In* (Baltimore: Johns Hopkins University Press, 1985).
31. Space constraints preclude an extensive review of the relevance of Marxist theory to world politics.
32. David A. Baldwin, ed., *Neorealism and Neoliberalism* (New York: Columbia University Press, 1993). This volume brings together realists, neorealists, and institutionalists who accept the assumption of rational egoists as a common beginning point for theory. They diverge along several dimensions, among the most important being the explanatory power of institutions in shaping state behavior.
33. Thomas Schelling, *The Strategy of Conflict* (New York: Oxford University Press, 1960).
34. Robert Axelrod, *The Evolution of Cooperation* (New York: Basic Books, 1984).
35. Ibid., 176.
36. Ronald H. Coase, "The Nature of the Firm," *Economica* 4 (1937): 386–405; Ronald H. Coase, "The Problem of Social Cost," *Journal of Law and Economics* 3 (1960): 1–44.
37. Robert O. Keohane, *After Hegemony: Cooperation and Discord in the World Economy* (Princeton, N.J.: Princeton University Press, 1984).

38. Joseph S. Nye Jr., *Bound to Lead* (New York: Basic Books, 1990).
39. Judith Goldstein and Robert O. Keohane, eds., *Ideas and Foreign Policy: Beliefs, Institutions, and Political Change* (Ithaca, N.Y.: Cornell University Press, 1993).
40. For example, see the Correlates of War Project, J. David Singer and Melvin Small, *Resort to Arms: International and Civil Wars, 1815–1980* (Beverly Hills, Calif.: Sage, 1982).
41. Wohlforth, "Reality Check."
42. Manus I. Midlarsky, ed., *Handbook of War Studies* (Boston: Unwin Hyman, 1989), xx. Midlarsky's emphasis.
43. Waltz, *Theory of International Politics*.
44. J. David Singer, "System Structure, Decision Processes, and the Incidence of International War," in Midlarsky, *Handbook of War Studies*, 20.
45. Bruce Bueno de Mesquita, "The Contribution of Expected-Utility Theory to the Study of International Conflict," in Midlarsky, *Handbook of War Studies*, 144.
46. Michael W. Doyle, "Liberalism and World Politics," *American Political Science Review* 80 (December 1986): 1151–69.
47. Bruce Russett, *Grasping the Democratic Peace: Principles for a Post–Cold War World* (Princeton, N.J.: Princeton University Press, 1993).
48. See, for example, Singer, "System Structure, Decision Processes, and the Incidence of International War," 20–21.
49. Waltz, *Theory of International Politics*.
50. No attempt is made to cover the vast and growing literature that can be associated with the constructivist research program. Valuable as a starting point is the edited volume by Peter Katzenstein, notably chapters 1 and 2, which cite most of the relevant literature up to its publication. Peter J. Katzenstein, *The Culture of National Security* (New York: Columbia University Press, 1996). For more recent analysis see John Gerard Ruggie, "What Makes the World Hang Together? Neo-Utilitarianism and the Social Constructivist Challenge," *International Organization* 52, no. 4 (1998): 855–85; and Alexander Wendt, *Social Theory of International Politics* (Cambridge: Cambridge University Press, 1999).
51. Ronald L. Jepperson, Alexander Wendt, and Peter J, Katzenstein, "Norms, Identity, and Culture in National Security," in Katzenstein, *The Culture of National Security*, 40.
52. Karl Deutsch, *Political Community and the North Atlantic Area* (Princeton, N.J.: Princeton University Press, 1957).
53. Thomas Risse-Kappen, "Collective Identity in a Democratic Community," in Katzenstein, *The Culture of National Security*, 357–99.
54. Alexander Wendt, "Anarchy Is What States Make Out of It: The Social Construction of Power Politics," *International Organization* 46, no. 2 (1992): 391–425. Milner also develops this line of analysis. Helen Milner, "International Theories of Cooperation among Nations," *World Politics* 44, no. 2 (1992): 466–96.
55. For example, see Michael Barnett and Emanuel Adler, eds., *Security Communities* (Cambridge: Cambridge University Press, 1998).

56. For examples, consult Martha Finnemore, *National Interests in International Society* (Ithaca, N.Y.: Cornell University Press, 1996); and Audie Klotz, *Norms in International Relations: The Struggle against Apartheid* (Ithaca, N.Y.: Cornell University Press, 1995).
57. Richard K. Ashley, "The Poverty of Neorealism," *International Organization* 38, no. 1 (1984): 225–86.
58. Robert G. Herman, "Identity, Norms, and National Security: The Soviet Foreign Policy Revolution and the End of the Cold War," in Katzenstein, *The Culture of National Security*, 271–316.
59. See the essays in Lebow and Risse-Kappen, *International Relations Theory and the End of the Cold War*, for examples of these interpretations of why the cold war ended, which putatively contradict competing explanations.
60. Katzenstein, *The Culture of National Security*, 23.
61. Walt, "The Renaissance of Security Studies."

SECURITY AND PEACE

Understanding, Production, and Work Style

Davis B. Bobrow

The most attractive accomplishment of security and peace studies and policies would be for them to become historical curiosities akin to alchemy, Victorian-era plumbing, or vanquished diseases. A second best would be signs of progress on that road marked by improved understanding and early diagnosis, and—even better—more available and less costly means for prevention and treatment, containment and cure. To extend the medical metaphor, we would then see in the present or in confident prospect reductions in the incidence and severity of insecurity, destruction, casualties, and deaths, and in the opportunity costs of measures to achieve such reductions.

From the second-best perspective, these are in some ways the best of times for security and peace studies and policies. In other ways, they are far from that and leave a lot to be desired. These two aspects of our current intellectual and policy situation suggest lessons that are sobering in their implications for the limits on our understanding of security and peace and even more so for the application of our understanding to produce those collective accomplishments. Of no less importance, this duality challenges us to adopt a work style appropriate both to what we have learned and produced and to our continuing limitations—and to socialize successor generations of security and peace experts into it.

The following pages begin with a crude summary of what seems to me to be "good news" about the point to which we have come and then turn to a "darker side" suggesting how far we have to go. These lead me to identify some persistent realities that should be squarely faced up to and to offer some suggestions on how we should deal with our unfinished agenda.[1]

The Good News

We can readily recognize the abundance of intellectual and policy effort devoted to understanding and producing security and peace over the last half century and six now widely accepted expansions in the scope and resources of the field.

First, even the most cursory review of our major journals shows in recent decades a cornucopia of "prisms" for considering security and peace that apparently go beyond traditional power-centered and thus competitive (realism) and normatively centered and potentially cooperative (idealism) perspectives. Prominent entrants in the security and peace theory sweepstakes now wear rational choice, institutionalism, critical security, gender, power transition, domestic politics, failed state, democratic peace, and ideational perspective colors.

The proliferation of prisms has been accompanied, particularly in the last two decades, by five additional expansions of scope and increases of attention and resources: issue domains, generic types of actors, relevant specific actors with asymmetric agendas and assets, technology-enabled interactions, and information and information-processing tools.

Discussions of security and peace have come to regularly encompass issue domains other than the political-military such as economic, environmental, demographic, public health, sociocultural continuity, and fundamental political forms.

That expansion has brought with it attention to a widening range of generic types of actors inside and outside of governments. Consider the now rather accepted inclusion of central government civil ministries, subnational public authorities, firms and in particular multinational corporations, nongovernmental organizations (domestic and transnational), expert ("epistemic") communities, international governmental organizations (regional and global, functionally specific such as international financial institutions or multipurpose such as the G-7).

The end of the cold war has also brought increased attention to a larger if changing number of specific actors (with proper noun names) with more asymmetric agendas and capabilities for pursuing security and peace. Those players and purposes often were not, at least in prevailing American frames, important in the bipolar construct or were only considered in relation to it with considerable distortion. Asymmetric agendas now and for the future combine with asymmetric assets and vulnerabilities derived from the expansion discussed next.

Technology innovation and diffusion have changed the world in terms of damage-inflicting capacity, communication, mobility, transparency, and financial and commercial globalization. Their joint effects have massively increased the variety, speed, reach, visibility, and relevance of interactions across borders. As a consequence, the behaviors and the perceptions, the independent and intervening variables if you will, that matter for actual and recognized states of security and peace have proliferated. Barriers to entry into and competition in security and peace arenas have been lowered while time to adapt to ease of entry in analytic or policy terms has shrunk.

A final type of expansion involves resources to help in coping with or even being aware of the sets of expansions just noted. Compared with several decades ago, researchers and analysts of security and peace matters are enormously advantaged in terms of the amount and timeliness of information. The costs required for exploiting and processing that information have been sharply reduced. Retrieval and pattern identification have been facilitated and with them the feasibility of promptly flagging anomalies and changes. And surely the expert cadres and skill repertoires applicable to problems of security and peace have grown enormously within and across functional disciplines and geographic area specializations.

In sum, those who would research, manage, and even teach security and peace matters have entered in a period of "riches" with respect to concepts, phenomena, information, and human capital. All that bodes well for the second-best accomplishment suggested earlier.

The Darker Side

One surely can recognize those riches and still have serious reservations about the extent to which our capacities to understand and produce security and peace have substantially improved. There are in general two reasons for such reservations. First, some of the expansions may be more matters of rediscovery or relabeling ("branding") than of genuine, progressive innovation. Second, the improvements may not have kept pace with the challenges posed by the six expansions. The first reservation implies that we may not be as absolutely better off in comprehending and dealing with security and peace problems as many think. The second implies that even if we are, those achievements may in a relative sense lag behind ramifying challenges to security and peace. I will briefly address the first reservation and then turn to the second.

To a significant extent, the first five expansions involve resurrection and relabeling rather than genuine discovery and innovation if we extend our recollections into (a) a more extended past than the several most recent decades and (b) a broader set of interpretations and policy emphases than those of the cold war superpowers. To deny this amounts to confusing cold war emphases in the American security and peace studies community with earlier and even contemporaneously different foci of attention.

Earlier periods and contemporary policy intellectual communities were not devoid of recognitions of the role of institutions and political forms national and international, ideas and problem-framing constructions, critiques of state power and its intellectual servants, or applications of economistic rationality. Security and peace were held to involve matters of economics and commerce, natural resource scarcity and control, identity-based aspirations and sociocultural survival concerns, natalist and public health issues, and domestically-oriented political opportunism.

In such frames, generic actors other than central government military departments were also treated as security-and peace-relevant subjects ranging from arms merchants to transnational financiers to religious faith movements and institutions. There surely was attention to multilateral institutions such as leagues and concerts. Specific, named actors other than the largest and most powerful states did not escape notice including networks. They were recognized to have on occasion asymmetric agendas and assets for inflicting harms on the conventionally more powerful involving resolve, agility, and guile. After all, use of the slingshot against the heavily-armed warrior goes back a long way. Finally, the current significance of new technologies and their applications is but the most recent of many such transformative waves.

Whatever one's views on their degree of genuine innovation, recent expansions or resurrections are to be applauded. Nevertheless, they do not necessarily outweigh the evolution of intellectual and policy challenges to security and peace.

More and different schools of thought make it less likely that important elements of the security and peace problematique will go unrecognized. They do not, however, guarantee that a wise synthesis will occur. Instead, they may defer it by focusing effort on deepening each school and finding grist for its narrow-purpose mill by treating only particular aspects of the other five expansions. That would not be unhelpful for the production of security and peace if the schools have harmonious implications for all or even most relevant parties, means, and ends—but that is questionable.

Consider, for example, two of the most intriguing, potentially powerful, and empirically relatively well-based contemporary perspectives—power transition and democratic peace theories. The first prescribes unipolarity globally and regionally and thus policies to achieve and maintain single-state dominance alone or through coalition leadership. It has an obviously realist core emphasizing shares of traditional power assets, and it focuses on security and peace at the level of states and combinations of states. It raises questions about the willingness of others to provide the leading state with the benefits it would want, or perhaps even need, to play such a role.

Power transition theory leaves open the possibilities of genuine conversion to the conventions espoused by the prevailing leading state. It also allows for the possibilities that others might be willing to do so only with a sigh so long as they see no attractive choice, or even adopt a deliberate stratagem of compliance to secure the assets to catch up with and eventually surpass the leading state globally or regionally. The first may well call for the leading state to be notably reliable and generous in its provision of security and peace to current and potential followers. That, however, poses a requirement of the domestic politics of the leading state, but why and how that requirement will be met lies outside of power transition theory. The second, as with the contemporary engagement of China, poses eventual security and peace risks. If a power transition is eventually inevitable, we are left to ponder the feasibility of transforming the probable successor prior to transition. Why should a realist-minded successor informed about power transition theory believe that transformation efforts by the current leading state are primarily intended to smooth a transition rather than avoid or postpone one?

Democratic peace theory (with its idealist core) in contrast prescribes creation of a world of essentially compatible, if somewhat competitive, states based on sufficiently common norms, interests, and domestic politics to damp security threats and buttress peace preferences. A "community of democracies" is held to be at least a latent security community for its members. While the focus is on state political forms, those recommended do offer in a probabilistic fashion conditions conducive to (but not guaranteeing) security and peace for subpopulations and even individual citizens. For security and peace, there are several significant problems since we begin from a world of substantial power inequalities and less-than-full democracies. One is that even though established democracies seldom war with each other, powerful democracies do on occasion coerce (threaten at least the nonmilitary security of) less powerful ones. How severe can class disparities between democracies be before ostensible security communities are rather imperial and tributary state systems? A second is the less than short and linear path to the sorts of democracy the theory envisions. Whatever one labels such part-of-the-way-to- (or from-) democracy cases, their elites may have incentives to engage in actions and rhetoric whose immediate consequences are to lessen the national, regional, and international degree of security and peace. Indeed, such a nonprogressive course may become more rather than less likely with the initial onset of plebiscitarian democracy.

In the current world, the policy and policy intellectual communities of the American leading state seems to simultaneously subscribe to the ideas of both power transition and democratic peace theory. That combination does not inherently lead others to attribute full respect for their security and peace to those who hold and act on such a vision. International audiences may instead see a realist wolf draped in an idealist democratic cloak.

Even if the illustrative theories were more compatible than seems to be the case, they—like most of our other candidate conceptual perspectives—provide quite incomplete prescriptions. Imagine our reaction to a doctor who told us to take a particular medication without saying how much of it, for how long a period of time, and without warning and countermeasures about potential adverse side effects. Our likely demurs would not be trivial, and might easily turn to anger and pursuit of compensation if the treatment turned out to at most partially deal with symptoms but not the root pathology that is at the source of our troubles. If "prisms" are equivalent to diagnostic specializations, that undesirable possibility may well be increased. Of course, our "patient" may find herself given conflicting diagnostic advice (as with the "too fast" and "too slow" postmortems on the recent breakdown of the Israeli-Palestinian peace process). That situation poses risks of "compromise" mixing of emphases depriving each of efficacy, and not just of a mistaken choice between alternatives.

What of the other five previously mentioned expansions? That in issue areas surely is warranted as it comes to more closely approximate the stocks and flows that pose threats to individual, group, national, and international safety, and that singly or in combination can generate movement toward conflict or cooperation. Yet that expansion may pose a particular danger, and certainly poses some very difficult questions. The danger is of course that of securitization with its basic features of threat from the behavior and intentions of foreign others, assertion of privileged claims on resources, and warrant for waivers from the checks and balances institutional and normative of otherwise appropriate political processes. Surely a multidimensional conception of threats (and thus of threat agents) to security in the first instance only multiplies rather than eliminates the classic security dilemma. It does indeed make cooperative security and (impure) public goods provision more needed, but the domain expansion does not in itself guarantee increased provision in general or in a particular domain.

As security and peace come to be conceived of in a multifaceted way, some difficult questions become more pressing. What are the dynamics of cause and effect for each facet? What about interactions between facets? Consider the difficulties of sorting out the cause-and-effect thicket of relationships between economic, environmental, demographic, public health, and democratic governance domains. Even if the general sign of relationships is understood, that does not suffice to direct intellectual and policy resource allocation at the margin. We still lack an encompassing metric across security facets to weigh trade-offs between them. Simply adding to the mercantilist duo of power *and* prosperity enlarges our agenda more than it clarifies how to pursue it in real time, actual space, and available budgets.

Expansion of the types of actors relevant to security and peace brings with it not only the benefits of checks and balances and multiple point-of-entry systems but their disadvantages as well. After all, the expansion of types rests on the view that no single one should be expected to fully control what happens about security and peace. What are some of the darker-side issues? One is that of whether similarity of security-and peace-related preferences (of outcomes, means, and processes) within a generic type of actor exceeds differences. To the extent it does not, focusing on the variety of types may be misleading. Suppose instead that each type is rather homogeneous for our concerns. We then need to consider the possibilities for, transaction costs of, and likely content of deals struck between types. Are such arrangements easier for some facets of security, and if so which ones? If so, do we need to guard against unduly focusing on them and slighting others more crucial for security and peace? Under what circumstances are the deals likely to have desirable characteristics of anticipation, specificity, bindingness, and sustainable commitments that would significantly enhance security and peace?

The warranted awareness of more and more varied particular specific actors with the associated increases of asymmetries in agendas, assets, and vulnerabilities imply that several kinds of problems for security and peace are more rather than less difficult. Analytically, identifying a security and/or peace Pareto frontier or near-frontier for the relevant parties becomes harder. Even if identifiable, the requisites for its pursuit mount in terms of temporally-synchronized internal policy climates, acceptable transaction costs, equivalent risk-taking, common perceptions of precedents, and compatible interpretations of events and moves in terms of confidence-building or lessening. Accordingly, our needs for understanding and prediction ramify in general and in terms of "local knowledge" about what may for many have been obscure actors.

In logic, those challenges could be lessened by defining some actors, assets, and vulnerabilities as exogenous to peace and security systems, a sort of intellectual nonrecognition policy. That would confine intellectual and policy challenges to what amount to preferred others and preferred policy means and strategies based on prior investments and achievements. In reality, that choice may not be available. Cognitive and affective stances by some parties to security and peace matters cannot by themselves forestall others from having and pursuing their particular security agenda and claims, using whatever seems to them to be their most advantageous means, or adhering to culturally rooted visions of a good peace or a good war.

That leaves us with needs for informed and creative adjustment and adaptation (not to be confused with appeasement or total relativism). Meeting those needs calls for extending knowledge and insight about a substantially increased number of specific actors and about the offensive, defensive, and deterrence possibilities associated with the universe of asymmetrically-available assets and pertinent vulnerabilities.

Interactions enabled by the new technologies surely can facilitate security and peace in important ways. They also challenge established intellectual and policy conceptions about security and peace. That applies to the importance of particular general variables such as geographic distance and the mass of an actor's economic and population base. That also applies to the degree of overlap between the set of sovereign states and the universe of security- and peace-relevant generic and specific actors. In each of these examples, declines in relative importance are for more stable, slow-to-change elements of security and peace problems with more established management repertoires. We then face more imminent and significant obsolescence of intellectual and policy structures unless we find ways to generate less fixed, routinized, and inertial institutions and analytic frameworks.

Even the sixth expansion, that in information availability and professional expertise, is not necessarily an unmixed blessing. The possibilities of professional tribalism in sociology of knowledge terms versus synoptic judgment may well be increased analogously to the darker prospect from prism proliferation. The availability of larger and larger volumes of information may be met primarily by gatekeeping selection and compression mechanisms (individual, organizational, and software) unrepresentative of the world marked by the other expansions. The users of information may be unaware of the biases built into those mechanisms, let alone able to hold gatekeepers accountable. Lower barriers to information dissemination may lend themselves to advertent (disinformation and information management) or inadvertent reductions in information quality.

Some Lessons (We Should Have) Learned

Any selection of lessons from the previous good news and darker-side observations is, of course, substantially personal and subjective, but then so are most efforts at brief retrospective and prospective treatment of a highly-active and socially-important basic and applied research field. With that caveat, here are mine.

Beyond an aura of desirability, security and peace are and will remain contested or captured concepts. There will not be consensus on their operational content, sufficient conditions, or an encompassing, umbrella metric to measure the degree to which security and peace exist or the extent and rate of movement toward or away from them. As Wolfers suggested some decades ago, the basic conceptions are "ambiguous." That ongoing contestation has two major foci. The first involves disagreement about what aspects of human affairs individual and collective must be present to label a situation as one of security or peace. The second involves disagreement about for whom those chosen aspects held to amount to security or peace have to be present. The second dispute goes on about levels of analysis categories (e.g., individual, group, nation) and sociological and economic markers (e.g., race, religion, cohort, and class)—as well as about the divisibility or indivisibility of security and peace in relation to different nation-states and groups.

Security and peace concepts can of course be captured at particular points in space and time. Such local and temporary consensus reflects and for a while may reinforce success by some fraction of actors and institutions in privileging their constructs of security and peace (and thus their claims for attention and resource priority). The resulting conventional wisdom givens for academic and policy specialist discourse amount to political outcomes more than natural laws, as is also the case for security-and peace-linked prevailing distributions of attention and resources. Political competition and distributional controversy domestically and internationally are and will be present far more often than not. Accordingly, so too will be efforts to contest and capture the operational meaning and the indicative leading, concurrent, and lagging indicators of security and peace.

At the same time, there is and will be widespread agreement that a necessary condition for security and peace is not met for those who are currently or in prospect targeted for physical coercion. Yet even that agreed principle has substantial ambiguity and controversy with regard to differentiating less-than-unconditional, unqualified, and interstate situations. Does the necessary condition include absence of physical coercion and coercive threats by governmental and movement elites against their own citizens and members or placing them in harm's way? Does posing threat to others tend to stimulate beliefs that the poser is also a target that has yet to attain security or peace? Whatever the answers to these questions, we have yet and are unlikely to achieve agreed rules to assess the degree to which the necessary conditions for security and peace are unmet—descriptive or normative accounting rules to weigh the present versus the future, the probability of pain being inflicted and its likely severity, or the shortfall for self relative to that for others.

As with positive conceptions of security and peace, those about their absence also become subjects for capture, a quest in which the contenders rarely start from a level playing field. The views and partisans advantaged tend to follow from interpreted historical legacies and recent experiences. Absent gross failures, dramatic anomalies, or pervasive fatigue, established interpretations tend to prevail in academic and policy circles. Already-accepted views and their resource-advantaged custodians can dominate interpretations. They are well positioned to both frame the agenda for security and peace studies and analyses, and then to draw certification from that frame. Established conventions about insecurity and nonpeace are extraordinarily resilient and evidence-resistant. While they may eventually lose credibility, they can for an extended period deprive alternatives of the momentum that would make them persuasive. The odds work against timely recognition of grounds for change and favor elaboration and interpretive bolstering and tuning of previously established insecurity and nonpeace conceptions.

The six expansions cannot be relied on, and may on balance interfere with, the achievement of domestically and internationally widely-agreed and timely understandings about the determinants of security and peace and the implications of policies to produce them. Rather than relying on help from those expansions, we should accept a continuing need to adapt to them.

More specifically, functional types of issues are not as readily separated from each other as tractability for analysis or policy bargaining would have us desire. Decomposability and issue-isolation is a matter of fragile and tenuous consent by multiple, varied parties (for example, dual-use technology transfer as a military or economic matter, or emissions reduction as an environmental or economic security matter). Specific problem-solving between a pair or small number of states is hard to contain from becoming a precedent in the minds of others (for example, U.S. "rewards" to influence North Korean nuclear programs).

A good fit between signals intended and signals interpreted becomes less likely with a potential security and peace negative spiral. That is hardly a new problem, but it may well already have been worsening with the multiplication of generically- and specifically-different actors and accelerated signal transfer and interpretation. Without subscribing to a thesis of civilizational conflict, one can accept one of civilizational and subcivilizational miscommunication. The signals an actor in the security and peace problematique sends and believes it has received are substantially affected by prior judgments about where it sits, how and by whom it was placed there, and the agenda and capabilities of the other parties in the communication chain. All too readily what is for one party a defensive measure will for another be an offense-enabling one; an effort at compromise based on strength be a sign of weakness or a trap; an act of acceptance and empowerment be a move to dominate. Whatever tenuous confidence we have had in the fidelity of signaling systems needs to be downgraded and signal strength and interpretation clarification given more attention.

The technology and information expansions warrant reduced confidence in the feasibility of segregating issue domains, narrowing precedents, and clearly signaling intentions, incentives, and disincentives. Even before the recent expansions, history provides substantial cautions about overoptimism in those respects.

It would make security and peace studies easier if highly general theories could be readily operationalized and specified for specific situations. It would also be welcome for security and peace basic research and applied analysis if there was some standard inventory of readily-known holdings that would allow us to calculate or simulate reliably (as distinct from statistically significantly) the outcomes and payoffs in particular cases of security conflict and competition and of pacts to transition along a hot war–cold war–cold peace–warm peace continuum. Such full or near clairvoyance would have moved us much closer to the most complete achievement with which this essay began than we actually have come.

For now at least, we should bear in mind that the acid tests of security and peace understandings and production (or insecurity reduction) take place in specific relational situations with varying contexts. There is then an imperative for situational specification. The evolution of those situations cannot be relied upon to conform to standard, easily measured portfolios of assets. Such assets are often neither universally applicable or actually employed. "Davids" can and do on occasion frustrate, penalize, and get at least some of their way over "Goliaths" for at least a while.

Strategic theories and the security and peace policies and capabilities derived from them necessarily assume that some imaginable relational situations are relevant and that others are not. Those assumptions may be warranted on historical or statistical grounds or on shares of assets already thought to be crucial. They do, however, leave their adherents open to unexpected and only belatedly-recognized developments. The cold war record is replete with instances that, at least for the United States and other advanced industrialized countries, were not even on their strategic-planning radar screens and whose local dynamics were not well understood in a timely fashion, or were even denied significance while insecurity mounted.

If anything, the expansions make timely awareness and understanding of security- and peace-relevant specific relational situations less rather than more likely for several reasons. The first is that there are many more and more varied possibilities that compete for attention and quick responses. Not surprisingly, all that makes reliance on general diagnoses and prescriptions rather than case-specific ones more appealing. Yet those general approaches may not fit well with particular relational situations however benign the intentions with which they are followed (e.g., the independence referendum for East Timor or democratization of Indonesia), and may even if only for a while trigger a loss in security and peace in being and in prospect.

There are nontrivial temptations for the defenders of any prevailing strategic or scholarly fashion to defend it against anomalous relational situations, or at least to attend primarily to those more readily accommodated within such fashions. If anomalous situations can no longer be ignored, processes go to work to treat them as matters to be dealt with briefly so that one can soon get back to core business, or to contend that they lack substantial security and peace relevance ("no vital national interest," no cumulative knowledge for an academic sect). In an internationalized, and perhaps globalized, era of security and peace, outsiders to local situations may even assume that apparent progress in the aspect salient to them can be equated with progress in security and peace from the perspective of each local party. The appropriateness of such judgments needs the most careful scrutiny especially for what amount to multiparty, nested relationships. Consider the Oslo process for various Palestinian and Israeli groupings or the recent regime change in Belgrade for Kosovar Albanians and Montenegrins.

Suppose we accept the basic loss-aversion stance of prospect theory with its associated propensities for risk-taking and cost-bearing. It follows that we need to understand what loss prospects are at work for the parties in particular relational situations rather than assuming them to conform to the roster envisioned by outsiders. We of course inhabit a world where adherents and mission custodians of prevailing strategic theories, policy packages, and academic schools have something to lose in material and nonmaterial (status and deference) terms. We should not expect such stakeholders "to go quietly" in the face of what are for them isolated and transient security and peace anomalies.

Finally, we should have learned to have serious reservations about the likelihood that even well-resourced governments or security and peace expert communities will be very good at anticipating and adjusting to discontinuities and asymmetries—especially ones that pose greater complications for security and peace be it as opportunities or threats. Several examples at different levels of generality are indicative.

Behavior during the period between World Wars I and II is not encouraging, and that period seems to me relatively if imperfectly comparable to the present. Like the present, it had radical changes in military technology in destructive capacity, spatial reach, and operational domain (air); attempts at multilateral arms limitation; embryonic supranational governance institutions; a communications revolution (radio); communal assertion after the collapse of imperial systems; new and fragile nation-states; democratic hopes; major nations seeking to regain what they held to be their rightful international standing and redress historical grievances; and economic shocks with contagious international effects.

Reliance on extrapolation from trends, essentially reliance on continuity, had at best a mixed record even during what some now think of as the relatively comprehensible and manageable cold war period. Contrary to claims for extrapolation (as in the Hart-Rudman U.S. Commission on National Security/21st Century), a projection from 1956 to 1981 would have missed or at best tardily recognized the Sino-Soviet split, nuclear parity with the Soviet Union, the economic rise of East Asia, great-power intervention failures (Vietnam, Afghanistan), and strategic arms control.

Even for the actor(s) receiving enormous American attention, the Soviet Union and associated Warsaw Pact, most analysts missed the dynamics leading to collapse and tended to overestimate military and military technoindustrial performance. Nor in retrospect was our after-the-fact comprehension of hallmark, critical events for academic learning and policy (and policy process) prescriptions about crisis management all that impressive. Consider the often-discussed Cuban missile crisis of 1962. For several decades, the national governmental parties had only an imperfect understanding of each other; American nongovernmental researchers knew little of significant U.S. actions of which the Soviet leadership was probably aware; and the highest American officials were probably unaware of some orders not complied with and some steps they had not authorized toward a general war posture. We can be misled by postmortems and not just by extrapolations.

It is important to recognize that the phenomena underlying cautions of the sorts just illustrated are far more intractable than is suggested by allegations of deliberate deception. Government officials do of course fail to tell the truth on occasion (e.g., the Tonkin Gulf incident and perhaps the more recent bombing of the Chinese embassy in Belgrade). Security and peace scholars are humanly prone to focus on evidence supporting what they sincerely view as conceptually, empirically, and normatively desirable interpretations. The more fundamental difficulty is that the truth often is hard to know about recent and current security and peace matters, and there were and are abundant incentives not to admit that given security and peace stakes.

Some Suggested Emphases

The previous good news, darker-side, and lessons learned opinions do not yield a complete set of recommendations for "best practices" for understanding and producing security and peace. They do, however, suggest several elements that should be emphasized.

The most general is humility and modesty of claims. Those principles should be put into practice by conceptual pluralism, attention to situational specifics, and acknowledgment of uncertainties and conditionalities. While in some ways banal, this suggestion stands in contrast to the often excessive claims of partisans in current "security culture wars."

A modest stance involves less attention to establishing the dominance of any single theoretical prism, issue domain, or generic type of actor. Instead, we would recognize that at some times and some places each of the diverse elements of those categories has some relevance—while no single element tells the whole story before or after the fact. Rather than advocating any one underlying strategic conception, we would recognize the situationally dependent implications of, for example, offensive dominance, robust defense, deterrence, coercive diplomacy, preventive diplomacy, and the cooperative avenues of public goods provision and unilateral and multilateral self-restraint. Rather than arguing about exclusivist superiority, we would start from the possibility of simultaneously relevant insights from, for example, realist, liberal, and constructivist perspectives. We would not opt for the primacy in general of any one of rational unitary actors, organizational routines, domestic politics, or intraelite relationships. Nor would we pursue contentions that for the present and future predominant importance lies with states or firms or networks; unilateralism or multilateralism; or regionalization or globalization. We would instead pursue the characteristics and incidence of situations with different mixes of the elements of each set.

Another aspect of modesty and pluralism calls for rejection of disciplinary dominance. That is, we should not equate the factors that explain, predict, or produce particular security and peace problems or outcomes with the turf of any single discipline. This enjoinder applies within and between the several social science disciplines and those of natural science and engineering. Substantial emphasis should go to bridging across types of expertise and informed appraisal of the limits of knowledge and consensus in each of them.

Beyond humility and modesty, three aspects of professional practice merit more emphasis than they often get. The first, science and technology (S&T) literacy, requires serious departures in the education of security and peace specialists, especially as conducted in most political science departments and international affairs professional schools. The other two are more immediately feasible in those venues.

Many possibilities for security and peace have an important S&T element be it in independent/intervening/dependent variable terms, or those of danger/safety/reassurance. While obvious with respect to weaponry in the so-called "old" military security agenda, it is no less true for the so-called "new" security agenda of information warfare, terrorism, trafficking, and peacemaking. S&T has substantial relevance for economic, environmental, demographic, and public health security.

For each of these, S&T literacy consists at a minimum of four sorts of understandings. The first consists of the vulnerabilities of advanced technologies to primitive technologies and their adaptive use. The second involves differences between technology performance in a controlled or favorable environment (the laboratory, prototypes, managed tests, conducive theaters or adversaries) and performance in the far messier and suboptimal real world. The third emphasizes time in terms of obsolescence rates relative to how long it takes to procure, field, and countermeasure innovations and trends. Finally, account needs to be taken of global diffusion of S&T competencies and capabilities to and through nonstate as well as state actors.

More optimistically, there are two emphases arguably well within our reach with more encouraging implications for understanding and producing peace and security or at least curtailing insecurity. While neither has been without its advocates, each has often been ignored or received only lip service. The most obvious area for greater emphasis would have us make more use of available intellectual resources and legacies. With regard to work in the past (a past of both centuries and decades), more awareness of legacy contributions would at least reduce energy consumed with results in which revival exceeds discovery. Greater attention should also be directed to security and peace analyses from experts outside of the American-centered research and policy communities and, in particular, their work primarily intended for and consumed by audiences outside of the United States, United Kingdom, Canada, and Australia.[2]

Finally, several themes in the legacy stock of security and peace studies seem to me to have particularly helpful uses for the future of security and peace studies. These themes, featured in the applied systems analysis approach of Albert Wohlstetter, merit greater attention because they face up to and engage the sorts of complexity provided by the expansions discussed earlier rather than trying to eliminate or evade it.

First, the systems approach treats a given security or peace problem as a relational situation involving subsystems interacting with each other over time. Each subsystem has both material (economic, geographic, S&T) and sociopolitical (human and organizational including belief systems) elements. Convenient as it might be, analyses are prone to misjudgments if they ignore or take for granted similarity or permanence of particular subsystems or their elements. International security and peace studies are not replete with lawlike regularities although there are some probabilistic relationships, rules of thumb, and heuristics. Those are not to be ignored, but their applicability to a particular system or subsystem needs to be established rather than assumed. One requirement for doing that involves careful situational operationalization of their terms.

Applications of the applied systems approach should feature "opposed systems design" and "end-to-end analysis." That holds for explanation and prediction about, as well as for prescription of interventions to affect, particular systems. The world of opposed systems design is not necessarily one of conflict, but it is one of differing and less than fully compatible preferences. Otherwise there would not be a security or peace problem.

As a system operates over time, the parties in it engage in a series of interactions based on recognitions and expectations about themselves and each other as seeking to achieve nonidentical preferences. Each resorts to instrumental strategies and moves that have an international element of blocking, countering, diverting, or shaping those of others. No party is assumed to be inherently passive or generally indifferent to outcomes or to the behavior of others in the system. Each party is assumed to have some latitude about what it can do by way of measure-countermeasure moves over time. That latitude can include types and arenas of behavior quite different in degree and kind from one party to another. The parties' benefit-to-cost or effectiveness-to-cost calculations need not be identical in terms of components, weightings of components, or discounting of the future relative to the present. Each party will try to adapt its instrumental behavior in light of its interpreted information about the past, current, and impending behavior of others and material factors in the system.

End-to-end analysis delineates the path or paths from the starting point taken for a security or peace relational situation to a historical or future outcome. An appropriate analogy is a process flow chart. End-to-end analyses recognize the intervening factors that can affect outcomes and examine their content and probabilities. As a work style, it guards against some of the distortions in choice pointed out by behavioral decision theory—unwarranted extrapolation from the ease or difficulty of initial steps along a path to chances of achieving later steps and then reaching a particular end point.

In combination, the applied systems approach, opposed systems design, and end-to-end analysis are well suited to accommodating and indeed being strengthened by the six widely-recognized expansions summarized previously (including that of multiple prisms). While initially developed for security and peace problems of a military and nation-state character, the recommended ensemble is not limited to such problems.

To conclude, the good news then is that of a style of work appropriate to the challenges of understanding and producing security and peace—if we choose to adopt it. The darker side is that the recommended style of work is very demanding in several ways. It calls for pooling knowledge and expertise across established borders of "schools," disciplines, and organizations. It does draw on and exploit general conceptual perspectives and historical patterns. Yet it treats them less as sources of conclusions and more as agenda setters for mustering, comprehending, and manipulating the empirical details of particular relational situations and changes in them. Given the variety, "hardiness," and resilience of security and peace problems, there is little reason to expect them to yield further to a less demanding professional work style.

Notes

1. The brevity of these reflections makes it only appropriate to note several caveats. My views are necessarily expressed in the form of oversimplified, stylized assertions lacking in desirable qualification and amplification. I have had to depart from the canon of extensive citations and thus scant giving credit where credit is due. Such omissions may be less serious because my concern lies more with a continuing and unfinished agenda than with compiling a roster of accomplishments. Finally, I in no way mean to imply that anything that follows is a fresh discovery, but only that the views presented tend for the most part to recommend a departure from one or another currently fashionable emphasis.
2. This de facto expert security community curiously is identical to the national members of a club of intensely cooperating government intelligence agencies—perhaps a recipe for compounding security parochialism.

CONVERGENCES BETWEEN INTERNATIONAL SECURITY STUDIES AND PEACE STUDIES

Louis Kriesberg

International security studies and peace studies are not a single subfield of international relations. Analysts in security studies and those in peace studies have generally viewed themselves and been viewed by others as working in quite different domains. Some persons in each area have been critical or dismissive of the efforts of those in the other. Nevertheless, many persons across both areas actually share significant concerns and questions, such as how to avoid or to limit wars and other violent conflicts. Furthermore, the work being done in each of these domains is increasingly overlapping. To enhance the possibilities of beneficial cooperation among analysts in these domains, the past relations and the current movements toward convergence should be examined. After doing so, I will discuss promising options for the future.

Earlier Relations

In previous decades, many persons working in security studies and many persons working in peace studies differed in several significant ways. For example, they tended to draw from different inter-

---

I thank the following persons who read earlier drafts of this paper and kindly gave me their comments: Eileen Babbitt, James Bennett, Volker Franke, and Nils Petter Gleditsch. I, of course, remain responsible for the observations and judgments made in this chapter.

national relations approaches. Persons doing international security studies tended to draw from the realist approach and those doing peace studies tended to draw from a liberal idealist or constructivist approach.[1] Realists generally assume that states are unitary actors seeking to maximize power. Liberal idealists, however, generally stress the importance of diverse domestic actors, transnational organizations, and normative factors. Realists emphasize the anarchic nature of the world system, and other approaches stress the varying degree of integration and the shared ways of thinking in the world or regions of it.[2]

Peace studies analysts have generally drawn from a wider variety of fields of inquiry than have analysts working in international security studies. Many workers in peace studies have been more receptive, for example, to the perspective and insights of feminist thinking in international relations.[3] The feminist attention to the manifold roles of women in sustaining social life fits well with the concern of many in peace studies about the ways people at the grass roots affect and are affected by so-called high politics. The emphasis among many feminists upon the distinctive qualities of women has contributed to studying the roles women have played in peace movements and the roles they might play in countering wars and overcoming large-scale violence.[4]

Some peace studies analysts have also been relatively attentive to the possible impact of religion and of culture on war and peace.[5] Analysts have shown how religious beliefs, organizations, and leaders have contributed to mitigating as well as to exacerbating violent conflicts. Additionally, some workers in the peace studies domain have been relatively attentive to transnational social movement organizations and to critical analyses of global political economy. The many trends constituting globalization have increased the power of multinational corporations, and the persons who control those organizations increasingly shape and use the global market for their benefit.[6] They also provide new opportunities for resistance and more egalitarian relations.[7]

Other differences are also noteworthy. International security analysts have tended to assume the perspective of one primary actor in an international conflict, typically their own country, while peace studies analysts tended to take a more global or systemic perspective. Persons in international security studies generally focused on military means while persons in peace studies stressed nonviolent methods.

International security analysts have examined in great detail, for example, the nature of nuclear warheads and delivery systems and their impact on military strategy.[8] Issues relating to deterrence and to nuclear proliferation have drawn great attention since the end of World War II. More recently, attention has been given to chemical and bacteriological weapons and to terrorism.

Finally, international security analysts tended to concentrate on avoiding war (negative peace), while peace researchers often stressed issues of justice and equity (positive peace) as well. Members of each camp also tended to differ in their institutional bases: those working in international security often were employed in institutes receiving foundation and government funds, while those in peace studies often were employed in colleges and in universities, and sometimes in nongovernmental social movement organizations.

These differences were particularly strong in the United States in the early decades after World War II. The differences arose in large part from varying career origins, intellectual traditions, and network associations. In the United States, an important tradition in peace studies, emphasizing nonviolence and social justice, initially developed in church-related colleges. The first peace studies program was established in 1948 at the Church of Brethren–affiliated Manchester College in Indiana. In the late 1950s, research-oriented centers began to be established, notably the Center for Research on Conflict Resolution at the University of Michigan.

Many of the people engaged in security studies flourished in college and university departments and international relations programs. They also were associated with academic and nonacademic institutes associated with the U.S. government and its armed forces—for example, RAND.[9] As I discuss later, the divergence in theory, research, and practice between people engaged in these two domains has hampered the members' work in each camp.

Some people, of course, did research and examined policy alternatives that in some ways bridged these differences. One arena of shared interests was the causes of war and of peace; indeed, analyses on this topic by Wright, Richardson, and Deutsch et al. were part of the important quantitative tradition in peace research and hence peace studies.[10] Work in this tradition has continued among both peace researchers and international security analysts, as illustrated by the work of Singer, Isard, Leng, and Vasquez.[11] They have tended to analyze factors that might account for variations in warfare over time and among different countries, often using quantitative data.

Those factors include systemic features such as the number of major powers in the system, state characteristics such as type of governance, and relationship factors such as trading interdependency.

Among other topics, considerable writing about crisis management and foreign policy decision making constituted areas where peace studies and international security studies have overlapped, with some variance in emphasis. Thus, some persons in the international security studies domain tended to assume that officials generally acted in terms of rational calculations of relatively fixed national interests, while analysts in the peace studies domain often emphasized group, normative, and emotional factors. Nevertheless, some analysts identified with each domain read and critiqued each other's work and influenced each other. This may be noted in work on the way officials from antagonistic states interact with each other in crises.[12]

Many professional associations also provided settings for informal and formal exchanges of ideas. For example, the International Studies Association has long included an International Security Studies Section and a Peace Studies Section, and members from each section sometimes participated together on the same panels. Within the American Sociological Association, the Section on the Sociology of World Conflicts was established in the early 1970s and its membership always has included students of peace and of military forces. The name of the section currently is Peace, War, and Social Conflict. The International Sociological Association included a Research Committee on Armed Forces and Society (RC01), and in 1980 that was reorganized to include sociologists studying international relations, peace, and conflict resolution; the name of the research committee was changed to Armed Forces and Conflict Resolution.[13]

The differences between the peace and security domains have not been as great in Europe as in the United States. Thus, many European peace institutes included work related to alternative military doctrines. In varying degrees this was the case for the International Peace Research Institute Oslo (PRIO), established in 1959; the Department of Peace Studies at the University of Bradford, England, established in 1973; the Peace Research Institute Frankfurt (PRIF); the Copenhagen Peace Research Institute (COPRI); and the Tampere Peace Research Institute (TAPRI). In such European centers, ideas were developed, for example, about nonoffensive defense, which many peace researchers argue contributed to changes in Soviet thinking and hence to the ending of the cold war.[14] Thus, the Soviet military posture was modified so that it would be recognized as defensive and not regarded as threatening offensive actions.

In many other countries in the world, international security studies and peace studies emerged only in the 1980s or 1990s. In the contemporary context, for reasons that I will discuss, the domains are becoming less sharply differentiated. Consequently, work in the relatively new centers of study reflects some of the changes that emerged after the cold war ended, including greater convergence between international security studies and peace studies.

From 1948 until the end of the 1980s, Americans both in security studies and in peace studies typically concentrated their attention on the cold war. The former generally viewed it as a military contest between two camps consisting of governments.[15] Persons working in international security studies emphasized military relations, particularly concerning nuclear deterrence and extended deterrence. They gave attention to the military hardware as well as the doctrines about their use. Some of them also studied foreign policy decision making and crisis management, particularly as conducted by high officials.[16]

Analysts working in peace studies examined social movements, such as peace movement organizations opposing nuclear weapons or engaged in people-to-people diplomacy.[17] They also analyzed the role of the military-industrial complex, particularly in the United States.[18] In addition, many of them examined the processes of socialization in families and schools and the influences of the mass media.[19] Some of these researchers were themselves associated with peace movement organizations.

Interestingly, analysts in both camps generally failed to anticipate the sudden transformation and ending of the cold war. Neither camp undertook intensive analyses about the possible explanations and implications of that failure. However, some persons in each domain offered reasons for the transformation in terms of the policies they had previously argued; those policies, they said, worked to prevent an escalation of the cold war and eventually to transform it.[20] Thus, security analysts contended that the long-standing militant containment policy of Democratic and Republican governments or the arms buildup and proactive anti-Soviet policy of President Ronald Reagan's first administration forced the Soviet leaders to yield and accept a new accommodation.

On the other hand, peace studies analysts pointed to other factors to account for the transformation of the Soviet Union's foreign policy, the ending of the cold war, and then the dissolution of the Soviet Union. They stressed the importance of the assurances given to the Soviet Union in the 1975 Helsinki Accords about the permanence of the borders established at the end of World War II. They also stressed the growing social exchanges and human ties fostered by détente, which continued despite the Reagan administration's lack of support for such activities.[21]

In short, many differences existed in past decades between persons working in peace studies and security studies. They differed in their research methodologies, in the importance accorded to particular values, in the questions they posed, and hence in the kinds of answers they tended to provide. These differences limited the work of persons in each domain, as they talked past each other. They too often ignored each other's ideas and findings, or when they did give them attention, it was to argue against them. If analysts in each domain gave more consideration to each other's work, they might have complemented each other's efforts and each enriched the other, as discussed in this chapter.

Contemporary Developments

In the post–cold war era, the domains of peace studies and international security studies have moved much closer together. Thus, security is now understood to refer to much more than military matters. It is widely thought to include concerns such as environmental degradation, refugee flows, and economic issues. Furthermore, large-scale violence directed against ethnic, religious, and other communal groups became matters of broadly shared international attention.[22] The roles of international governmental organizations and of nongovernmental organizations in preventing and stopping highly destructive conflicts rapidly expanded. Many of those organizations also increasingly became engaged in peacebuilding after such conflicts.[23] These and related developments are due to profound global changes and associated changes in ways of interpreting the transformed world. Partly because of these new circumstances, the analysts in both domains have also undergone many changes in the questions they pose and the answers they offer.

Global Changes

In recent decades, as is widely noted, the world has been undergoing profound and rapid changes. This is evident in the increasing economic integration, ever more swift and intensive communication, and many other global trends. Consequently, the world is becoming more homogenized, but with various people resisting and some reacting violently against that very development.[24] Furthermore, multinational business corporations, transnational social movement organizations, and international governmental institutions are increasing in number, size, and resources.[25] All this contributes to reducing state sovereignty.

These interacting developments have profound significance for peace and security studies. Conflicts marked by large-scale violence within states greatly increased in the 1990s but show some signs of slackening since then.[26] These conflicts have often been between peoples mobilized by appeals to different ethnic, linguistic, religious, or other communal identities. Although these conflicts may seem to be domestic, external connections generally are significant; they are manifested in the growing engagement of diaspora groups, the impact of the violence on neighboring countries, and the support given to one side by officials in other governments who seek to advance their own interests.

As a consequence of such developments and the other global trends previously noted, international norms about human rights are increasingly shared. The demand to take action to stop gross violations of human rights has become widespread and insisted upon by many states and international organizations, nongovernmental as well as governmental. The visibility of such human rights violations and the normative insistence to stop them have resulted in numerous interventions by international organizations such as the United Nations. These interventions, unlike earlier UN interventions, were not contingent upon the concurrence of the combating parties.[27] This has given a new legitimacy to the use of force in international settings.[28] Yet the costs in deaths and protracted engagement have diminished the willingness of many governments to undertake such interventions. In any event, the increased relative significance of large-scale internal conflicts has raised the salience of domestic conflicts for security studies workers and violence management for peace studies workers.[29]

Changes among Peace and Security Analysts

Many changes in the activities, institutional settings, and ways of thinking among persons in the security studies and peace studies domains have occurred since the 1970s and especially since 1989. These changes have tended to bring security analysts and peace analysts into closer association.

The development of problem-solving conflict resolution ideas and practices has affected greatly both security and peace studies.[30] This has been particularly so in the United States since the early 1970s.[31] By the end of the last century, the ideas and applications of problem-solving conflict resolution had spread and evolved in most parts of the world. This development provides a newly-shared language and way of thinking for persons working in peace studies and international security studies. Even tough-talking diplomats are now likely to assert that they are striving for win-win outcomes.

The growth of the field of conflict resolution, in conjunction with the other previously noted developments, has affected the practice of people in both international security and in peace studies. Peace researchers are much more likely themselves to conduct and to associate with people who engage in peacemaking and peace-building work. This includes arranging and facilitating conflict resolution workshops and dialogue groups, providing conflict resolution training, and consulting about conflict management systems. Such work is undertaken by a wide variety of organizations, such as the Carter Center of Emory University, CDR Associates, the Fellowship of Reconciliation, the Mennonite Conciliation Service, Search for Common Ground, and the United States Institute of Peace (USIP).

In a complementary fashion, persons engaged in international security studies are increasingly engaged in studying how to prevent large-scale violence and to build stable peace.[32] They strive to do so using a wide array of nonviolent methods, including economic sanctions and diplomatic mediation. The Institute for Defense Analysis in Alexandria, Virginia, in conjunction with the United States Institute of Peace, has designed a computer-based peace-building/postsettlement transition simulation to help examine alternative strategies. Persons in international security studies increasingly work with their own and foreign governments to foster reconciliation and institutions to manage conflicts, as they are involved with activities relating to peacekeeping, nation-building, and peace-building. Furthermore, they increasingly associate with persons in nongovernmental organizations—for example, those providing peace-building services, advocating the protection of human rights, and giving humanitarian assistance.[33]

As a result of all these developments, more people are engaged in the practice of peace-building, and persons with backgrounds in the international security and the peace studies camps more often interact with each other. In addition, more venues for such interactions have been established—for example, the United States Institute of Peace, founded in 1984. Intellectual exchange is fostered by journals such as *Security Dialogue* and *International Security*. Conflict resolution courses and programs are increasingly being introduced in traditional international relations programs. Furthermore, programs in civilian institutions provide training for military and other national defense executives and managers, as in the national security studies courses provided by Syracuse University's Maxwell School of Citizenship and Public Affairs and Johns Hopkins University's Paul H. Nitze School of Advanced International Studies. Finally, the curricula at military service academies, the command and general staff colleges, and the war colleges increasingly reflect a broader range of perspectives and of security tasks, such as peacekeeping.[34]

Future Developments

In anticipating the future, I will stress likely developments that I regard as desirable. I anticipate that new subfields will develop that cut across the domains of security and peace studies. Some of these subfields will focus on substantive issues. For example, they are likely to relate increasingly to different conflict stages: prevention, limiting and interrupting violent conflict escalation, terminating violence, and postconflict peace-building. In addition, they are likely to focus on particular ways of conducting and terminating conflicts; such methods include mediation and negotiation, constructive ways of conducting a struggle, contributing to conflict transformation, and fostering domestic conditions and institutions that are conducive to peace. Finally, some issues relating to general theoretical and analytical approaches will affect the work of most people in peace studies and security studies.

One substantive subfield that has rapidly grown relates to early warning and preventive diplomacy. At first, the emphasis was on forecasting the outbreak of intense violence and providing information officials might use in anticipating their responses to such violence and its consequences. This work drew on the international security approach. Subsequently, the emphasis shifted to developing policies for averting and limiting such violent outbreaks. This emphasis upon preventive diplomacy drew relatively more on the peace studies approach.[35]

A major subfield focuses on interrupting and stopping violence. The matter of particular interest here is the role of external actors, whether international governmental organizations, nongovernmental actors, or national governments. Thus, there is important new work on sanctions. For example, targeted, or "smart," sanctions have recently been stressed, but even their effectiveness is in question for certain goals.[36]

Another expanding substantive subfield relates to peacekeeping and postconflict peace-building. Several issues are currently receiving considerable attention, and that is likely to increase among peace and security analysts. Peacekeeping by the UN and by regional international organizations has expanded greatly after the end of the cold war.[37] Military personnel are increasingly trained in peacekeeping operations and how to avert conflict escalations.[38]

Currently, increasing attention also is being given to sustaining agreements that have been reached.[39] Particular attention is more and more given to building institutions that would reduce intercommunal conflicts and provide channels for their nonviolent management.[40] This includes various forms of federal structures, autonomy, and power sharing. It also includes democratic processes providing basic political rights. Increasingly, too, attention is being given to the civil society needed to sustain democratic processes and institutions.

The finding that democracies do not make war against each other has become a matter of great interest and the subject of considerable research. Workers in peace studies and security studies are examining the nature of that relationship and of the relationship between democratic polities and foreign intervention.[41] Nongovernmental organizations that provide humanitarian relief, medical care, and other services are proliferating. They are working in some of the same areas as do national governmental organizations and international governmental organizations. Consequently, inefficient use of resources and inappropriate competition sometimes arise. Ways to achieve a more effective division of labor and better coordination are increasingly being discussed.[42]

Practitioners and analysts alike are giving great attention to attempts at reconciliation between antagonists, and this attention is likely to grow. The issues are complex, since the very concept is multidimensional. In moving toward reconciliation, one or more party in a fight is likely to seek justice, truth, security, and kindness, perhaps even forgiveness.[43] Various groups may emphasize one or another of these dimensions at different times. Consequently, balancing the achievement of various dimensions of reconciliation is difficult and occurs in varying sequences and degrees among different groups in the opposing communities.[44]

Aside from various substantive subfields within which persons working in peace studies and in security studies will act in some degree cooperatively, some general issues will affect people working in these domains. For example, policy-relevant work is likely to be increasingly done for and with nongovernmental actors and not directed only at government officials. Academics may well spend some time engaged in nonacademic work, while persons engaged in applied work are likely for a time to take academic appointments. This engagement will most likely affect not only the questions asked but also the kind of answers sought and found. Thus, attention is likely to be given to relatively malleable factors, to agency rather than to structural conditions.

In addition, the increased interaction and overlap between persons in these domains may have a salutary effect on theory, research, and practice in each. Much international relations theorizing has been directed at what others have written, with too little reference to evidence relevant to the ideas. Advocates of particular approaches may overstate the case in order to get a hearing for matters that they feel have been given too little attention. But that can result in having the ideas dismissed, and that further escalates the debate. So driven, the debates become difficult to resolve.

Attention to the shared questions is a way to transform such debates. Attention also needs to be given to the information that would help answer the questions that are posed. The information may be qualitative or quantitative, but in either case, it has an external referent about which experientially-based consensus is possible. Thus, the discussions about the finding that democracies do not make war on each other have relied heavily on a variety of empirical analyses.

Finally, some persons in these domains are likely to undertake analyses that help synthesize the ideas and practices of international security studies and of peace studies. Some such work is being done, and more is needed.[45] The synthesizing work obviously requires focusing on policy-relevant issues. One such focus relates to the dilemmas associated with advancing human rights and justice while also settling fights and ending violence. Not all values can be maximized at the same time, and this poses dilemmas as the pursuit of a good goal may result in many bad consequences. Improving knowledge about the likelihood of various consequences of different strategies will contribute to resolving the dilemmas.

Such knowledge, however, cannot be precise for any single case. We mortals will have to rely on good judgment in each case.[46] Yet, insofar as good information and understanding is widely shared, good judgment is more likely to occur and be able to be followed.

Conclusions

I anticipate that convergence between security studies and peace studies will continue as the range of the peacemaking and peacebuilding agenda grows broader and more complex. Work in each domain has already benefited by the increasing overlap between the domains. The policy questions addressed and the repertoire of answers offered by persons in each domain have expanded. Peace studies workers increasingly recognize that atrocities occur, that violence takes many forms, and that there are times for acting with urgency. Security studies workers increasingly recognize the growing importance of cooperating with nongovernment actors and of expanding reliance on nonmilitary options.

Progress is being made. One important sign of and contributor to that progress is the increased range of voices joining the conversations about peace and security. As previously noted, this is the case for the increasing engagement of women in peace and security studies and the growing application of feminist thought in those domains. They are providing new insights and important perspectives.

In addition, work by persons in and from regions of the world previously excluded or ignored from conversations are now included. Thus, many centers of peacemaking and security studies are being established in more and more countries in the developing world. In South Africa, for example, some centers have done significant work for many years and are now broadening their range of work. The Centre for Intergroup Studies, for instance, was founded in Capetown in 1968, under the leadership of Hendrik W. van der Merwe; it focused on conflict resolution within South Africa, helping to develop channels of communication among the major groups there. Now, as the Centre for Conflict Resolution, with Laurie Nathan as the executive director, the scope of activities has been expanded to include facilitation and mediation among disputing parties in Burundi and elsewhere in Africa.

Although the closer relations between workers in international security and in peace studies have many benefits, there also are risks. One risk for peace researchers is that they become co-opted by high officials and lose their special relations with and perspectives derived from persons at the grass roots. A risk for security studies workers is to adopt words from the peace studies field but without incorporating the overall context.

Many differences in orientation are likely to persist, as they should. Thus, some people will work more closely with high-ranking officials in governments and international governmental organizations. Others, however, will work more closely with nongovernmental and grass-roots organizations as, for example, do Lederach and Galtung, Jacobsen, Brand-Jacobsen, and Tshudie.[47]

The time frames of workers in these fields are also likely to continue to differ. Some persons, frequently they are political leaders, operate in terms of the short term, dealing with the crisis at hand. Others, frequently working in religious institutions or advocacy organizations, work in particular communities and countries for decades. Persons in peace studies often stress long-term structural factors, including education, culture, and class structure.

Such differences sometimes will be a source of opposition and tension, but they are needed. Unfortunately, the division of labor may be manifested in a highly competitive and destructive manner. To minimize such conduct, certain truths need to be reiterated. The matters of concern in peace studies and international security are so complex that no single approach can provide a full treatment and a comprehensive understanding. No one can do everything, so a division of labor can be quite useful. The division of labor, however, can and should function so workers in each domain recognize the insights and knowledge of workers in the other domain. That can be constructive and helpful for members of each community in performing their tasks.

Notes

1. Peter L. Berger and Thomas Luckman, *The Social Construction of Reality* (New York: Doubleday, 1966); Hans J. Morgenthau, *Politics among*

Nations (New York: Knopf, 1948); Kenneth N. Waltz, *Theory of International Politics* (New York: Random House, 1979); Alexander Wendt, "Anarchy Is What States Make of It: The Social Construction of Power Politics," *International Organization* 46, no. 2 (1992): 391–425.
2. Kenneth N. Waltz, "Structural Realism after the Cold War," *International Security* 25, no. 1 (2000): 5–41.
3. Cynthia Enloe, *Bananas, Beaches, and Bases* (Berkeley and Los Angeles: University of California Press, 1989); Elise Boulding, *Cultures of Peace: The Hidden Side of History* (Syracuse, N.Y.: Syracuse University Press, 2000); Betty A. Reardon, *Sexism and the War System* (Syracuse, N.Y.: Syracuse University Press, 1996).
4. Harriet Hyman Alonso, *Peace as a Woman's Issue: A History of the U.S. Movement for World Peace and Women's Rights* (Syracuse, N.Y.: Syracuse University Press, 1993); Tamra Pearson d'Estree and Eileen F. Babbitt, "Women and the Art of Peacemaking: Data from Israeli-Palestinian Interactive Problem-Solving Workshops," *Political Psychology* 19, no. 1 (1998): 185–209; Simona Sharoni, *Gender and the Israeli-Palestinian Conflict* (Syracuse, N.Y.: Syracuse University Press, 1995); Carolyn M. Stephenson, "Gender Differences in Conflict Resolution," in *United Nations Expert Group Meeting on Political Decision-Making and Conflict Resolution: The Impact of Gender Difference,* UN Document EGM/PDCR/12996/EP4 (Santo Domingo, Dominican Republic: United Nations, 1996); Anna C. Snyder, "Conflict and Consensus-Building at the 4th UN World Conference on Women: A Study of International Nongovernmental Cooperation" (Ph.D. diss., Syracuse University, Syracuse, N.Y., 1998).
5. Douglas Johnston and Cynthia Sampson, eds., *Religion, the Missing Dimension of Statecraft* (New York: Oxford University Press, 1994).
6. William I. Robinson, *Promoting Polyarchy: Globalization, U.S. Intervention, and Hegemony* (New York: Cambridge University Press, 1996).
7. Jackie Smith, Charles Chatfield, and Ron Pagnucco, eds., *Transnational Social Movements and Global Politics: Solidarity beyond the State* (Syracuse, N.Y.: Syracuse University Press, 1997).
8. Bernard Brodie, ed., *The Absolute Weapon* (New York: Harcourt Brace, 1946).
9. Fred Kaplan, *The Wizards of Armageddon* (New York: Simon and Schuster, 1983).
10. Quincy Wright, *A Study of War* (Chicago: University of Chicago Press, 1942); Lewis F. Richardson, *Statistics of Deadly Quarrels* (Pittsburgh: Boxwood Press, 1960); Karl W. Deutsch, Sidney A. Burrell, Robert A. Kann, Maurice Lee Jr., Martin Lichterman, Raymond Lindgren, Francis L. Loewenheim, and Richard W. Van Wagenen, *Political Community and the North Atlantic Area* (Princeton, N.J.: Princeton University Press, 1957); Carolyn M. Stephenson, "Peace Studies, Overview," in *Encyclopedia of Violence, Peace, and Conflict,* ed. Lester Kurtz (San Diego: Academic Press, 1999), 809–20.
11. J. David Singer, Stuart A. Bremer, and John Stuckey, "Capability Distribution, Uncertainty, and Major Power War, 1820–1965," in *The Cor-*

relates of War I: Research Origins and Rationale, ed. J. David Singer (New York: Free Press, 1979), 265–97; Walter Isard, Understanding Conflict and the Science of Peace (Cambridge, Mass.: Blackwell, 1992); Russell J. Leng, "Influence Strategies and Interstate Conflict," in Singer, The Correlates of War, 124–57; John Vasquez, The War Puzzle (Cambridge: Cambridge University Press, 1993).

12. For example, see Glenn H. Snyder and Paul Diesing, Conflict among Nations: Bargaining, Decision Making, and System Structure in International Crises (Princeton, N.J.: Princeton University Press, 1977); Richard Ned Lebow, Between Peace and War (Baltimore: Johns Hopkins University Press, 1981); Michael Brecher, Crises in World Politics (Oxford, England: Pergamon, 1993); Margaret G. Hermann and Charles F. Hermann, "Who Makes Foreign Policy Decisions and How: An Empirical Inquiry," International Studies Quarterly 33, no. 4 (1989): 361–87; Robert Jervis, Perception and Misperception in International Politics (Princeton, N.J.: Princeton University Press, 1976).

13. In the late 1970s, the idea of broadening the scope of RC01 was raised by some International Studies Association members interested in finding a hospitable research committee for their activities. Exploring options for this group, I was encouraged by Morris Janowitz, a leading figure in RC01, to join that research committee and broaden its scope. Gwyn Harries-Jenkins, then chair of RC01, agreed, and the scope and name of the committee was formally changed. Sociologists studying military forces predominate in the membership of the committee, but those studying conflict resolution and nonviolence also belong and participate in panel sessions and other committee activities.

14. Jorgen Dragsdahl, "How Peace Research Has Reshaped the European Arms Dialogue," in Annual Review of Peace Activism, 1989, ed. John Tierman (Boston: Winston Foundation for World Peace, 1989), 39–45.

15. Many peace researchers, particularly in Europe and in the Third World, examined imperialism and economic dependency. For example, see the frequently cited article by Johan Galtung, "A Structural Theory of Imperialism," published originally in the Journal of Peace Research in 1971; it is reprinted in Johan Galtung, Peace and World Structure: Essays in Peace Research (Copenhagen: Ejlers, 1980).

16. Snyder and Diesing, Conflict among Nations; Graham T. Allison, The Essence of Decision: Explaining the Cuban Missile Crisis (Boston: Little, Brown, 1971).

17. John Lofland, Polite Protestors: The American Peace Movement of the 1980s (Syracuse, N.Y.: Syracuse University Press, 1993); Sam Marullo and John Lofland, eds., Peace Action in the Eighties (New Brunswick, N.J.: Rutgers University Press, 1990).

18. Dieter Senghass, Rüstüng und Militarismus (Frankfurt: Suhrkamp, 1972).

19. James William Gibson, Warrior Dreams: Violence and Manhood in Post-Vietnam America (New York: Hill and Wang, 1995).

20. Louis Kriesberg, International Conflict Resolution: The U.S.-USSR and Middle East Cases (New Haven, Conn.: Yale University Press, 1992);

Richard Ned Lebow and Thomas Risse-Kappen, eds., *International Relations Theory and the End of the Cold War* (New York: Columbia University Press, 1995); William Curti Wohlforth, *The Elusive Balance: Power and Perceptions during the Cold War* (Ithaca, N.Y.: Cornell University Press, 1993).
21. Mary Kaldor, "Who Killed the Cold War?" *Bulletin of the Atomic Scientists* (July–August 1995): 57–60.
22. Walker Conner, *Ethnonationalism: The Quest for Understanding* (Princeton, N.J.: Princeton University Press, 1994); Donald L. Horowitz, *Ethnic Groups in Conflict* (Berkeley: University of California Press, 1985).
23. Larry Dunn and Louis Kriesberg, "Mediating Intermediaries: Expanding Roles of Transnational Organizations," in *Studies in International Mediation: Essays in Honour of Jeffrey Z. Rubin*, ed. Jacob Bercovitch (London and New York: Macmillan and St. Martin's, 2002).
24. Benjamin Barber, "Jihad vs. McWorld," *Atlantic Monthly*, March 1992, 53–63.
25. Smith, Chatfield, and Pagnucco, *Transnational Social Movements and Global Politics.*
26. Ted Robert Gurr, *Peoples versus States: Minorities at Risk in the New Century* (Washington, D.C.: U.S. Institute of Peace Press, 2000).
27. Otara A. Otunna and Michael W. Doyle, eds., *Peacemaking and Peacekeeping* (New York/Oxford: Rowman and Littlefield, 1998).
28. Andrew J. Goodpaster, *When Diplomacy Is Not Enough: Managing Multinational Military Interventions* (New York: Carnegie Commission on Preventing Deadly Conflict, 1996), 1–38.
29. Noted in personal communication by Eileen Babbitt.
30. Persons working in the problem-solving conflict resolution approach tend, in varying degree, to emphasize ways in which adversaries in a conflict shift from seeing each other as engaged in a struggle in which what one side gains is at the expense of the other to seeing a mutual problem for which they seek a solution that has some mutual benefit.
31. Louis Kriesberg, "The Growth of the Conflict Resolution Field," in *Turbulent Peace,* ed. Chester A. Crocker, Fen Osler Hampson, and Pamela Aal (Washington, D.C.: U.S. Institute of Peace Press, 2000), 407–26.
32. Carnegie Commission on Preventing Deadly Conflict, *Final Report of the Carnegie Commission on Preventing Deadly Conflict* (New York: Carnegie Corporation, 1997); Arie M. Kacowicz, Yaacov Bar-Siman Tov, Ole Elgstrom, and Magnus Jerneck, eds., *Stable Peace among Nations* (New York/Oxford: Rowman and Littlefield, 2000).
33. Alice Ackermann, *Making Peace Prevail: Preventing Violent Conflict in Macedonia* (Syracuse, N.Y.: Syracuse University Press, 2000).
34. Volker Franke pointed out some of these developments in a personal communication.
35. David Carment and Patrick James, eds., *Peace in the Midst of Wars* (Columbia: University of South Carolina Press, 1998); Michael S. Lund, *Preventing Violent Conflicts* (Washington, D.C.: U.S. Institute of Peace Press, 1996).

36. David Cortright and George A. Lopez, eds. *Economic Sanctions: Panacea or Peacebuilding in a Post–Cold War World* (Boulder, Colo.: Westview, 1995); David Cortright and George Lopez, with Richard W. Conroy, Jaleh Dashti-Gibson, and Julia Wagler, *The Sanctions Decade: Assessing UN Strategies in the 1990s* (Boulder, Colo.: Lynne Rienner, 2000). Evidence against the effectiveness of economic sanctions has been reported for a long time by peace researchers and others. For example, see Peter Wallensteen, "Characteristics of Economic Sanctions," *Journal of Peace Research* 5, no. 3 (1968): 248–67.
37. Robert A. Rubinstein, "Cultural Aspects of Peacekeeping: Notes on the Substance of Symbols," *Millennium* 22, no. 3 (1993): 547–62.
38. David Last, "Organizing for Effective Peacebuilding," in *Peacekeeping and Conflict Resolution*, ed. Tom Woodhouse and Oliver Ramsbotham (London: Cass, 2000), 80–96.
39. Fen Osler Hampson, *Nurturing Peace: Why Peace Settlements Succeed or Fail* (Washington, D.C.: U.S. Institute of Peace Press, 1996).
40. John McGarry and Brendan O'Leary, eds., *The Politics of Ethnic Conflict* (London: Routledge, 1993).
41. Nils Petter Gleditsch and Havard Hegre, "Peace and Democracy," *Journal of Conflict Resolution* 41, no. 2 (1997): 283–310; Margaret G. Hermann and Charles W. Kegley Jr., "The U.S. Use of Military Intervention to Promote Democracy: Evaluating the Record," *International Interactions* 24, no. 2 (1998): 91–114; Bruce Russett, "The Democratic Peace: And Yet It Moves," *International Security* 19 (spring 1995): 164–75; Bruce Russett and John R. Oneal, *Triangulating Peace: Democracy, Interdependence, and International Organization* (Princeton, N.J.: Princeton University Press, 2001).
42. Louis Kriesberg, "Coordinating Intermediary Peace Efforts," *Negotiation Journal* 12 (October 1996): 341–52; John Paul Lederach, *Building Peace: Sustainable Reconciliation in Divided Societies* (Washington, D.C.: U.S. Institute of Peace Press, 1997).
43. Michael Henderson, *The Forgiveness Factor* (London: Grosvenor Books, 1996); Martha Minow, *Between Vengeance and Forgiveness* (Boston: Beacon Press, 1998); Eugene Weiner, ed., *The Handbook of Interethnic Coexistence* (New York: Continuum, 1998).
44. Louis Kriesberg, "Paths to Varieties of Inter-Communal Reconciliation," in *From Conflict Resolution to Peacebuilding*, ed. Ho-Won Jeong (Fitchburg, Md.: Dartmouth, 1999).
45. Hugh Miall, Oliver Ramsbotham, and Tom Woodhouse, *Contemporary Conflict Resolution* (Cambridge, England: Polity, 1999).
46. Isaiah Berlin, "My Intellectual Path," *New York Review of Books*, May 14, 1998, 53–60.
47. Lederach, *Building Peace*; Johan Galtung, Carl G. Jacobsen, Kai Frithjof Brand-Jacobsen, and Finn Tschudi, *Searching for Peace* (London and Sterling, Va.: Pluto, 2000).

ACCOUNTING FOR INTERSTATE WAR

Progress and Cumulation

J. David Singer

This turn of the millennium certainly offers us another opportunity—and incentive—to get more serious about trying to explain, and perhaps reduce the incidence of, that brutal, stupid, and destructive form of collective behavior known as war. In almost every epoch and almost every corner of human civilization, we find the politicians and the priests calling for an end to such barbarous behavior. But time after time, their prescription is to demand that the other party give up its aggressive behavior and meet the demands of our reasonable and accommodating brethren.

This recurrent pattern is nicely captured by Mark Twain in "The War Prayer," penned in response to the U.S. intervention in the Philippines in 1898, rejected by *Harper's Bazaar* in 1905, but finally published in November 1916 as the drumbeat for war against Germany had begun to accelerate. In praying, "Grant us the victory, O Lord our God," Twain then laid out the corollary, unspoken prayer: "Oh Lord our God, help us to tear their soldiers to bloody shreds with our shells; help us to cover the smiling fields with the pale forms of their patriot dead; help us to drown the thunder of their guns with the shrieks of their wounded, writhing in pain. . . .We ask it, in the spirit of love, of Him Who is the Source of Love."

Some Promising Auguries

Can we perhaps do better than this sanctimonious and self-serving hypocrisy, which hardly seems to move us closer to the day when war begins to lose its legitimacy, when its counterproductivity becomes fully evident, and when human groups back away from lending psychic and material resources to its preparation? Some might say that such a process is already under way, thanks to the devastation wrought by the two world wars, the advance of weapons technology, the repugnance with which we witness the genocidal conduct associated with the last half century's wars in the Balkans, sub-Saharan Africa, and Southeast Asia. Along with Mueller and Levi we might reasonably adopt so sanguine an outlook, but the indicators to the contrary are difficult to ignore.[1]

The land mines still planted along boundaries from Korea to Kosovo taking scores of casualties every month, the steadily-increasing worldwide trade in light weapons, the obscene U.S. military budget, and the presence of more than thirteen thousand strategic warheads on high alert among the nuclear powers all remind us that the preparedness for war, the willingness to threaten war, and the ease with which political elites mobilize and carry out military actions are very much with us. As I write these lines at the beginning of a new year and a new millennium, the pope in Rome and some of his counterparts elsewhere are calling on us to desist from armed violence, but as Mark Twain reminded us in his prayer for our soldiers, more of the world's religious leaders are busily calling the faithful to the barricades and encouraging their propensities for yet another holy war.

Another of the weak reeds that some of us cling to is that of the "Kantian peace," the proposition that as international trade continues to increase, and as more societies are governed by democratic/republican regimes, such tendencies will conduce to a diminishing incentive to the mobilization for and conduct of war. The problem with this particular hope is twofold. First, even though world trade is increasing, a closer look shows that the worldwide level of intrastate commerce continues to grow at a somewhat faster rate. Second, the data-based evidence suggests that—even if intersocietal trade *were* on the increase—the pacifistic consequences are far from clear. While Polachek, Russett, and O'Neal all interpret the data in this fashion, scholars such as Barbieri conclude otherwise.[2]

When we shift from trade to regime types, we find the same uncertainties. The U.S. foreign policy establishment likes very much the idea that the fraction of the world's national regimes has become increasingly democratic, and that this reflects a tide of the democratic peace. But if we look closely at the coding criteria, there is not much hard evidence to support the alleged expansion of democracy.

Yet another slim reed is that known as the "evolution of cooperation." In a computerized tournament attracting some of the top game theorists, the most successful strategy for inducing cooperative behavior on the part of refractory members of a social system turned out to be "tit for tat." In these simulations, most players start off with largely cooperative moves and continue to reinforce such behavior all around. But since any human system will contain some noncooperative members ("rogue states"?), the problem is one of modifying their behavior, and in the tit-for-tat strategy, we punish them by responding with similar noncooperative behavior. The charming premise is that such conflictful responses will show them the error of their ways and lead our "defectors" into more cooperative behavior patterns.

The problems are threefold. First, how often in history have we seen most states in the global or a regional system behaving in a cooperative fashion? Perhaps the Congress of Vienna system held for a while, but by 1854 Europe had experienced the Franco-Spanish, Russo-Turkish, Austro-Sardinian, Schleswig-Holstein, Roman Republic, and Crimean Wars. Second, every social organization is a coalition, and there will almost always be some members of the coalition with incentives to initiate or perpetuate sharp conflict, thus not exactly contributing to the evolution of cooperation. Third, and most critical, it is almost axiomatic that the way to escalate a dispute is to react to hostile and uncooperative behavior by responding in kind; at the very least, the strategy might call for tit *minus one* for tat. This approach to war reduction might—given these problems—attract no attention at all were it not for the highly desirable characteristic that it requires no strengthening of international institutions, thus avoiding the state sovereignty issue, and no need to generate a worldwide shift in norms. So much for peace on the cheap.

Retrospect and Prospect

Given this pessimistic reading, let me step back from the contemporary scene for a moment and look both backward and forward in our effort to get a better handle on the explanation of war. We might think of four stages in the history of our effort to explain—and perhaps limit—the frequency of war. The first runs from the earliest appearance of armed, organized combat up through the end of World

War I, in which we saw a growing body of literature that was interesting, diverse, and insightful, but resting largely on assertion, speculation, and anecdote. The second stage—marked largely by the work of Richardson and Wright in the interwar period[3]—illustrated the possibility of using scientific method in our quest. The third stage, perhaps best exemplified by the Correlates of War Project beginning in the early 1960s, went the next step, combining a rigorous methodology with an explicitly agnostic, multitheoretical orientation, and might be called the "natural history" stage.[4] The dominant concern was/is to ascertain what goes with what: under what conditions do which behaviors culminate in which outcomes on the war-peace spectrum? This current stage is already beginning to blend into the fourth, in which the results of our systematic historical empiricism might permit the articulation and testing of more formal and mathematized models that will rest less and less upon the untested and often naive premises found in their opening rounds.

Premises: Epistemological and Empirical

Bearing in mind that we are now well into the third stage—the natural history stage—but barely into the fourth stage in our search for the explanation of war, it might be the propitious moment to stop and evaluate some of the empirical and epistemological assumptions that ought to guide our investigation. Leaving aside for the moment our *ethical* assumptions, let us look more closely at the assumptions from which we might want to work on the epistemological and empirical dimensions.

Let me begin with an epistemological assumption that will cause only a modest amount of grief in these precincts but could lead to howls of anguish in the Modern Language Association; the reference is, of course, to the syndrome known as "deconstruction," which is usually associated with those schools of thought that could be called "the posties," embracing the postmodern, poststructural, postbehavioral, and most germane to us, postpositivist outlook. I make no pretense of being on intimate terms with colleagues of those persuasions or familiar with the distinctions among them. As I understand this fairly recent orientation—and it may go back to Karl Mannheim[5]—developing a science of human behavior just is not possible for several reasons: (a) there may not even *be* any empirical social reality; it is nothing more than imaginings given credibility by the language we use to describe these fictitious happenings; (b) even if there is social reality, we can never apprehend it because every human being is the product of his or her cultural identity, gender, age, profession, education, and accumulated personal experiences; and (c) the representations of reality that we generally accept are "socially constructed," created and imposed on societies by the elites as an instrument of control.

A milder—and less nihilistic—version of the "mission impossible" school doesn't deny the existence of an empirical reality but argues that we positivists define it too narrowly. For example, Alker suggests that our "data" must include not only the alleged historical and empirical phenomena that we attempt to describe and explain but also the reports about alleged observations of such phenomena, sometimes referred to as a call for more hermeneutics and less exegesis, as in biblical studies.[6] Coming closer to the perspective of our small but growing "epistemic community"[7] are those in the tradition of the late Hedley Bull who—with a touching faith in their own observational accuracy and perfect recall—question the need for all this scientific paraphernalia and assure us that the classical methods of the historian will do just fine.[8] These traditionalists might want to listen to Mannheim more attentively; a good scientist attends to rigorous methods of observation, measurement, analysis, and inference simply because we *do* take some of the latter's warnings seriously.

In order to rectify all these failings of the contemporary scientific scene, we are offered quite a variety of dubious epistemologies. Already familiar to the quantitative world politics community is Dessler's effort to draw from the physical sciences such platitudes as the need to "identify the mechanisms through which specified outcomes occur" or "the real structures that produce the observed phenomena."[9] And at the end of this thoughtful essay, we are left with no guidance toward this end beyond the strictures of "scientific realism"[10] and the belief that causality does indeed obtain in the referent world. This line of reasoning will of course lead to the articulation of increasingly ambitious "theories" that are, in truth, little more than speculative models that rest on problematic and far from operational and thus testable premises. One variant of this approach is the "analytic narrative" in which one combines a case study with a formal—if preoperational—model and then moves back and forth in the hope of making the facts and the model increasingly congruent.[11] This would not be such a bad idea if it were applied to a population of cases that constituted an explicit class of cases, and then it sought to bring the model and most of the cases into harmony. But doing it a case at a time is virtually guaranteed to be a decades-long exercise in futility. Of more ancient vintage is the "structured, focused comparison,"[12] which, on closer examination, may be focused but typically fails on the comparison dimension because the model is not expressed in terms that are sufficiently precise and operational to permit their application to a population of putatively comparable cases. The net effect is a series of individual case studies each examined via models that are roughly similar but will end up applying rather different criteria and coding rules, resulting in something only weakly structured, focused, and comparative. So much, then, for the ambitious enterprise by which we might eventually hope to bring the ideographic and the nomothetic into some sort of harmony. It is exactly because of the inevitable tension between the immanent vagaries of our individual crises, wars, alliances, treaties, institutions, and so on on the one hand and the scientific aspiration to find a *general explanation* of some class of phenomenon on the other that all of these proposed methods are nothing more than the thoughtful cogitation that all scientists engage in as they mull over the separate cases about which they hope to generalize and the model that they hope will permit such a generalization. And, to put a realistic spin on this, there will almost always be a fair number of cases that just do not fit—at least in the earlier stages of the investigation. We may have quasi-deterministic models in our minds, but the natural world most certainly will defy us by its stochastic indeterminacy and ubiquitous equifinality!

Closely related is the doomed effort to ascertain/demonstrate "causality." In my view, this is a chimera invented to help persuade us that we really can know how the world truly works, and it might best be replaced with the concept of *explanation*. That is, as we uncover more and more regularities and covariations—and thus generate an increasingly rich and credible *description* of the ways in which all sorts of events and conditions go together empirically, we will arrive at increasingly-accepted *explanations*, and as these persuasive "stories" are combined with what we think we know about individual and group behavior, the closer we will come to legitimate theories—in the sense of codified knowledge that commands the assent of our most capable colleagues.

Considerably more unnerving, and further down the self-styled "scientific realist" path, is an approach that is called "evolutionary epistemology" intended to resolve the realist-versus-relativist impasse that arose out of the alleged passing of positivist and empirical methodologies. These recurrent debates over epistemology in the social sciences need not surprise us, given how poorly scientific method is taught and how dubious is the status of the social sciences in the academic world. Further, when we read those philosophers who tend to support and illuminate the scientific approach to social phenomena, we find that many of them are as confused as they are inaccessible; I find Hempel and Popper, not to mention Harre and Lakatos, not very helpful.[13] Like religion, philosophy of science should be kept out of reach until we are sufficiently mature and experienced to be adequately immune to their all-too-plausible blandishments!

Turning from the doubters to the doers, let me articulate some of the more relevant empirical-epistemic assumptions about the "nature of" the universe and the social systems—sometimes called "artificial" for reasons that still baffle me[14]—of concern to us, and ways of comprehending these systems. A central axiom is that the global system and the social groups it comprises evince highly regular and thus recurring patterns, but we have only begun to discover them and confirm their existence. There are lawlike regularities, but we still have only a dim grasp of them. And despite the existence of all these regularities, they are far from deterministic; while certain types of states respond over and over to the same stimuli in the same context in the same way, there are plenty of exceptions, giving us statistical distributions rather than deterministic and perfectly uniform law. Further, when we find extraordinary regularities, it is worth noting that the "causal path" between background conditions and behavioral outcomes can vary considerably; there are several ways to go from a given set of initial conditions to a well-specified outcome.

Such regularities can take several forms, of which the simplest is a trend line in the magnitude of a given attribute of a given system; inasmuch as every social system is an evolving one, rates of change in such an attribute are also subject to change over time. Moreover, cyclical patterns are often found, usually not in fixed intervals of real time offering true periodicity, but in the form of recurring sequences or the order in which events and conditions follow one another over and over.

In my judgment, we are not likely to uncover fully-deterministic regularities not only because all the systems and subsystems that we study are evolving, and in sequences that may well be irregular, but also because there is an *inherent randomness* in their behaviors and interactions vis-à-vis one another. Of course, the magnitude of such stochastic phenomena will diminish as we reduce (inter alia) measurement error, erroneous simplifying assumptions, misspecifications of our models, and the factors subsumed under the error term. But it will never be reduced to zero; as asserted previously, this residual randomness is inherent in the universe.

In sum, our search for the lawlike regularities in matters of war and peace will advance erratically as a result of both empirical findings and theoretical insights; we will not get very far relying on only one or the other, despite pendulumlike fashions; systemic, data-based investigations are rarely "barefoot" or "dustbin" empiricism, nor is the construction of formal models merely "intellectual gymnastics." In our search for an explanation of interstate war, we may discover empirically that two, three, or more subtypes arise out of systematically different conditions and processes, but we can always increase the goodness of fit by adding more differentiating variables; if not careful, we end up with a different model for each of the eighty-odd interstate wars since 1816, looking no different from our colleagues of the "No two wars are alike!" school.

Extension and Recapitulation

While most of the foregoing discussion is addressed to the study of interstate war, it should come as no surprise that a good part of it might be extended to the general field of world politics.

Semantic Problems

And a good place to start that extension might be with the semantic side of things. Note, first, that I label our field "world politics" rather than international relations, or worse yet, IR. These initials are also widely used to denote such fields of investigation/speculation as information retrieval, infrared, interocular response, interrogatory reaction, and so forth. More seriously, given the variety of actors that we study—ranging from individuals and agencies to regions and the global system—"international" misses a lot. Equally important, we cannot be satisfied with nothing more than "relations" in the sense of bonds, links, connections, and relationships. How about the *behavior* of the many entities of interest as well as the *interactions* among them? Relations might be trade partners, alliance members, neighbors, rivals, and so on, whereas it is interaction patterns that help to create such relations, and these relations, in turn, help generate such interaction patterns.

Other semantic carelessness can stand in the way of cumulative research. Consider, for example, how often we still use the archaic concept of nation-state, when few such can be found in today's system of territorial states; rather, some of them are multinational and perhaps more are subnational, in which a given "nation" is divided into several states. That short-lived Wilsonian ideal of self-determination for each nation organized and legitimized as a coterminous state that arose out of the dismemberment of the pre–World War I empires began to crumble on the eve of World War II, and was barely visible at the dawn of the nuclear age. Or consider the traditional concept of bipolarity or multipolarity, clarified and examined in the post-Napoleonic epoch to reflect the number of discernible clusters of states, typically bound together by military alliance, trade relations, shared diplomatic representation bonds, or perhaps certain cultural or political similarities.[15] But with the emergence of the "cold war" rivalry, many of us[16] began to forget history and to think of polarity in terms of simply the number of major powers in the system, on the dubious if inarticulate premise that around each single major or superpower we will always find a cluster of bound-together states. What happens when—as on the eve of most European wars from the Congress of Vienna to the Rome-Berlin-Tokyo axis—we find several major powers in the *same* pole?

Another case is that of the traditional distinction between collective defense and collective security, with the former designating a typical military alliance arrayed against another coalition or even a single identified "revanchist" state. Collective security, on the other hand, was used to describe regional or nearly-universal organizations designed to preserve the status quo, regardless of which of its members might turn out to be the ultimate threat to order.[17] Either out of ignorance or an effort to enhance the legitimacy of the cold war alliances, such arrangements as NATO, the Warsaw Pact, and the UN were all increasingly described as collective *security* systems even though the first two are collective *defense*, and only the UN deserves to be called a collective security organization. Another example of more recent vintage is "ethnic conflict." Whether the opposing groups are different in terms of language, religion, ethnicity, social class, or region, and whether they reside in the same territorial state or are more or less separated by one or two boundaries, the journalists are calling the hostility, enmity, or violence "ethnic." At the least, we should use interethnic, interreligious, and so on, and thus avoid the foolish and simpleminded implication that it is the *difference* between the groups that *accounts* for the conflict.

Finally, it is difficult to exaggerate the mesmerizing effect of calling military spending a "defense budget"; that label reduces the citizen's or journalist's interest in asking where that money goes. Do the following U.S. military adventures qualify as "defense": Spanish-American War, Cuban invasions, Vietnam, Panama, Chile, Guatemala, Nicaragua, Afghanistan? In this context of how we understand military preparedness as defense, worth noting is the recently created U.S. Pentagon "Agency of Threat Reduction," perhaps recognizing that most of the Defense Department's resources go for threat enhancement, threat enlargement, and intimidation.

Moving back from the specific to the general, one of the more debilitating semantic failures is that of how we understand two of our most central concepts: (a) theory and (b) data. Looking first at the notion of data, most of the writing in our field can barely differentiate between data and what might more clearly be called anecdata. In the more disciplined works of social science, *data* refers to a series of observations on years, places, events, or conditions generated by the application of a careful and precise and operational set of procedures, permitting us to compare the value or magnitude of that factor across these several observations. But among laymen, politicians, and prescientific scholars, almost any or all impressions, facts, narratives, reports, or recollections are honored with the label *data*. Seeing this careless usage suggests that quite a few of us have arrived at our anecdotage even before leaving graduate school!

Similarly, all too many of us seem quite willing to use the word *theory* for any effort to generalize ranging from a piece of folklore, a charming hunch, an off-the-wall hypothesis, or an axiomatic equation reflecting nothing more than an assumption that seems plausible. This is especially unfortunate because it gives equal status and privilege to these rather casual propositions and to a body of knowledge that (a) rests upon a set of generalizations that (b) have been operationally articulated, (c) put to a fairly stringent empirical test, (d) are logically consistent, and (e) can provide a reasonably coherent story that explains why a certain empirical regularity occurs across a particular class of comparable cases. Why, one might ask, would we use the same word to describe the vague ideas with which we begin an investigation and the disconfirmable explanatory scheme with which the investigation is concluded?

The Ethical Conundrum

Turning from the ways in which our semantic carelessness and disagreements have hobbled the effort to build a coherent and cumulative science of world politics, we might next address a number of ethical issues. Let me begin with the pernicious distinction between positive theory and normative theory. In the preceding paragraphs, I suggest what seems to be a reasonable understanding of theory in the scientific—or "positive"—sense to mean a coherent body of knowledge that helps to explain a well-defined set of empirical/historical regulations and patterns. What, then, is "normative theory"? In common usage, the distinction is between what *is* and what *ought* to be, and while this is clearly a distinction worth making, it hardly makes sense to use the same word to describe both.

When we address normative—and thus, ethical—issues, it seems to me that we need to rely heavily on "positive theory," while avoiding the tendency to conflate the two. Most scholarly writing on matters ethical tends to begin—and end—with an elaboration as to what kinds of behavior are acceptable under which empirical conditions, leading to two problems. First, and most obvious, is the inability of our ethical specialists—or in the current jargon, diplomatic "ethicists"—to operationally define the specific acts or the specific conditions under which such acts should be proscribed. Second, and perhaps even more disabling, is the reluctance to examine the *consequences* of a given class of behavior under a given class of conditions. For example, some would condemn and others would condone the use of military force by an outside actor in response to a serious violation of the human rights of a citizenry by its own government or a faction thereof.[18] Typical of this dilemma were the situations in Yugoslavia and Rwanda. As the Serb forces laid siege to Sarajevo and Dubrovnik, Western governments vacillated and quarreled while Russia and China argued for nonintervention. Pacifist elements called for negotiation while the assault continued, and in the absence of meaningful intervention, the Milosevic forces grew in strength and brutality such that the "ethnic cleansing" campaigns against Moslems, Albanians, and Croatians inter alia escalated until the U.S. and the NATO allies finally and belatedly intervened with massive bombing attacks that lasted nearly three months. The result was several thousand casualties, a near-rupture in Chinese relations, "ethnic cleansing," and continued genocide against Moslems in Kosovo. In my judgment, much of this tragedy could have been avoided had the Western big three pushed the UN Security Council to authorize a small ad hoc air strike against the Serb forces in early 1991. Even had the United Kingdom and United States (along with Turkey, Israel, and Sweden each providing fewer than five aircraft) taken out the Serb artillery sites in the first days, my prediction was that the ethnic cleansing campaign would never have been instituted. The point, of course, is that foreign intervention—by itself—could not be evaluated in moral terms, except in light of the likely consequences, and to make such a contingent forecast required more than a series of op-ed arguments. The history of world politics can be traced through such amateurish debates, with predictably inconclusive results. The dynamics of world politics are inevitably so complex that easy and consistently accurate predictions will be agonizingly rare. Thus, we need to combine norms as to (a) what actions fall where on an ethically acceptable–unacceptable scale, and (b) what are the most probable *consequences* of such actions, along with (c) where *those* predicted consequences fall on the ethically acceptable scale. In other words, the ethical problem cannot be separated from the scientific problem, and the latter rests largely on the extent to which we employ scientific method to examine such classes of historical cases and ascertain the "lessons of history."[19]

The Level-of-Aggregation Question

Since the appearance of the level-of-aggregation issue as a major concern among our more visible theorists,[20] we have debated which level of social aggregation is most likely to lead to the more powerful explanations of war and other crucial dynamics in world politics, and with the beginning of the cumulative quantitative research programs in the mid-1960s, the issue has taken on increasing salience. While both of us converged around the significance of the system level at that time, it may have been less an awareness of the implications than suspicion that the autonomy of the state—tending to ignore the powerful constraints of the system's structure and outline—was seriously exaggerated. Whereas Waltz continued to assert that the most potent factor in world politics was system structure—by which he often meant simply the distribution of material capabilities[21]—a good many of us, having once asserted the system's importance, moved on to a more nuanced position. For instance, I began to look in a fairly systematic way at the national security and foreign policy decision process,[22] concerned with the ways in which both the system-dominant attributes and the subsystem-dominant ones interacted[23] to perpetuate the menacing state of anarchy.

But the more we attended to the state level of aggregation and the decision process, the more evident it became that our research priority was premature. Many of the early "peace research" scholars took too literally the UNESCO dictum that it is in the minds of men that wars begin, failing to appreciate how unlikely we were to get at the decision rules until we had a far fuller grasp of the kinds of behavior patterns that were generated by certain classes of decision makers in response to certain classes of conditions and events. In other words, it soon became clear that in order to comprehend the "throughput" of decision making, we needed to know much more about the ways in which the input covaried with the output. This is because the myriad sets and combinations of decision rules would offer endless possible models, whereas knowing which inputs were correlated with which outputs could drastically reduce that variety by ruling out a good many of the possibilities.

Following that reasoning, the scientific research community moved rapidly away from the more psychologically-oriented projects and attended more and more to system level/macrolevel studies, producing a rather impressive range of findings, nicely summarized in Geller and Singer.[24] But not surprisingly, this emphasis gradually came under criticism, not only because it could tell us rather little about the decision rules that might link up certain regional or global conditions and events with the incidence of war or other interaction patterns of interest at the several levels of aggregation. Furthermore, this particular paradigm inhibited the examination of process-oriented or dynamic models, with the Bremer and Cusack volume bringing together much of that criticism and promising examples of the more dynamic paradigm.[25] There was, of course, another and equally critical concern: the widely-shared belief that any interesting set of international outcomes could barely be accounted for by variables at any one or two levels of aggregation, no less using only bivariate statistical analyses. Worth noting here is that my 1961 article on the "level of analysis problem" was intended only to emphasize the distinctions and not to say that a given model needs to be restricted to a single level of aggregation.[26]

Not surprisingly, then, the priority today is toward the multilevel and multivariate model, reflecting the consensus that outcomes of theoretical or policy interest just cannot be explained by one or two factors at one or another level of social complexity. Too many psychological, domestic, regional, dynamic, and system-level phenomena are unfolding and interacting within the same "causal" sequence, and it is essential that we keep an eye on most of them at the same time, while some of them can be held constant and others are "allowed" to change their values and magnitudes sequentially or simultaneously.

Conclusion

As I consider the six profound questions that our editors asked us to address, I hope that this essay does a responsible job. But space and time preclude a truly thorough and original treatment of that assignment. Perhaps, then, the editors will permit me, in place of an original conclusion, to reprint a short—and allegedly humorous—summary of where our field stands scientifically, and how come. It was written nearly three decades ago, appeared in *Political Science* in 1975 under the title "Cumulativeness in the Social Sciences: Some Counter-Prescriptions," and with permission of the original publisher, reappears here to illustrate the extent to which our field is still plagued and stymied by some of the same bad habits that seemed back then to stand in the way of cumulative progress. Are we hard-wired for failure?

In every social science, there tends to be a recurrent and cyclical preoccupation with the lack of cumulativeness. Some attribute this to the familiar "absence of theory" and lay it at the doorstep of "barefooted empiricism." Others might see the culprit lurking in the conceptual morass that often passes for theory and would suggest that grand schemata that *are* not—and usually *cannot*—be tested will hardly make for greater cumulativeness.

There seems to be more than a germ of truth in both of these suspicions, but let me suggest a third possible source of our disappointment. I refer to certain norms and practices found among *both* the theorizers and the empiricists: those folkways that we pick up in college and graduate school and are seldom able to shake in the postdoctoral years. On the assumption that an awareness of them and their implications may lead to their gradual extinction, I itemize here a few of what may be our less attractive foibles. While some of them may be peculiar to the field of world politics, most seem to be found all across the discipline.

Terminology

1. If our discipline is concerned with global politics, be sure to call it "international relations"; then we will all know that we're interested only in the *relations* among *nations*, and not the attributes, relationships, and interactions of all sorts of entities.
2. As long as you precede your efforts with the phrase "It doesn't matter what we call it, provided we define our terms," feel free to ignore all conventional definitions.
3. Any time you happen across an isolated fact or a welter of verbiage, be sure to label it "data."
4. If we already have a well-accepted word for a generally understood concept, be sure to coin a new one; don't be transparent when you can be prismatic or refractory.
5. When you're not sure which dimensions of a phenomenon you're trying to describe, refer to "the nature of ———."
6. If you're referring to any observed or hypothesized regularity, call it "structure."
7. If you have trouble differentiating among hunches, suppositions, convictions, preferences, and findings, just call them "theories."
8. If you're using the word "relationship," don't let on whether you mean covariation of variables, similarities between entities, bonds and links between entities, or something else.
9. When using the word "paradigm," don't let on whether you mean model, research strategy, a set of axioms, epistemological criteria, or something else.
10. When using the word "parameter," don't let on whether you refer to the isomorphism between the sample and the population, a constant, a slowly changing variable, a nonmeasured variable, a boundary condition, or something else.
11. If you are unable to articulate an idea clearly, begin to crank out a large number of examples; we'll eventually figure out what you're driving at.
12. Whenever you refer to physics, chemistry, or biology, call them the natural (or exact) sciences; then it'll be clear that we're in an unnatural or inexact science.

Taxonomy and Typology

1. As you shift from one research problem to another, be sure to change your taxonomy in subtle and unreported ways; this reduces the probability of integrating the results.
2. When discussing roles, relationships, or interactions, avoid identifying the social entities that play these roles or experience these relationships and interactions; otherwise, you'll be taken for a stodgy "institutionalist."

3. When constructing a typology, don't use categories that are mutually exclusive, logically exhaustive, or rest on explicit dimensions.
4. When focusing on conflictful interactions, be sure to say that you're dealing with "the exchange system."
5. If you're concerned with the impact of unemployment on national foreign policies, emphasize that you're examining "the economic system," and if unemployment happens to fall unevenly among different ethnic groups, note that this requires study of "the cultural system"; the more "systems" you examine, the less you'll worry about putting your findings together.
6. When one or two attributes of a system show change over time, insist that "it's a completely new system."
7. If the folklore has it that the *mitrailleuse* or satellite surveillance or public diplomacy has affected the course of world politics, insist that it has led to different and successive systems.

Epistemology

1. If you disagree with a colleague's epistemology, tell him how they "do it in physics."
2. If it is suggested that certain attributes of a social system can be described by observing the distribution of certain attributes among its subsystems, mutter something about "the ecological fallacy in reverse."
3. If a given piece of work doesn't spell out—in mathematical form of course—all the possible relationships among variables that might obtain, observe laconically that "barefooted empiricism remains far from dead."
4. If a colleague's work strikes you as too deductive, remind him of the importance of all those chemists in their labs, and if too inductive, quote Einstein or Bohr.
5. If a colleague's work shows a strong preoccupation with reproducibility and precision, alert others to his or her "indifference to theory."
6. If, after years of urging that insight and intuition have no place in science, you discover the limits of hyperpositivism, announce that science is a failure.
7. If a colleague is not persuaded by the logic and evidence you adduce, invoke a carefully selected metaphor from everyday life; any discontinuities between child rearing and strategic deterrence, or between driving a car and running a foreign office, will be graciously overlooked.

Research Strategy

1. When undertaking a new investigation, don't bother to read prior studies in that area; until you came along, no one else did it right.

2. If your methodological repertoire is limited, emphasize that you only employ those methods "appropriate" to the specific inquiry at hand.
3. When you're stymied on the measurement of one of your critical variables, put that project aside and write another essay on what Thucydides *really* meant.
4. When another's study explicitly focuses on the interaction effects of predictor variables A and B, quickly note his or her "indifference" to variable C.
5. When beginning a new set of investigations, don't be misled by the plausibility of alternative models; pick one that you like and get on with the derivation of "nontrivial deductions."
6. If your model has no recognizable similarities to the referent world, remind your critics that models are supposed to be "useful, not truthful."
7. When a colleague strays into other disciplines for new concepts or models, alert others immediately to these dilettantish tendencies.
8. If you find a colleague working on a given class of problems for several years, point out his or her "lack of breadth."
9. When drawing analogies from interpersonal to international relationships, never go to the findings of psychologists; their experimental evidence might be inconsistent with your argument.
10. If another project has invested considerable effort in identifying a population of nations, intergovernmental organizations, or other actors, be sure to either ignore their listing or quibble about that South Pacific island that was omitted.
11. When our critics point out the absence of cumulative knowledge about world politics, press the button that says, "After all, we're an infant discipline."
12. If several people, at the same institution or not, are unoriginal enough to be working on the same problem (such as the causes-of-war problem), be sure to observe that they are mere replicas of one another. And if they're working within a common paradigm, ask whatever happened to creativity.

Reportage and Communication

1. When publishing more than one paper on a given problem, don't indicate where it falls in your sequence of reports, or whether it represents an extension, refinement, or revision of earlier reports; a little mystery is good for your scholarly reputation.
2. Since it's too much trouble to revise a manuscript to incorporate the comments and suggestions you solicited from others, just tack on the necessary footnotes; the tightness of your reasoning is less critical than the illusion of exhaustive scholarship.
3. If your paper is on the casual side, don't worry about identifying sections and subsections in it; merely insert a numeral—preferably Roman—on every fifth page.

4. In writing up a nice and tight empirical study, don't waste time putting it into a larger context; get right down to the matter at hand.
5. Be sure that the title of your article or book promises considerably more than is delivered.
6. If you've picked up a good idea or insight from someone else's work, be sure to write it up as something brand new and creative.
7. If you're a panel discussant, paraphrase all the authors' caveats and self-criticisms, being sure to imply that they were oblivious to such problems.
8. Never specify or reiterate the spatiotemporal domain to which you hope to generalize; all propositions are universal.
9. Avoid the rigid tendency of making your opening and closing paragraphs consistent with each other, and in any event, don't let either of them be consistent with the actual operations you carried out.
10. Be sure that the major query of a study is carefully camouflaged, and that the outcome variable remains shrouded in mystery; otherwise, another researcher might be able to refute your findings.
11. Rather than spell out the case for the validity of your indicators, allude to your "auxiliary theory"[27] and get on to the important matters.
12. When your student turns in a paper that is incoherent, disorganized, grammatically improper, and replete with errors of spelling and punctuation, ignore such trivial weakness and assure him or her that we're scientists, not literary critics.
13. To use your time efficiently, never consider undertaking the construction of a data set, but follow others' work closely, and as soon as you hear of a potentially useful set, request it from the drone who put it together; that kind of scut work is inappropriate for creative scientists.
14. If, with the support of a public or private funding agency, you generate a useful and high-quality data set, refuse it to others until you've milked it dry; you can always say that the set is not yet complete or clean.
15. If someone proposes the creation of a new journal, or a section in an existing journal, devoted to data making and index construction, cite Conant to the effect that empiricism is not science but is merely a poor substitute for good theory.
16. If someone suggests a different way of printing and distributing journals, remind him or her that we've always done it this way.
17. If you've read a colleague's paper and can't figure out what the hell he did or why, be sure to praise its "heuristic value."

Ideology and Policy

1. When a colleague's work is addressed to some minor social inconvenience, such as war, hasten to note his or her indifference to poverty or injustice.

2. If a colleague's empirical findings are inconsistent with your ideological premises, point out that "it is no accident" that his or her research is supported by————, or that his nation is the richest (or poorest) in the world, or that he is not a she, an underdog, an African, or untenured.
3. When a colleague uses the same coding categories to describe both Soviet and American diplomatic actions, tell others that you don't worry about his patriotism, but . . .
4. When you're challenged as to the accuracy of your facts on the Chinese ABM, tell the critics, "If you knew what I know, and had a Q clearance, you'd believe me."
5. If a taxpayer asks whether your research will lead to an improvement in U.S. policy, remind him that you're a scientist, not a politician.
6. If the question of policy implications should arise, put on your other (citizen's) hat and note that social scientists are not different from barbers.
7. When you're trying to account for the difference between the infantry's and the cavalry's share of the defense budget, invest a minimum of twelve man-years, and when you're trying to account for the differences between crises that end up in war and those that do not, write a learned essay over the Easter holidays.
8. When examining the ratio between Yale and Harvard men in the Navy Supply Corps, break out your entire methodological armamentarium, but in examining the ratio of military to civilian fatalities, rely heavily on an exegesis of the "just war" doctrine; that's what "normative theory" is for.
9. If, after extolling the virtues of "value-free" science for years, you discover that ethical considerations might just be relevant, denounce scientific method as a hoax perpetrated by the establishment in order to preserve the status quo; allusions to the Karls (Marx and Mannheim) should wrap up the argument.

The Clincher

Finally, if by some remote chance, we begin to gather scientific momentum and there is a real danger that cumulativeness and codification might get out of hand, allude to Kuhn and call for a new paradigm.

Notes

1. John Mueller, *Retreat from Doomsday: The Obsolescence of Major War* (New York, Basic Books, 1989); Werner Levi, *The Coming End of War* (Beverly Hills, Calif.: Sage, 1981).
2. Solomon Polachek, "Peace Economics: A Trade Theory Perspective," *Peace Economics, Peace Science, and Public Policy* 1, no. 2 (1994): 12–15; Bruce Russett, *Grasping the Democratic Peace: Principles for a Post–Cold War World* (Princeton, N.J.: Princeton University Press,

1993); O'Neal et al., "The Liberal Peace: Interdependence, Democracy, and International Comfort, 1950–1985," *Journal of Peace Research* 33 (1996): 11–28; Katherine Barbieri, "Economic Interdependence: A Path to Peace or a Source of Interstate Conflict?" *Journal of Peace Research* 33 (1996): 29–49.
3. Lewis Richardson, *Arms and Insecurity: A Mathematical Study of the Causes and Origins of War* (Pittsburgh: Boxwood Press, 1960); Quincy Wright, *A Study of War* (Chicago: University of Chicago Press, 1942).
4. J. David Singer, "The Etiology of Interstate War: A Natural History Approach," in *What Do We Know about War?* ed. John Vasquez (Boulder, Colo.: Rowman and Littlefield, 2000).
5. Karl Mannheim, *Essays on the Sociology of Knowledge* (New York: Oxford University Press, 1952).
6. Hayward R. Alker, *Rediscoveries and Reformulations* (Cambridge: Cambridge University Press, 1996).
7. Peter Haas, "Do Regimes Matter? Epistemic Communities and Mediterranean Pollution Control," *International Organization* 43, no. 3 (1989): 377–403.
8. Hedley Bull, "Strategic Studies and Its Critics," *World Politics* 20, no. 4 (1968): 593–605.
9. David Dessler, "Beyond Correlations: Toward a Causal Theory of War," *International Studies Quarterly* 35 (1991): 343, 345.
10. Roy Bhasker, *A Realist Theory of Science*, 2d. ed. (London: Routledge and Kegan Paul, 1986).
11. Robert H. Bates, *Analytic Narratives* (Princeton, N.J.: Princeton University Press, 1998).
12. Alexander L. George, "Case Studies and Theory Development: The Method of Structured, Focused Comparison," in *Diplomacy: New Approaches in History, Theory, and Policy*, ed. Paul G. Lauren (New York: Free Press, 1979), 43–68.
13. Carl G. Hempel, *Philosophy of Natural Science* (Saddle River, N.J., Prentice Hall, 1966); Karl Popper, *Logic of Scientific Discovery* (New York, Basic Books, 1959); Rom Harre, *The Method of Science* (London: Wykeham, 1970); Imre Lakatos and Alan Musgrave, *Criticism and the Growth of Knowledge* (Cambridge: Cambridge University Press, 1970).
14. Herbert Simon, *Science of the Artificial* (Cambridge: MIT Press, 1969).
15. William L. Langer, *European Alliances and Alignments, 1871–1890* (New York, Knopf, 1950); Edward V. Gulick, *Europe's Classical Balance of Power* (New York: Norton, 1955).
16. Glenn Snyder and Paul Diesing, *Conflict among Nations* (Princeton, N.J.: Princeton University Press, 1977).
17. Inis L. Claude, *Power and International Relations* (New York: Random House, 1962).
18. Laura W. Reed and Carl Kaysen, eds., *Emerging Norms of Justified Intervention* (Cambridge, Mass.: American Academy of Arts and Sciences, 1993).
19. J. David Singer, "Conflict Research, the Security Dilemma, and Learning from History," in *Behavior, Culture, and Conflict in World Politics*,

ed. William Zimmerman and Harold Jacobson (Ann Arbor: University of Michigan Press, 1993).
20. J. David Singer, "The Level-of-Analysis Problem in International Relations," *World Politics* 14, no. 1 (1961): 77–92; Kenneth N. Waltz, *Man, the State, and War: A Theoretical Analysis* (New York: Columbia University Press, 1959).
21. Waltz, *Man, the State, and War*; Kenneth N. Waltz, *Theory of International Politics* (Reading, Mass.: Addison-Wesley, 1979).
22. J. David Singer, "Inter-Nation Influence: A Formal Model," *American Political Science Review* 57, no. 2 (1963): 420–30.
23. Morton Kaplan, *System and Process in International Politics* (New York: Wiley, 1957).
24. Daniel S. Geller and J. David Singer, *Nations at War: A Scientific Study of International Conflict* (Cambridge: Cambridge University Press, 1998), chs. 5 and 6.
25. Stuart A. Bremer and Thomas R. Cusack, eds., *The Process of War: Advancing the Scientific Study of War* (New York: Gordon and Breach, 1995).
26. Singer, "The Level-of-Analysis Problem."
27. Herbert M. Blalock, *Social Statistics* (New York: McGraw-Hill, 1979).

NOTES FROM THE UNDERGROUND

A Tale of Three Perspectives

Linda B. Miller

The invitation to participate in a millennial reflections panel on international security and peace studies and to publish these remarks arrived at a propitious moment. The public opportunity to reappraise my own academic career as I was already doing privately meant a chance to ruminate in a way that might have value for younger scholars at earlier stages of their careers. And since my own trajectory closely parallels that of the International Studies Association (ISA) in terms of time, such an overview should be of general interest to the membership.

In that spirit, I offer what I have titled "Notes from the Underground." Such a literary title signifies not only my origins as an undergraduate student of literature and history before I embarked on the professional study of political science and international relations (IR) in graduate school, but also my nearly four decades of teaching undergraduates, primarily women, in liberal arts colleges, "the underground" in relationship to major research universities, where much of the research and writing on international security originates. I have held research appointments at a number of U.S. institutions (Princeton, Harvard, Columbia, Brown), which has kept me up-to-date with major findings and alleged paradigm shifts. In many ways, then, I have had the best of a variety of worlds, with the usual balance of successes and disappointments, of recognition and underappreciation in roughly equal measure.

More recently, I have added a third perspective to the first two of student and teacher, that of editor of an official ISA journal, *International Studies Review*. I am struck by the ways in which these three perspectives—student, teacher-researcher, and editor—have built on each other, in part, as Bob Jervis reminds us, because we tend to fit new data into existing categories, and, in part, because we do construct our own autobiographies, perhaps at the risk of not being able to get out of them.

In this supposedly new age of "narratives" and "discourses," we should examine our perspectives periodically to see not only what needs to be discarded but also what should be retained, whatever its origins. I am not surprised that much of what I learned as an undergraduate in the late 1950s at Harvard is relevant in 2000, especially the need for multidisciplinary insights, for knowledge of people and places as the essence of politics. More surprising, given the pedestrian quality of graduate education at Columbia in the early to mid-1960s, some of what I learned there is equally vital, especially the idea that national and by extension international security is, in Arnold Wolfers's phrase, "an ambiguous symbol."[1] The important role of history as the database for international relations rather than the hard sciences was a self-evident truth. How else could patterns in human behavior over time and space be discerned and analyzed?

Over the decades of teaching and writing, I think I have learned as much from my students as I have from my own research, at least when I reflect on the matter away from the drudgery of paper grading! In my years in the classroom at Barnard, Wellesley, Harvard, and Brown, I have repeatedly stressed the importance of clear thinking. I have urged students to find an individual voice, shorn of the slavish obeisance to higher authority that mars so much of the scholarship that comes my way now as an editor. The students' demand that theory must explain something, not just parade itself as categorical, especially if it is parsimonious, has attained the stature of a congenial commandment. Since many of these students come to the study of international relations from non-American backgrounds, the idea that their experiences and their governments and societies must be part of any informed conversation is assumed, though it still seems to be controversial in some of the parochial professional literature. Similarly, students instinctively weigh the interplay of domestic and international factors in their analyses of security and insecurity. Classical political theory, Western and non-Western, as a rich source of complex questions is sometimes a hard sell in the classroom, but it is a superior antidote to the current events sprawl that may have brought students to the class in the first place. Recently, pathbreaking work in comparative political theory[2] has rejuvenated the prospects for giving students a richer understanding of human nature on which theories of security rest, albeit uneasily.

So embedded in my own approach are these bedrock views that debates about their validity seem strained and artificial. Yet as an editor I confront daily the lengthy efforts to reinvent these wheels before getting to the heart of a manuscript's arguments. Particularly persistent are the endless acknowledgments or references to texts like Kenneth Waltz's *Theory of International Politics* that have shaped the field but threaten to distort it by narrowing the agenda of acceptable questions to investigate more than twenty years after publication.[3] In a changed world, this tendency is a serious impediment in a field that likes to think of itself as "cutting edge" rather than derivative.

Students who are able to cultivate a toleration for ambiguity are comfortable with the notion that the state may be both "obsolete" and "obstinate," to use Stanley Hoffmann's trenchant formulation.[4] Often, they have little difficulty understanding that globalization may actually stimulate national identity or, better, a plethora of local identities.[5] They are frequently able to distinguish between tribalism that stems from a lack of diversity within societies or little contact with the outside world and the fear of the "other" that demagogues exploit as a means of obtaining and perpetuating political power. Although they are intrigued with the possibility that democracies might not go to war against each other now, they are persuaded that this observation might be limited to the North Atlantic–North American region rather than constitute a law of global politics in the twenty-first century.

At the best of times, the models or guideposts we employ may lead to "generic knowledge," in Alexander George's phrase,[6] if we are alert to politics on the ground as the true test of IR theorizing. This organic connection between theory and practice is often buried in the self-styled "great debates" that have roiled the field of security studies periodically. Strikingly, my students majoring in the natural sciences have been the most critical of efforts to apply "scientific" methods to the social universe of social science. They are equally surprised that there is any controversy over whether ideas as well as material factors matter in the drama of large events like the end of the cold war. Just as they accept the blurred lines between comparative politics and international relations, they take constructivism on board in the same critical fashion they bring to realism and idealism, to neorealism and liberal internationalism. Eclecticism in the pursuit of truth or as a way of ensuring the legitimacy of "multiple pathways"[7] is not a cop-out.

It is not necessary to romanticize the common sense of undergraduates, to insist on the wisdom of babes, as providing a sounder basis for advanced study than the serious work of scholars who have asked the right questions and never been satisfied with easy answers or sloppy methods. No, I cite these examples and others that follow because we often go astray when we insist on the primacy of theory, its supposed elegance and coherence, when we know that these intellectual constructs are just that. Theories do not and cannot on their own delineate the range of choice and consequence, let alone the sequence of cause and effect, of international relations in its many and wondrous parts. Theory alone cannot tell us when it is appropriate to speak truth to power, though it may make such speech more penetrating when it does take place.

Clearly, attention to other disciplines has its hazards as well as its advantages. Political scientists who have struggled to incorporate the dictums of economics into their toolkits, to insist on rational choice assertions as most appropriate to the study of political phenomena, have been too slow to accept revised thinking about the limits of this technique. Economists who now see the benefits of psychology in understanding rationality's limits are leaving political scientists behind the curve, although "emotion," along with "cognition," is now attracting some IR scholars as a fruitful, if still tenuous, research topic. Economists who have been investigating the utility of biologically driven evolutionary theories for several decades are now meeting equally skeptical political scientists, so the infatuation with natural science models may be diminishing somewhat.

We have been here before. Political scientists clung to obsolete hard science methods long after physicists had left the Newtonian world far behind. What keeps political scientists in thrall to the theories of other disciplines for too long is not the superior wisdom of these approaches so much as the dogmatic belittling of those social scientists who are inherently suspicious of disciplinary imports. That unfortunate deformity, coupled with a tendency of American graduate education in political science to embrace fads, produces the next generation of a professoriate that is increasingly specialized and doctrinaire.

The implications of this dreary trend are explored at length in two recent issues of *International Security*, the leading U.S. journal. What is striking about the exchange between Stephen Walt and a variety of other scholars is the debate about whether formal models should be judged in part by their utility in analyzing the "real world" as opposed to such criteria as logical consistency.[8] Unwilling to concede any ground on this point, despite the wealth of examples that show formal models as dramatically flawed with respect to empirical tests, the quantifiers are condemned to ex post facto interpretations of events like the end of the cold war that nonformal scholars have already explored and incorporated into their own less rigid theories.

What is the way forward? Not surprisingly, my preferences reflect the three perspectives I have outlined. Since indiscriminate borrowing from other disciplines continues to be such a dubious undertaking, I recommend that we encourage cross-fertilization based on linkages between political science and other social sciences that respect the core of those subjects. Expressed more concretely, large events in the contemporary political world, like the collapse of territorial empire, the upsurge in ethnic conflict or genocide, or the insistence on identity, might be analyzed by groups of scholars brought together by a belief that each of their disciplines has something needed to complete an empirically-rich picture of the phenomena, especially when the events themselves take place in areas of the world less well-known to U.S.-based security researchers.

Fortunately, such efforts are already under way and reaching publication in book form, notably the Borderline series of the University of Minnesota Press. In volume 14, for example, anthropologists, steeped in cultural studies, explore the state in conjunction with political scientists who investigate culture in ways reminiscent of earlier scholarship on war and peace before the cold war and its restricted research agenda took over mainstream IR scholarship. A fruitful result of this collaboration appears in chapter 11, where Hugh Gusterson argues that authors in *International Security* not only failed to prepare their readers for the end of the cold war, a tall order to be sure, but did so by insisting that debates over weapons systems were more worthy of discussion and financial support from foundations than mere speculation about transformative historical change that they could not imagine.[9]

A final reason for proposing group research where scholars cross disciplinary boundaries with their training and intuition intact, rather than projects where some concepts must be ranked lower due to their disciplinary origins, reflects the increasing interest in normative "theories" that promise not policy relevance but serious reconsideration of accepted practices in world politics and domestic affairs associated with the imperatives of hegemony derived from five decades of cold war theory and practice. In security studies, this hegemonic bent has crippled U.S. scholarship much as the same tendency has produced some tarnished outcomes in American foreign policy.

Renewed interest in ethics and international affairs, long treated as irrelevant to the main struggles of world politics, has revealed the poverty of much previous scholarship, with its pretensions and self-referential discourse. Only when we acknowledge that "foreign policy is an inherently moral activity" and that "the national interest is an inherently moral category"[10] will we begin to reposition the study of international security in a more secure intellectual context. Only then will the construction and assimilation of norms move to the center of our vision from the periphery where it languished during the cold war. Only then will the newer debates about globalization and governance as security issues attract the sustained interest they so richly deserve.

Even as the first fruits of this intellectual journey are reaching publication, a growing insistence that our studies must try to repair the world—*tikkun olam*—is apparent. What such a reconnection between theory and practice will accomplish is admirable: a restoration of security studies so that it fulfills the overarching goal of my three perspectives, a liberal art in the fullest meaning of the term.

Notes

1. Arnold Wolfers, *Discord and Collaboration* (Baltimore: Johns Hopkins University Press, 1962), ch. 10.
2. Roxanne Euben, *Enemy in the Mirror* (Princeton, N.J.: Princeton University Press, 1999).
3. Kenneth N. Waltz, *Theory of International Politics* (Reading, Mass.: Addison-Wesley, 1979). For a spirited defense of structural realism, see Kenneth N. Waltz, "Structural Realism after the Cold War," *International Security* 25, no. 1 (2000): 5–41.
4. For a restatement and reappraisal of this term, see Stanley Hoffmann, "A Retrospective on World Politics," in *Ideas and Ideals,* ed. Linda B. Miller and Michael J. Smith (Boulder, Colo.: Westview, 1993), ch. 1.

5. See G. Pascal Zachary, "Get over It," *Foreign Policy* (September–October 2000): 62.
6. Alexander L. George, "Knowledge for Statecraft: The Challenge for Political Science and History," *International Security* 22, no. 1 (1997): 44–52.
7. Donald Puchala, "Marking a Weberian Moment: Our Discipline Looks Ahead," *International Studies Perspectives* 1, no. 2 (2000): 141.
8. Michael Brown et al., eds., *Rational Choice and Security Studies* (Cambridge: MIT Press, 2000).
9. Jutta Weldes et al., eds., *Cultures of Insecurity* (Minneapolis: University of Minnesota Press, 1999).
10. David Welch, "Ethics and Foreign Policy," *Georgetown Journal of International Affairs* 1, no. 1 (2000): 79.

INTERNATIONAL POLITICAL ECONOMY

REFLECTIONS ON THE FIELD OF INTERNATIONAL POLITICAL ECONOMY

Helen Milner

Introduction

The academic field of international political economy (IPE) is a relatively young one. As an established part of international relations (IR), it rose to prominence in the late 1960s and early 1970s. Scholarly writings that would now be called IPE date back much further,[1] but they were not widely-recognized as part of a distinct field until the 1970s.[2] This means that the field is only about thirty years old. The period of oil shocks in the developed countries beginning in the early 1970s provided a strong impetus to the organization of the field. It brought to the fore a set of questions that either had not been addressed in IR before or had been dismissed as unimportant. Concern with these "new" issues energized scholars and prompted the founding of the field.

The key questions at that time dealt with five issues central to IR: the use of economic instruments of statecraft, especially relative to military force; hegemonic stability theory and the decline of the United States, or more broadly of the West; the role of domestic politics; dependency theory and development; and the importance of international institutions. The questions that animated the field were ones such as the following: (1) was military force still useful given the new (or renewed) importance of economic resources? (2) had the United States lost its hegemony, especially in becoming so dependent on foreign oil from a group of less-developed countries?

(3) why did the advanced industrial countries, which were fairly similar in their domestic structures and international positions, respond so differently to the oil shocks? (4) were the lesser-developed countries all bound to remain peripheral, dependent economies trapped in low-growth trajectories? and (5) did this period of monetary and real economic shocks elevate the importance of international institutions, such as OPEC, the International Monetary Fund, the World Bank, and the International Energy Agency, in world politics? Since then, research in the area has grown greatly, and the field has become well-established within American and European political science departments.[3] However, a number of the issues occupying the heart of the field have changed. As I argue below, hegemonic stability theory has largely faded, and the other issues identified earlier in this paragraph have taken on new and different casts in light of the field's current preoccupation with the causes and consequences of globalization.

Definition of the Field

What is IPE? This is less clear than ever. Defining the field is not obvious and is often done in two distinct ways. On the one hand, it is defined as everything that is *not* part of security studies in IR; on the other it is more narrowly defined (as at its inception) as dealing with either economic independent or dependent variables—e.g., economic factors as causes or economic outcomes as consequences. In this latter, narrower sense IPE is defined as only those issues related to the interaction of politics and economics, or states and markets. To be part of IPE, a study must have either an economic independent or dependent variable. The definition of the field matters since it helps to adumbrate the central issues that demarcate the enterprise.

In the first, more expansive definition, IPE includes basically all issues not in security studies. Fundamentally, this seems to mean any issue where the use of military force either does not occur or is not a likely event or a central preoccupation. Many interpret the field in this broader sense and include a vast array of issues and approaches in IR. IPE tends in this version then to become the study of a huge range of phenomena that often have very little to do with economic factors, either as causes or outcomes. These include the study of international institutions—whether or not they involve economic issues—environmental issues, human rights, the role of women and minorities, and international cooperation of any sort.

Some go even further and extend IPE far beyond the confines of IR or even these broad issues. Tooze, for instance, argues that "international political economy as a focus of inquiry extends beyond the problematic of conventional international relations. . . . An IPE problematic will initially ask questions about assumptions and values. IPE developed as a critique of existing orthodoxy through exposing the implicit assumptions and values in accepted approaches."[4] Or as Strange claims, "The whole point in studying IPE rather than international relations is to extend more widely the conventional limits of the study of politics, and the conventional concepts of who engages in politics, and of how and by whom power is exercised to influence outcomes. Far from being a subdiscipline of international relations, IPE should claim that international relations are a subdiscipline of IPE."[5] Others desire to broaden the field even further. Amoore et al. call not only for the "historicization" of IPE but also for considering "how time and history condition the mode of analysis appropriate to the social sciences, and how human subjectivity infuses the theory/practice relationship that in turn shapes our understanding of the world. In other words, we have to go beyond questions of methodology to embrace a substantive concern with the historicity of knowledge itself before we can genuinely construct a historicized IPE. Such a concern raises the issue of 'reflection' as a key problematic to consider in any attempt to historicize IPE."[6]

Is this expansion of the field useful? While all of the topics mentioned above are important, they do not seem to be relevant solely or even largely to IPE. The role of norms and values, "critical" theory, reflectivity, methodology, epistemology, and ontology all are relevant to IR, political science, and social science more generally. When researching the relationship between economics and politics, all of these issues can be important; and when done in the context of this relationship, they are part of IPE. But they are not intrinsically or largely the domain of IPE.

Neither are other important areas of IR. IPE should not be conflated with research into international institutions or cooperation. IPE is not just about cooperation or about international institutions. The field of IPE may include these if they relate to economic factors or issues, but not all institutions or cooperation involve economic dimensions. Studies of the UN, for example, are not intrinsically part of IPE; they are only if they include some economic component. Furthermore, IPE also involves the study of conflict, both militarized and not; it is not just concerned with cooperation. The economic causes of war and peace or the economic consequences of military conflict, for example, certainly fall within the realm of IPE. Moreover, much of IPE does not necessarily involve international institutions; a great deal of economic interchange has little to do with formal international institutions or cooperation. IPE and the study of international institutions and/or cooperation are different subjects, although they do overlap when they involve economic issues.

The narrower definition of IPE is more heuristic. It assumes that economic factors are an inseparable part of the field. The interaction of politics and economics, or more narrowly markets and states, becomes key in this approach. It involves showing how political factors like government policy choices influence economic outcomes, especially the operation of markets; and conversely, it entails showing how economic phenomena may alter the way politics operates, often by changing the preferences and/or capacities of the actors. The mutual interaction of these two then is the central distinguishing feature of the field. Without an economic component, I would argue, the phenomena are not properly part of IPE. So political studies about topics that have little or no economic aspect should not be considered IPE.[7]

How then is IPE related to IR? Is IPE just a subfield of IR? Or does its reach extend into IR but also beyond? I maintain here that the latter is the case. IPE overlaps with important parts of IR, but it also branches out into other fields, drawing both methodological tools and substantive questions from them. It certainly has strong links, for instance, with economics and comparative politics.

Indeed, the early work in IPE was very much geared as a response *against* economists: it consisted largely in showing economists that they had to add political variables to their models. The scholarship of Robert Gilpin on multinationals, that of Benjamin Cohen on imperialism, and the work of Susan Strange on the nature of the international monetary system are all examples of research that rejected economists' explanations of these phenomena and emphasized the effects of politics. They challenged economists' explanations of international trade, production, and finance that ignored politics. Gilpin's book demonstrated that one had to consider the role of power in shaping markets and the operation of multinational corporations.[8] Cohen's book on imperialism also challenged economists by arguing that the balance of power among leading states was the central cause of this phenomenon.[9] Susan Strange highlighted the role of American and British power in shaping the international monetary system.[10]

These authors challenged economists' arguments about the international economy, showing that one could not adequately understand these topics without knowledge of political factors.

What is the state of this relationship between the two fields now? Today parts of the field are tightly linked to the discipline of economics. This is especially true in studies of economic policymaking. Some, like Strange herself, have argued that there is too much dependence—and perhaps even an uncritical reliance—in IPE on economics and its models. Nevertheless, a wide range of scholars use economic models as a basis for understanding the preferences or likely behavior of actors, and in so doing fuse the two fields.[11] Others continue the earlier tradition of showing economists that they must add political variables to their explanations.[12] And others, of course, reject "economic approaches" out of hand as being ahistorical, decontextualized, and conservative, as some of the earlier authors cited claim.

So what should be the relationship between IPE and economics, especially international economics? Some argue that we should jettison economic theorizing entirely, that rational choice models simply cannot give us much understanding of important political (and social) phenomena. Strange, echoing many others, claims that economics "as a discipline tends to exaggerate the rationality in human behaviour.... How much more has international economic history shown that political choices on economic policies have seldom been motivated by carefully reasoned assessments of quantifiable economic costs and benefits, but rather by political aims and fears, and sometimes by totally irrelevant considerations and irrational emotions."[13] This complete rejection seems an extreme position for a field that wants to explain many of the same things that the economics profession has been working on for a century or more. If one takes a less extreme view, however, what are the possibilities? Should we just be adding political variables to economists' models? Or should we be rewriting their models by adding political content to economic theories? Interestingly, the latter is what economists themselves are starting to do, as I shall discuss later.

How are IPE and comparative politics related? More and more IPE work is comparative and domestic in flavor. Although much IPE scholarship earlier was comparative in spirit,[14] it is now very hard to separate the two areas. Integrating the two fields seems to be an important avenue for future progress. Studies in IPE could benefit from more use of the theory and knowledge of domestic politics developed in comparative politics. It is imperative to a better understanding of IPE topics, like trade, money, and development, to use models of domestic politics that explain how policy is made. Understanding where actors' preferences come from and how they are "aggregated" formally or informally into actual policy choices, for instance, is a fundamental element of comparative politics that bears strongly on IPE questions. Incorporating variables from traditional comparative politics, such as domestic political institutions, could provide fruitful new ways to explore IPE issues. Some of this has occurred as scholars explore variables such as the nature of electoral rules, the party system, the legislative process, and the number of veto players for explaining policy choices, as Rogowski and Simmons have done.[15] Fruitful collaboration between comparative politics and IPE has been and will continue to be a source of progress for the field.

As the diagram in figure 1 suggests, IPE has links with a number of fields. Its reach extends into and beyond IR. And it certainly has links with comparative politics and economics. As I elaborate later, the field is ever more tightly linked to comparative politics. It is difficult today to distinguish the fields of comparative and international political economy. In part because of globalization, much of the most interesting work involves the crossover area where scholars look either at the way in which domestic politics affects the international economy or at how international economic factors shape domestic politics.

Figure 1. The field of IPE

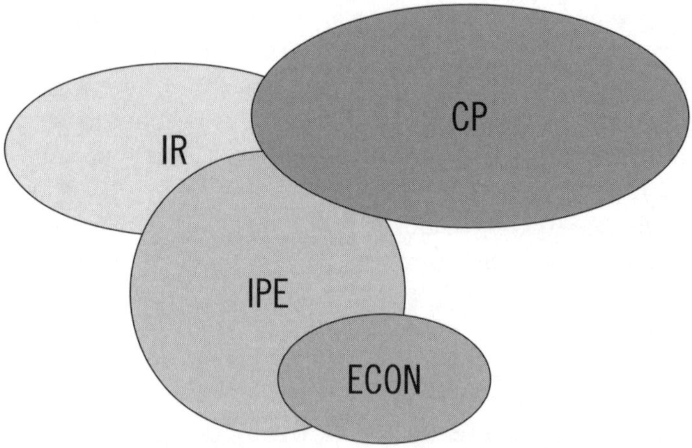

Key Issues

Why does the definition of the field matter? Defining the field is important because it focuses attention on a common set of critical questions and issues. The narrower definition proposed earlier has the advantage that it draws researchers to concentrate on a well-defined series of topics. In the field of security studies, for example, most researchers agree that the central topic is war; the search for its causes, consequences, and prevention provide a unifying set of issues in the field. In IPE, there is probably no such single focus of attention. But there are two or three topics that have long dominated the field's agenda: economic development and its cognate, differential rates of economic growth; the effect of domestic politics on the international economy and vice versa; and conflict and cooperation among states in the international economy.

First, the issue of economic development and differential growth rates has long been a central one. Why some countries (or regions) grow faster than others has been a motivating research question for many studies since the field's inception. Political scientists have tended to focus on the political determinants of economic growth and development. This is limited not just to studies of current developing countries[16] but also to studies of how the West became the center of the industrial revolution and the consequences of its economic superiority,[17] as well as to studies of the political prerequisites of economic growth for developing and transition countries.[18] In addition, many studies of economic policy-making by political scientists have sought to understand policy choices largely because of their impact—often indirect and untested—on the differential economic growth rates of countries.[19]

A second traditional issue that defines the field is the impact of the international economy on domestic politics and vice versa. The older literature on interdependence and the more recent work on globalization are examples.[20] Dependency theory also examined this question as well as the former one about economic growth.[21] The interaction between domestic and international political economy is a major area of interest that persists today.

A third topic that has long defined the field's range of interests has been the examination of conflict and cooperation among states in the international economy. Attention to the role of international institutions in maintaining good economic relations among states and in fostering greater cooperation has been a central issue.[22] The literature on trade wars, competitive devaluations, and other forms of economic conflict has also been prominent.[23] This research area also includes studies of economic sanctions and statecraft,[24] as well as research on the ways in which economic assets can help countries achieve their political goals against the will of other countries.[25] The central questions all relate to the interaction of politics and economics among states in the international system. The political, economic, and social causes and consequences of differential economic growth rates for nations are the central focus when the field of IPE is more narrowly defined.

What are the main research agendas in IPE today? They continue to concern these three central questions by which the field is defined, but they have also been refashioned over time, both as a result of accumulating knowledge in the field and changes in the world. The main research agendas have altered since the 1970s, although many of the new themes have evolved from older ones. Previously, in the 1970s and early 1980s the main themes, as pointed out earlier, concerned economic versus military sources of power; hegemonic stability theory; the role of domestic politics in policy-making, especially the role of state-society interaction in this process (e.g., strong versus weak state and societal arguments); dependency theory and development; and the role of international institutions in promoting economic cooperation, especially among the G-7 countries. Changes have occurred in the field's focus of attention. Some themes, like dependency theory and hegemonic stability theory, have been overtaken by world events. Others, like the domestic politics and international institutions ones, have been transformed from their earlier incarnations into new ones associated with the rise of globalization. World events have affected the focus of the field, although they have not completely altered it. Despite these real-world changes, a number of the older themes are still (indeed, even more) relevant and pursued by scholars in IPE.

The wave of democratization and economic liberalization that began in the mid-1980s and accelerated after the end of the cold war has helped to remake the agenda in the development area. Combined with the problems that dependency theory had in dealing with the increasing heterogeneity in economic performance and status of the once-developing countries, these changes drew attention away from the earlier issues. Currently the impact of democratization, and regime type more generally, on development is a key topic, and the interaction of economic and political reform has become central.

Dependency theory has largely been discarded, but concerns over the impact of capitalist world markets on small developing countries—as well as on large countries—persist. Although the logic of dependency theory is no longer accepted by many, worries about how small countries can achieve stable and high levels of economic development, especially when buffeted by very powerful global economic pressures, are still at the forefront of research and policy concerns.

Hegemonic stability theory (HST) has suffered a similar decline in attention within the field. A dominant research agenda in much of the 1970s and 1980s, the theory eventually ran into both empirical and theoretical difficulties. While never empirically "falsified," HST proved to have numerous difficulties explaining the more specific changes in stability and openness in the international economy.[26] In addition, the revival of the United States and the relative decline of many other potential challengers, like the Soviet Union and Japan, since the late 1980s alleviated worries over the loss of hegemony. Finally, the challenges to the theory's logic were never successfully rebutted.[27] Since the late 1980s scholars have been therefore less interested in the theory, in spite of the newer concerns over American "hyperpower" by non-Americans.

The issue of globalization has captured the heart of the field's attention over the last decade. The phenomenal growth of world trade and capital flows has prompted renewed attention to the whole topic of international economic integration. Both the causes of and consequences of a global market for nation-states have become hotbeds of research. This new focus has transformed several earlier themes pursued by the field; research on the relationship between domestic and international political economy, on the role of international institutions, and on the foundations of power in world politics has been modified over time. Globalization as a process has cast increasing doubt on the traditional separation of the domestic and international levels of analysis. The mutual interaction between the two is dramatically evidenced today, and research on this interaction—often in the form of two-level games—has burgeoned.[28] Very few studies of comparative political economy these days can avoid including research on the impact of global markets, as they might have a decade ago.[29] In addition, scholars have begun examining more carefully the impact of domestic politics on the prospects for international integration. In particular, issues about how regime type (democracy versus autocracy) affects economic reform, growth, and liberalization have gained prominence.³⁰ Moreover, research about the roles of international institutions has also been altered perceptibly. The growing need for these institutions to stabilize and organize the increasingly-integrated world economy has put notable pressure on them. Research into what role they can hope to play, whether they act as independent agents, and what structures and procedures will be most efficacious is of great interest today.³¹

The literature on economic cooperation and conflict has also been subtly transformed. International institutions have gained in importance both in scholarship within the field and in policymakers' eyes. The great momentum in European integration that began in the early 1980s, for instance, has generated renewed attention to this area but in a different guise than earlier. Applications of theories of international cooperation and domestic political institutions to explain European Union integration are booming areas of research today.³² These recent themes, then, centered on globalization—e.g., the interaction of domestic and international factors, two-level games in foreign economic policy-making, regime type and economic policy (effects of democracy on policy, crises, political and economic reform, and development), and the political economy of European integration—constitute some of the main, new centers of gravity in the field.

Methodological Debates

What is the state of methodological debates in IPE? I would argue that they tend to mirror those in IR and political science generally. The two debates of central importance involve the use of rational choice techniques similar to those in economics and the value of large-N versus small-N (or case) studies. Many scholars question the value of rational choice techniques that derive from economics, as already noted.³³ Even more doubt arises over the utility of *formal* rational choice models, although in truth there are only a few IPE scholars who use formal models.³⁴ Again the definition of IPE matters; using formal rational choice techniques is not enough to make you a scholar of IPE in the more narrow definition of the field proposed before. Moreover, as I claim elsewhere, ironically IPE is less formalized than security studies for better or worse.³⁵

Is the assumption of rational choice in general useful in IPE? The issue here relates to both rationality and choice. Some scholars, like Strange, argue against the likelihood of rational behavior, while accepting that actors in IPE may have some latitude for choice. Others object to the formulation as one of choice; they see constraints on actors (usually from the system or existing norms) as preeminent. Others, of course, reject both tenets. It seems harder to abandon or argue against the assumption of (some) rationalism in IPE than in other areas not concerned with the economy. Given the tight connection to economics and the fact that actors here are often making decisions about economic variables—where costs and benefits are frequently measurable—the assumption of rationalism seems more tenable. This is perhaps why there exists much less work on psychology in IPE than in other areas of IR; and, I would argue, less in the constructivist mode—at least in IPE defined more narrowly. Consideration of the costs and benefits in taking actions as impressed by the operation of markets means that agents here are often calculating with some element of reason; and the only reason to calculate is if they have some degree of choice.

Does formalism help? Sometimes it may, and sometimes it may not. If one wants to communicate or collaborate with the economists, it is essential. And if one believes that being very clear about the assumptions one uses, and how they logically must lead to one's conclusions, then the formal statement of arguments is imperative. If one cares less about communicating with economists and if the clear statement of one's precise assumptions is not possible, then formalism may be less useful. In areas where our theories of politics are poorly developed, there is likely to exist little understanding of the causal relationship between variables, let alone any precise knowledge of how different assumptions lead to different causal relations. In these situations formal models may not be very helpful, and may even be misleading. The theorist may not comprehend the restrictive nature of her specific assumptions and hence see the particular formal model as more general than it is. The utility of this approach, as with others, depends on the question at hand and the state of the field.

Does rational choice explain everything about IPE? Certainly not. There is plenty of room for other approaches, and more to be gained from combining different approaches than in limiting them. Most economists, let alone political scientists, recognize this. As one volume assessing the contributions of Nobel Prize–winning economists to political science has pointed out, "one theme pervades [the Nobelists' reflections]: a chafing dissatisfaction with the standard neoclassical paradigm of economic analysis.... There is no dissatisfaction evident with the fundamental postulate of neoclassical economics—that the unit of analysis on which all else is built is the individual choice.... Nevertheless... the neoclassical paradigm... is being not just picked at but massively reworked by those dissatisfied with its assumptions as a basis for analyzing human behavior."[36] As economists are discovering, there are interesting models of nonrational behavior that can be applied. The essential element is that these models themselves have to be rigorous, formally stated, and/or empirically testable for the economists to find them useful. The work on prospect theory begun by Kahneman and Tversky has been one of the most notable diversions from rationalist models.[37] Movement away from rational choice to more cognitive models seems increasingly likely. But movement away from the postulate of agent's choice will clearly not be led by economists or psychologists; it is more likely to come from scholars in the fields of political science and sociology, and especially from either systems theory or constructivism, where choice and agency are less important.

In terms of empirical methods, what are the debates in the field? Again, I think they are the same as elsewhere in political science. The central issue seems to be how valuable are case studies versus large-N analysis. What is the value of large-N studies that use statistical techniques to analyze data? Several objections to them reappear: scholars wonder about the noncomparability and uniqueness of cases, the inadequacy of quantitative measurement of variables, and the overestimation of the precision of findings. Their contributions include greater confidence in the external validity of claims, and less concern about selection biases.

How useful are case studies? Objections involve their low external validity and weak generalizability, as well as serious worries about replicability and selection bias. The contributions of case studies lie in their ability to help scholars think through a theory and its causal mechanisms. Often they can offer some evidence when no better data can be found or provide some critical test of a new idea. They also can be used to show the internal validity of the argument explored. Both methods then are useful for different tasks. When it is especially hard to adequately quantify some variables and/or our predictions from theory are clear, cases may be very helpful. But case studies alone may have serious biases in them. It is probably ideal to combine the two approaches. One can then flesh out the logic of the argument in the cases and determine if it has some external validity in the large-N analysis.

Some Conclusions

Is there consensus in the field of IPE on substance and methods? This depends at least on how one defines the field. The more narrowly it is defined, the more strongly one probably can answer this in the affirmative.

Finally, how extreme are the cross-national differences in conceptions of the field of IPE? Are there significant differences at least in European and American views of the field? Waever in the *International Organization* retrospective volume argues that there are, and that Europeans will never adopt the social "scientific" approaches common in the American community.[38] I would dispute this. It is true that the European academic community in IR has been less enamored with such approaches, although this is not true in other fields. The methods of economics and the natural sciences are as "scientific" in Europe as in the United States, so any differences in political science have nothing to do with the European academic culture. Indeed, I would argue that the field of political science in general in Europe has many of the same kinds of divisions over definitions of the field, its methods, and its theories as in the United States.

As a concluding point, it is apparent that economists are increasingly taking over areas of IPE and comparative political economy. They are adding political variables to their models, combining international and domestic levels, and moving into the study of international institutions.[39] If IPE scholars do not respond, economists shall monopolize the field for better or worse. There are at least two ways the field could respond to this. One is to move away as quickly and dramatically as possible from the central tenets of economics and thereby establish the autonomy, if not antinomy, of IPE to economics. The other way is to engage in more economically-sophisticated work in the field, taking on the economists on their own ground and demonstrating once again that to understand IPE requires more than just knowledge of economics. This path requires that political scientists have a thorough knowledge of the economics of their research area and integrate their findings with those of economists; it fosters an interdisciplinary brand of IPE. These paths are not mutually exclusive, of course. Both may serve to contribute to our knowledge of the international political economy.

Notes

1. For example, Albert Hirschman, *National Power and the Structure of Foreign Trade* (Berkeley: University of California Press, 1945); Jacob Viner, "Power and Plenty as Objectives of Foreign Policy in the 17th and 18th Centuries," *World Politics* 1, no. 1 (1948): 1–29.
2. This claim is not without dissenters: "the unwillingness of [IPE's] foremost American advocates to seriously acknowledge that political economy as a rigorous discipline goes back to the opening decades of the seventeenth century (generally attributed to Montchretien in 1615), rather than beginning in 1968 with Richard Cooper, is confirmed when perusing most standard texts." Peter Burnham, "Open Marxism and Vulgar International Political Economy," *Review of International Political Economy* 1, no. 2 (1994): 221.
3. The organization of political science departments in other areas of the world, such as China or Russia, is less well-known. Whether they have established IPE positions and research centers would be an interesting question to address.
4. Roger Tooze, "Perspectives and Theory," in *Paths to IPE*, ed. Susan Strange (London: Allen and Unwin, 1984), 7.
5. Susan Strange, "Wake Up Krasner, the World Has Changed," *Review of International Political Economy* 1, no. 2 (1994): 218.
6. Louise Amoore, Richard Dodgson, Randall Germain, Barry Gills, Paul Langley, and Iain Watson, "Paths to a Historicized International Political Economy," *Review of International Political Economy* 7, no. 1 (2000): 54.
7. One could of course argue, in terms dear to economists' hearts, that all phenomena are "economic" in that they involve costs and benefits and the operation of markets.
8. Robert Gilpin, *U.S. Power and the Multinational Corporation* (New York: Basic Books, 1975).
9. Benjamin Cohen, *The Question of Imperialism* (New York: Basic Books, 1973).
10. Susan Strange, *Sterling and British Policy* (London: Oxford University Press, 1971).
11. For example, Helen V. Milner, *Resisting Protectionism* (Princeton, N.J.: Princeton University Press, 1988); Ronald Rogowski, *Commerce and Coalitions* (Princeton, N.J.: Princeton University Press, 1989); Jeffry Frieden, "Invested Interests: The Politics of National Economic Policies in a World of Global Finance," *International Organization* 45, no. 4 (1991): 425–51.
12. For example, Beth Simmons, *Who Adjusts?* (Princeton, N.J.: Princeton University Press, 1994); Stephen Haggard and Robert Kaufman, *The Political Economy of Democratic Transitions* (Princeton, N.J.: Princeton University Press, 1995); Sylvia Maxfield, *Gatekeepers of Growth* (Princeton, N.J.: Princeton University Press, 1997).
13. Susan Strange, "International Economics and International Relations: A Case of Mutual Neglect," *International Affairs* 46, no. 1 (1970): 310.

14. For example, Peter Katzenstein, ed., *Between Power and Plenty* (Madison: University of Wisconsin Press, 1978); Peter Katzenstein, *Small States in World Markets* (Ithaca, N.Y.: Cornell University Press, 1985); Peter Gourevitch, *Politics in Hard Times* (Ithaca, N.Y.: Cornell University Press, 1986).
15. Ronald Rogowski, "Trade and the Variety of Democratic Institutions," *International Organization* 41, no. 2 (1987): 203–24; Simmons, *Who Adjusts?*
16. For example, Stephen Haggard, *Pathways from the Periphery* (Ithaca, N.Y.: Cornell University Press, 1990); Haggard and Kaufman, *The Political Economy of Democratic Transitions*; Michael Shafer, *Winners and Losers* (Ithaca, N.Y.: Cornell University Press, 1994).
17. For example, Douglass North and Robert Thomas, *The Rise of the Western World* (New York: Cambridge University Press, 1973); Robert Gilpin, *The Political Economy of International Relations* (Princeton, N.J.: Princeton University Press, 1987); Immanuel M. Wallerstein, *The Modern World System* (New York: Academic Press, 1974); Charles Tilly, *Coercion, Capital, and European States* (Cambridge, England: Blackwell, 1990).
18. For example, Adam Przeworski, *Democracy and the Market: Political and Economic Reforms in Eastern Europe and Latin America* (New York: Cambridge University Press, 1991); Joel Hellman, "Winners Take All: The Politics of Partial Reform in Postcommunist Transitions," *World Politics* 50, no. 2 (1998): 203–34.
19. For example, Katzenstein, *Small States in World Markets*; Simmons, *Who Adjusts?*; Robert Wade, *Governing the Market* (Princeton, N.J.: Princeton University Press, 1990); Geoffrey Garrett, *Partisan Politics in the Global Economy* (New York: Cambridge University Press, 1998).
20. For example, Robert O. Keohane and Joseph Nye Jr., *Power and Interdependence* (Boston: Little, Brown, 1977); Edward Morse, *Modernization and the Transformation of International Relations* (New York: Free Press, 1976); Robert O. Keohane and Helen Milner, eds., *Internationalization and Domestic Politics* (New York: Cambridge University Press, 1996); Garrett, *Partisan Politics in the Global Economy*.
21. For example, James Caporaso, ed., *Dependence and Dependency in the Global System*, special issue of *International Organization* 32, no. 1 (1978); Wallerstein, *The Modern World System*; Fernando Henrique Cardoso and Enzo Faletto, *Dependency and Development in Latin America* (Berkeley: University of California Press, 1979).
22. For example, Ernst Haas, *The Uniting of Europe* (Stanford, Calif.: Stanford University Press, 1958); Keohane and Nye, *Power and Interdependence*; Robert O. Keohane, *After Hegemony* (Princeton, N.J.: Princeton University Press, 1984); Stephen Krasner, ed., *International Regimes* (Ithaca, N.Y.: Cornell University Press, 1983).
23. For example, John Conybeare, *Trade Wars* (New York: Columbia University Press, 1987); Kenneth Oye, *Economic Discrimination and Political Exchange* (Princeton, N.J.: Princeton University Press, 1992); Barry Eichengreen, *Golden Fetters: The Gold Standard and the Great*

Depression, 1919–1939 (New York: Oxford University Press, 1992); Simmons, *Who Adjusts?*; Marc Busch, *Trade Warriors* (New York: Cambridge University Press, 1999).

24. For example, Hirschman, *National Power and the Structure of Foreign Trade*; David Baldwin, *Economic Statecraft* (Princeton, N.J.: Princeton University Press, 1985); Lisa Martin, *Coercive Cooperation* (Princeton, N.J.: Princeton University Press, 1992); Dan Drezner, *The Sanctions Paradox* (New York: Cambridge University Press, 1999); Jonathan Kirschner, *Currency and Coercion* (Princeton, N.J.: Princeton University Press, 1995).

25. For example, Gilpin, *U.S. Power and the Multinational Corporation*; Gilpin, *The Political Economy of International Relations*; Paul Papayoanou, *Power Ties: Economic Interdependence, Balancing, and War* (Ann Arbor: University of Michigan Press, 1999).

26. For example, Stephen Krasner, "State Power and the Structure of International Trade," *World Politics* 28, no. 3 (1976): 317–47; David Lake, *Power, Protection, and Free Trade* (Ithaca, N.Y.: Cornell University Press, 1988).

27. For example, John Conybeare, "Public Goods, Prisoners' Dilemma, and the International Political Economy," *International Studies Quarterly* 28, no. 1 (1984): 5–22; Arthur Stein, "The Hegemon's Dilemma," *International Organization* 38, no. 2 (1984): 355–86; Duncan Snidal, "The Limits of Hegemonic Stability Theory," *International Organization* 39, no. 4 (1985): 579–614; Joanne Gowa, *Allies, Adversaries, and International Trade* (Princeton, N.J.: Princeton University Press, 1994); David Lake, "Leadership, Hegemony, and the International Economy," *International Studies Quarterly* 37, no. 4 (1993): 459–89.

28. For example, Helen V. Milner, *Interests, Institutions, and Information* (Princeton, N.J.: Princeton University Press, 1997); Lisa Martin, *Democratic Commitments* (Princeton, N.J.: Princeton University Press, 2000).

29. For example, Alexander Hicks, *Social Democracy and Welfare Capitalism* (Ithaca, N.Y.: Cornell University Press, 1999); Torben Iversen, *Contested Economic Institutions* (New York: Cambridge University Press, 1999).

30. For example, Haggard and Kaufman, *The Political Economy of Democratic Transitions*; Dani Rodrik, "Democracies Pay Higher Wages," *Quarterly Journal of Economics* 114, no. 3 (1999): 707–38; Edward Mansfield, Helen V. Milner, and B. Peter Rosendorff, "Free to Trade," *American Political Science Review* 94, no. 2 (2000): 305–21.

31. For example, Lloyd Gruber, *Ruling the World: Power Politics and the Rise of Supranational Institutions* (Princeton, N.J.: Princeton University Press, 2000); B. Peter Rosendorff and Helen V. Milner, "The Optimal Design of International Institutions: Why Escape Clauses Are Essential," *International Organization* (forthcoming).

32. For example, Matthew Gabel, *Interests and Integration* (Ann Arbor: University of Michigan Press, 1998); Geoffrey Garrett and George Tsebelis, "An Institutional Critique of Inter-Governmentalism," *International Organization* 50, no. 2 (1996): 269–300.

33. For example, for some debates see Jon Elster, ed., *Rational Choice* (New York: New York University Press, 1986); James Coleman and Thomas Fararo, eds., *Rational Choice Theory: Advocacy and Critique* (Newbury Park, Calif.: Sage, 1992); Donald Green and Ian Shapiro, *Pathologies of Rational Choice Theory* (New Haven, Conn.: Yale University Press, 1994).
34. For example, Stephen Walt, "Rigor or Rigor Mortis?" *International Security* 23, no. 3 (1999): 5–48.
35. Helen V. Milner, "The Analysis of International Relations: Formal Models in International Political Economy," in *The Analysis of International Relations*, ed. Detlef Sprinz and Yael Wolinsky (Ann Arbor: University of Michigan Press, 2001).
36. James Alt, Margaret Levi, and Elinor Ostrom, eds., *Competition and Cooperation* (New York: Russell Sage Foundation, 1999), xv.
37. Daniel Kahneman and Amos Tversky, "Prospect Theory," *Econometrica* 47, no. 2 (1979): 263–91.
38. Ole Waever, "The Sociology of a Not So International Discipline," *International Organization* 52, no. 4 (1998): 687–728.
39. For example, Kyle Bagwell and Robert Staiger, *Domestic Policies, National Sovereignty, and International Economic Institutions*, NBER Working Paper Series, no. 7293 (Cambridge, Mass.: National Bureau of Economic Research, 1999); Giovanni Maggi, "The Role of Multilateral Institutions in International Trade Cooperation," *American Economic Review* 89, no. 1 (1999): 190–214; Torsten Persson and Guido Tabellini, *Political Economics* (Cambridge: MIT Press, 2000).

Some Thoughts on International Political Economy in the Context of Public Policy Education

Robert T. Kudrle

In the early 1980s I tried to develop an approach to international economic relations for Humphrey Institute public policy students that would combine parsimony with comprehensiveness; I was also serving on the editorial team of *International Studies Quarterly*. Both activities led me to think more systematically about the connections between economics and politics than I had done before. I saw no advantage in abandoning the basic theory that seemed reasonably successful in my own discipline of economics, and I had to consider the students. Public policy students with an interest in international affairs care little about the disciplinary origin of a satisfying approach, still less whether insights come from American government, comparative politics, international politics, foreign policy, or public policy. Here economics holds a distinct—some would argue, meretricious—advantage: microeconomic subfields employ the same tools and a common language, and our students must learn microeconomics for policy analysis.

My natural starting point was "political economy" as William Riker rather narrowly defines it: the application of microeconomics to political phenomena.[1] In other words, instead of using two completely different approaches to politics and markets, insofar as possible, the same approach would be used. Elsewhere in this volume, Helen Milner has noted two other common uses of the term when preceded by "international," ones that focus on subject matter rather than method. The broadest usage sweeps up virtually all of international relations not connected with military force; the one she prefers is restricted by economic considerations as dependent or independent variables.[2] By stressing method rather than substance, I sidestep that dispute. As a practical matter, however, the greatest traction from the approach outlined here comes where economic variables loom large; I have applied it mainly to explore the sources of foreign economic policy.

None of the prevailing theories of international policy at that time was grounded in the methodological individualism upon which virtually all of economics is built. Instead, there was a consistent attempt to link foreign economic policy to broad prevailing international relations approaches, almost invariably Marxism, liberalism, and realism.[3] With Davis Bobrow, I sketched the barest outline of what an analysis of foreign economic policy might look like when approached from a standpoint based on microeconomics.[4]

The Basic Approach

The economist confronting political phenomena asks what actors want and what incentives they have to act collectively. Most public policy products (law and administration) are either pure (e.g., defense) or impure (e.g., law enforcement) public goods based on the criteria of nonexhaustibility and nonexcludability. This starting point naturally treats foreign policy as a species of public policy rather than as something utterly different. In terms of linkage to the political science literature, this implies immediate attention to comparative politics and policy.

In international affairs, citizens appear concerned about public policies that serve certain fundamental goals that must be sought as collective goods. These goals may be regarded as guiding individuals' policy preferences in the absence of the special personal stakes that drive domestic policy preferences in the simplest public choice models. The inductively identified goals should not be capable of further reduction or summarization and they should be universal among modern states. The most fundamental appear to be autonomy, security, and prosperity. Autonomy deserves first consideration because some desire to be *maître chez nous* lies at the heart of an internally stable state. A desire for autonomy is very closely akin to common definitions of nationalism.[5] At the nation-state level ambitions may vary widely from, at minimum, a desire to maintain a sense of national distinction to, at maximum, an attempt to avoid any substantial foreign influence.[6] Protection from foreign violence is sought within that context. A state's security challenge can really only be considered in the context of autonomy because various approaches to security pose varying autonomy costs. The weighing of such costs depends on how the group or dominant elements in it view other nation-states. Prosperity can be considered simply the maximization of national wealth because modern nation-states command redistribution policies.[7]

A fourth goal, standing, appears to be less universally important, yet it clearly drives much foreign policy behavior, especially by large states. Standing refers to international rank and influence upon, or regard from, those in other states.[8]

Some might question the sufficiency of the goals. Concern about the environment is included with prosperity because the high-income countries, at least so far, value the natural world primarily as contributing to income, broadly construed, rather than for its own sake. Others might assert that just as altruism plays an important role within states, an international counterpart should be recognized. Foreign assistance as a percentage of national product in most countries declined in the 1990s from an already small base, however.[9]

By making multiple goals explicit, the investigator is forced to consider how governments pursue trade-offs and synergies among them. Fungible resource allocation in the service of nonprosperity goals may be paid as an ordinary price in reduced consumption of other goods and services, but depending on the circumstances, some policies directly barter contributions to one goal for diminished service to another, while other policies promise positive payoffs for more than one goal. The broad outlines of difference in the foreign economic policies of a number of high-income countries seemed satisfactorily interpretable in these terms during the cold war.[10]

The emphasis in economics on maximization and efficiency focuses attention on the opportunity costs involved in the pursuit of national goals. It also forces a clear distinction between preferences and constraints.[11] The relation between them involves consideration of (temporary, moving) equilibria—however imperfectly achieved from some national interest standpoint—and predicts changed policy in response to shifts in either the effective preferences or the constraints. Constraints include the structure of the international system and the place of the state in it, the levels of income and technology of system members, and the degree of congruence of purpose in various dimensions of the state in question with that of other states. Unpacking the latter involves consideration of strategic interaction and bargaining for large states ("price makers") and adjustment for others ("price takers"). Cartel theory suggests hypotheses about the importance of size distribution of states for stability.[12]

One can envision a rational benevolent *dictatrix* considering her utility function with its several national goals and pursuing an optimal policy by bringing multidimensional indifference and (not necessarily everywhere concave) production surfaces together to produce an optimum. Such a seemingly absurd abstraction can be valuable if it contributes to a clearer understanding of the slippage between various constructions of the "national interest" and existing policy. This highlights not just the role of special interests but also broader problems of the gathering and processing of information and the aggregation of preferences. It also raises the traditional concern in economics for efficiency. How and why are changes in internal and external conditions failing to register in policy change? How much of the observed situation can be explained by bargaining or strategic interaction at two or more governance levels and by previous commitments? Most fundamentally, how and why are preference aggregation and choice mechanisms skewing policy away from the apparent desires of the typical citizen?

Comparing actual foreign economic policy with some vision of ideal policy serving some definition of the "public interest" requires a conception of the latter, and that implies judgments, not just about political economy and the traditional autonomy and security concerns of political science, but about economic issues per se. It also demands some guesses about the distribution of preferences because the valuation of autonomy, standing, and security cannot be directly observed. A comprehensive public policy curriculum for IPE must address all of these subjects.

Rational ignorance also plays a central role in the positive theory of policy determination from this perspective.[13] The private good of information processing and evaluation by the individual compared with its perceived value presents a formidable barrier to intelligent choice, especially where the transparency of a policy's impact is low. In such circumstances political leadership channeled by existing domestic structures plays a particularly important role in determining policy stasis and change.[14] Interests tend to loom in intensity with stakes relative to agent numbers, as suggested in the broad-brush collective action literature. A satisfactory economic approach must carefully consider both collective action and specific mechanisms of collective choice.[15]

Until quite recently, economists paid little attention to the origin of preferences. Economic historians, however, cannot avoid the issue, and Douglass North sketched the rudiments of a theory of ideology and ideological change congenial to the economic model.[16] Such ideology includes both a set of cause-and-effect beliefs and some standards of fairness. It serves to overcome otherwise rational antisocial behavior (free riding), and the state's enormous investment in legitimacy reflects its importance. Individuals' ideologies change when experience becomes sufficiently inconsistent with the previously accepted ideas. The same logic makes institutional change (in the sense of formal structures of governance) viscously endogenous.

Recent Research in IPE

I applied this approach in writing only informally and intermittently over the years after it was first developed.[17] Much international relations scholarship of the past fifteen years or so, however, appears highly congenial to it. The role of policy ideas and their diffusion across time and space has been explored as never before.[18] The research agendas in liberal institutionalism emphasize rationalism in a way readily-recognized and appreciated by economists.[19] Recent writing that links domestic and international politics often employs creative models that economists understand and admire.[20] And whatever the mix of qualitative and quantitative analysis, the newer writing typically pays great attention to formal scientific argument.[21]

Game theory changed the landscape in political science because it was formal and in economics because it was formally strategic.[22] Both disciplines now acknowledge the importance of the subject, but there is intense disagreement in both about its value relative to other research activities.[23] Game theory plays a significant but modest role in the curriculum of public policy schools, and this is likely a stable equilibrium for the foreseeable future. In a tightly packed curriculum, game theory's payoff appears mainly heuristic. The professional value of training beyond first principles remains to be demonstrated.

One very simple application of game theory links domestic and international policy-making by construing decision makers as simultaneously involved in "games" at both levels at the same time. As Putnam so memorably puts it, "Any key player at the international table who is dissatisfied with the outcome may upset the gameboard and conversely, any leader who fails to satisfy his fellow players at the domestic table risks being evicted from his seat."[24] This approach provides an important approach for the development of explicit, high-level international agreements with large attentive domestic constituencies. Yet other important agreements take a very different form, as Slaughter has stressed.[25] Large parts of international economic life are now governed by "policy networks" that develop formulas for international cooperation on a broad range of issues based on common experience or best-practice technique, completing bypassing negotiations at levels above the most directly affected parties and their immediate regulators.

Policy networks suggest a mode of international governance far removed from the world of realism (despite the typically greater influence of those with the highest stakes and greatest experience). More generally, the economist considering IPE will likely conclude that realism's focus on defending the primacy of the security goal leaves an ever-greater part of the policy space for persuasive consideration by others. Economists' instincts admittedly push toward excessive attention to prosperity issues, but opportunity cost is always on their minds. They will therefore always want to know when, how, and why security concerns are traded off against other goals. They will also want to know when a quest for relative economic gain can be clearly distinguished from a desire for a greater share of an absolute gain, the policy preferences of special interests, or sector-specific security concerns.

As has been widely noted, the increased attention to economic variables and methods by political scientists has taken place at the same time that economists have begun routinely addressing political issues.[26] Explicitly interdisciplinary work has sometimes produced impressive results. A notable contribution to IPE includes a sophisticated survey of factor specificity as a source of protectionist politics.[27] The findings stress answers that turn on the structure of the economy but, even more importantly, the structure of the political system.

Many articles in the major economics journals now focus on arenas other than markets. Although much of this work is presented even less accessibly than most models in political science, some of it can be easily explained. An example is the tenacity of trade protectionism, which is a highly-inefficient societal transfer. Fernandez and Rodrik offer a persuasive explanation in some circumstances: despite confident estimates of aggregate gains, even by dominant groups, uncertainty about the identity of gainers can prevent reform.[28] Another important contribution is the recent revisionist account of reciprocity in the General Agreement on Tariffs and Trade provided by Bagwell and Staiger.[29] In sharp contrast to the emphasis on mercantilist impulses stressed by most commentators, this interpretation develops the possibility that reciprocity is embraced to avoid the terms of trade deterioration that uncoordinated liberalization can produce.[30]

Marxism has never been much appreciated by economists on theoretical or empirical grounds, and most recent critical theory also appears uncongenial (as is its intention). Much of constructivism, however, which has enlisted some fine scholars from the Marxist tradition, appears to complement the rationalist scholarship or to contest it in promising ways (as argued by some of its leading practitioners).[31] Moreover, some of the same empirical territory is now being addressed from viewpoints grounded in economics by directly including the views and behavior of others in utility functions.[32] However innovative the latter may be, the results will doubtless appear meager to those from other traditions. The parsimony that economists prize can survive only limited contextualization.[33] As in the past, problems of affect and cognition will be reinterpreted, ignored, or minimized. Persuasion, for example, will typically be treated as information rather than arousal.

The economic approach does not deny some importance for factors not explicitly considered but simply asks how much is lost from their exclusion. For example, constructivists claim that changes in underlying preferences, as opposed to strategies in their pursuit, cannot be endogenized.[34] The ratio of the latter to the former may be higher than it appears, however. One example can illustrate the claim. Current changes in thinking about organized labor in many countries reflect concern that prevailing institutions limit general prosperity by reducing the adaptability of the economy as well as its level of employment and output. Policy changes that would increase efficiency by lodging benefits directly with individuals rather than through the workplace—if those changes were bolstered by other policy modifications that preserved social minima and the overall level of material equality—would satisfy those who saw the historic norms of "the rights of labor" as instruments of those objectives, while leaving others highly dissatisfied. More generally, the economic approach will track international norm transmission largely as a combination of information, experience, rational ignorance, and the concentration and diffusion of stakes—whether the latter be material or ideal.

No review of recent scholarship relevant to the approach outlined at the beginning of this paper can ignore the burgeoning rational choice literature in comparative politics. Although it treats issues broader than IPE, the work is "based on microfoundations, in which the collective outcome is derived, albeit often perversely, from choices made by individuals."[35] While much of this work focuses on purely domestic political developments, Bruno Frey has developed an application of public choice that traces individual aspirations within international organizations.[36]

Another large body of writing relevant to the approach outlined here grows from the work of Oliver Williamson and the "New Institutional Economics," which is characterized by the twin claims that institutions matter and that they can be analyzed by the tools of economic theory.[37] Williamson has developed a four-level scheme for analyzing social institutions that embed political economy phenomena in constraints with varying adjustment periods.[38] Much of the research discussed in this article can be usefully considered in this framework. Most fundamental are customs, traditions, norms, and religion that have historically had alteration periods that vary between one hundred and one thousand years. Much of the constructivist project and parallel work on norms by lawyers and economists explore this first level. Next are the broadest institutional rules of society in which change usually takes place between a decade and a century. Positive political theory in both political science and the law[39] can address issues at this level of analysis, which includes the functioning of both domestic and international institutions. The last two levels deal with most of the phenomena of economics. The third level deals with private governance structures that adapt over a decade or less and includes developments such as integration and new forms of contracting. Some or all of the development of publicly sanctioned international policy networks belongs here too. Fourth and finally, there is the continuous operation of markets.

Those employing rational choice in political science and the law sometimes have difficulty mastering phenomena in the last two of Williamson's categories, while naive economic approaches to public policy determination often ignore institutional variation and sometimes never move beyond simple analogies suggested by the last two levels alone.

Recent research by Irwin and Kroszner employs several elements of the scheme sketched at the beginning of this paper to analyze a major reorientation of American foreign economic policy.[40] After identifying private interests, ideology, and institutions as the principal contending (and obviously potentially-complementary) approaches to policy change, the authors consider each to interpret the growth of Republican support for the Reciprocal Trade Agreements Act during the 1940s.[41]

While Irwin and Kroszner focus on the broad determinants of policy, Bates, De Figueiredo, and Weingast employ methodological individualism and goals similar to those noted at the beginning of this paper to analyze popular Serbian support for Milosevic during the 1990s.[42] Although security trumps other concerns in a way that is familiar and reassuring for realists, explicit trade-offs among security, autonomy, and prosperity at the level of the citizen are not. In this study, rationality is attributed to behavior that is treated elsewhere as atavism.

IR and IPE as Social Science

Eichengreen suggests that there has not been enough "systematic, standardized" use of data with theory in the international relations literature by comparison with economics and that case studies are too idiosyncratic to cumulate to greatest advantage.[43] But consider the relative difficulties. Most standard scholarship in microeconomics deals with fairly straightforward measures as dependent, independent, and endogenous variables. In sharp contrast, broader social phenomena are fraught with complex and often invisible connections.

As Olson has stressed, indivisibilities in the consumption of nonmarketed goods sharply separate available measures from changes registered in utility functions.[44] Moreover, governments typically produce goods that are either nonexclusive or have large economies of scale in production. In both cases, the output eludes satisfactory measurement, is produced with unknown levels of efficiency, and is consumed with a valuation that can only be roughly estimated. These problems would remain even if organized interests did not participate in the political process and voters with single-peaked preferences decided issues in referenda. Such considerations imply that the sometimes clear boundaries between markets that justify exploration with partial equilibrium analysis in economics frequently blur when political phenomena are confronted. And even when a political issue appears neatly-bounded, the number of potentially-relevant variables about which there is adequate information, and especially appropriate measurement, is usually small. There is frequent resort to proxy. The number of policy environments, typically states, and the dangers of uncontrolled but perhaps critical changes in the relevant environment over time sharply limit the number of data points in either cross sections or time series (usable panel data are sometimes available). Light specification invites a poor fit, omitted variable bias, or both, while more complete specification increases multicollinearity and spends usually meager degrees of freedom. Causation is often contested, and the data seldom permit satisfactory tests for endogeneity.[45]

Conceptual, measurement, and data considerations mean that largely-qualitative analysis remains essential in careful political analysis, including IPE, and it will necessarily play a relatively larger role there than in economics for the indefinite future. There is also the ever-present danger of a loss of important elements of a conceptual approach through premature or excessive formalization.[46] This does not suggest that a qualitative research project need be less scientific; it may, however, be less conclusive. I say *may* because, when political and economic research are evaluated as description, explanation, and prediction on *major* issues, the marked superiority of economics can often be questioned.[47]

Looking to the Future

The previous discussion treated the nation-state as a given and assumed the collective pursuit of all goals through its agency. This considerably oversimplifies the past and provides a poor guide to future politics and policy. The economic approach to policy expects changing behavior in responses to changing constraints. Self-conscious groups not coterminous with the boundaries of the nation-state have always produced internal autonomy tensions. The reductions of external security threats in many parts of the world have doubtless eased central government fears about responding with accommodation. On the other hand, modern technology has generated economies of scale and learning effects that have pushed the optimum market size ever upwards for much economic activity. Hence the quest for prosperity propels autonomy-compromising coordination—if not heavier governance—as seen in the World Trade Organization as well as myriad economic integration schemes.[48] Some elements of autonomy may be strengthened as others are ceded in regional ventures. This can be seen as a trade of less "internal" for more "external" autonomy in a multistate effort.[49] For example, the European Union (EU) certainly exercises more bargaining power in the world than could any of its nation-states acting alone. Europe also provides an example of identification-pooling for the pursuit of standing.[50] Europe's rank in the many dimensions of human activity was widely recognized to exceed what any single state could achieve alone. Finally, alliances and collective security arrangements have always implied a trade-off of autonomy for security.

Although I have expressed skepticism about the severity of globalization's current threats to central areas of national policy such as growth and taxation,[51] globalization will increasingly affect attitudes and identities relevant to the fundamental goals. This will complicate spheres of autonomy demand as well as the group identification for which the psychic income of standing is relevant. The focus of security efforts will migrate upward. Domestic support for altruistic policy beyond the state's borders will likely expand. These and other changes will likely lead to a sharing of policy-making authority by the Westphalian state with both "lower" and "higher" levels of governance.

Shifts in political power among levels of government are well-advanced in Europe, but every serious integration initiative forces a rethinking of the relation of the goals with respect to types of policy and levels of governance. More generally, the forces of globalization challenge the linkages between the goals and the governance structures that have served them in the past. I also argue that the direction and speed of integration, with its melding of foreign and domestic public policy, cannot be understood without attention to trade-offs as they are perceived by individual citizens. This suggests the seminal importance of the approach taken to Serbian politics by Bates, De Figueiredo, and Weingast.[52] Parallel analysis appears well-suited to individuals facing political choices in less dramatic circumstances.

Europeans are currently experiencing a double dose of economic and social change as globalization and European integration interact with each other. But the two sets of changes should not be lumped together. Europe is engaged in an experiment with true economic integration based on a special history containing elements of both common identity and hideous conflict. This has legitimized a centralizing political counterpart to European economic integration that lacks a parallel in most of the rest of the world.

Dani Rodrik has recently provided a schematic approach to the development of the global economy that can be used to illustrate the qualitatively distinct characteristics of the European project, although that was not his purpose.[53] Rodrik claims that we now face a political economy "trilemma" of the nation-state, mass politics, and integrated national economies.[54] By the third term, Rodrik means the kind of integration in which Europe is currently engaged: goods, services, and all factors of production, especially labor. He claims that one of three choices must be made. The state must severely limit its policy activities so that much authority is focused above, where mass politics can deal with it directly. Alternatively, mass politics must be prevented from effectively addressing much of what really matters—one way of casting the "democratic deficit." If neither of the first two paths is chosen, the gains of complete integration must be sacrificed. The last point needs a careful look. Outside of Europe, one sees little popular interest in those gains. Rodrik cites John Helliwell's research that the U.S.-Canadian border reduces economic efficiency much more than might be guessed from a look at tariff rates or residual investment controls after the North American Free Trade Agreement (NAFTA).[55] As Rodrik suggests, much of this inefficiency doubtless stems from the difficulty of international contract enforcement and could be overcome only with greater legal centralization. But the example also suggests why the trilemma may be more apparent than real outside of Europe. There is no significant Canadian opinion favoring joint governance with the United States to gain that last quantum of economic efficiency—however surprisingly large it is alleged to be (and the Canadians are paying most of the inefficiency price). The autonomy cost of increased prosperity is so high as to block consideration of significantly stronger common governance.[56] On the other hand, the trilemma does well-characterize the current European situation, created as it has been by both economic and noneconomic forces. Its challenges offer cautionary lessons to the rest of the world.

Rodrik's model treats economic integration as a multidimensional phenomenon with no apparent qualitative breakpoints. It can be considered from another perspective, one that I think highlights how goal conflicts will limit the embrace of full international integration. I have argued elsewhere that the importance of the state can be largely gauged in one major dimension: the extent to which it can control its membership and can effectively claim tax authority over their income and wealth.[57] To the extent that the state cannot substantially control permanent population movements across its borders and that it cannot tax the income and wealth of its residents, either because of lack of transaction transparency or jurisdictional mobility, the state withers. If unskilled immigration cannot be controlled, state redistributional efforts can be neutralized. In addition, if the state cannot effectively tax human and nonhuman capital, its redistributive capacity drops sharply. Both possibilities threaten a critical element of national sovereignty: the ability to shape the state's after-tax distribution of income.

The long-run impact of policy innovations can often scarcely be described. The current level of European economic integration appears to lag very far behind the legal structure that enables it. The rest of the world should watch with special care how Europe deals with the closely-linked issues of internal migration and fiscal policy.

Cultural differences continue greatly to inhibit labor mobility within Europe. Yet other factors are also at play. Although many of the most successful politicians of the left as well as the right claim allegiance to markets, some unknown part of current European labor immobility must be assigned to the restricted role of labor and housing markets. If market forces in these dimensions become much more important, interstate mobility could accelerate. The almost certain accession of more low-income countries will put some downward pressure on earnings, particularly of the unskilled, even if the populations do not move. That tendency would be considerably magnified by migration because the nontradable sector would be directly affected. Forecasting here begins to take on the character of science fiction. Nevertheless, the U.S. experience suggests a very impressive example of path dependence: the remarkable potential of chain migration to cause rapid influx of culturally-alien newcomers from minor initial causes.[58] Such developments could raise both prosperity and autonomy threats. And it appears that any control over migration from new states into the EU will be limited to a fixed period after accession. There is no provision in EU doctrine or policy for the migration equivalent of the "escape clause" in trade law.

Fiscal tensions will loom much larger in Europe's future as well, and the present level of decentralization lacks long-run viability. The European tax base remains overwhelmingly national, and some member-states have never been effective at direct tax collection. The challenge has now been greatly increased. EU citizens can now easily shift themselves and their tax liabilities from one jurisdiction to another. And if they don't actually move, tax havens can hide their income anyway. Even if current tax transparency problems were solved,[59] some possible dynamics can alarm. Imagine a future attempt by a high-income EU nation-state to ameliorate an income distribution or an unemployment problem born of unfavorable technological change, the departure of industry for cheaper labor, or unskilled immigration. It might try to raise tax rates on local "winners"—those who own high amounts of human and nonhuman capital. But the "winners" can legally abandon that state, thus exacerbating its problems. Of course, cultural viscosity prevails now, but how strong will it remain over time? Only greater tax coordination within the union—so far resisted in the name of state autonomy—appears as a solution.

Regional integration schemes outside of Europe have a very different character. They have been built almost entirely on prosperity aspirations although external autonomy and security advantages have sometimes been claimed. Political integration of any kind has usually been rejected from the outset, and the uncontrolled movement of persons across borders has not been embraced. NAFTA, for example, specifically eschewed political innovation and was sold to the American public partly as a means to prevent unwanted immigration, not to open labor markets.[60]

The motivations for the more than thirty regional trading blocs that sprang up in the 1990s were doubtless quite varied, but the aspirations of citizens and leaders alike were certainly parallel to those underlying NAFTA more than those of the EU. Enlarging goods and services markets appeared to increase a state's commitment to a stable environment for business and hence to increase attractiveness to direct investors (although the level of binding commitment that has been achieved so far in most such arrangements has been modest). Citizens in most such schemes almost certainly prefer increased prosperity at the lowest possible price in autonomy foregone. In no case does a powerful parallel political agenda propel continuing integration, as was the case in Europe. Therefore, if we assume attentive constituents, integration proponents will succeed as they can argue for efficient trade-offs among the goals. This emphasis on opportunity cost inherent in the economic approach, as well as its emphasis on maximization and equilibrium, may grow in value for IPE scholarship.

Nearly all international economic interaction and the policies that condition it can be considered in three categories: exchange, penetration, and constraint. Economists and political scientists have studied the first category mainly by focusing on the way by which trade—in both goods and capital—changes the wealth and security positions of various states. This has been the focus of most of international economics and much of international politics and political economy. In some of the formulations of research reviewed earlier, the interactions have no effect beyond changes in wealth positions. In sharp contrast, penetration issues stress a broader range of interactions that are epitomized by the literature on the multinational corporation. The social impact of a permanent foreign presence generates issues well beyond those of mere commerce, and much of that presence has been regarded with ambivalence or hostility. Finally, many of the concerns associated with "globalization" involve international factors mainly as they constrain the operation of domestic policy. Concerns about the changing incidence of certain taxes in response to increased capital and labor mobility illustrate those issues. The broader agenda reduces the overall importance of increased scholarly understanding of the domestic politics of purely exchange issues and increases the need to examine much more of the comparative politics and public policy literature in political science. For the same reasons, additional subfields of economics are rising in importance for the study of the policy aspects of IPE. Public finance, labor economics, and environmental economics are growing in importance as international taxation, immigration, and the global environment have joined trade, investment, and finance issues as foci of major attention.

Nothing in the approach sketched above should be interpreted as denigrating insights from approaches to IPE not considered in this paper. I have merely reported on a framework devised largely for the non–political scientist and nonspecialist, whose interest is typically in policy analysis and who already knows the fundamentals of microeconomics. It aims to order existing knowledge and to probe its limits. I am encouraged that the approach appears increasingly consistent with much of the best social science scholarship.

Notes

1. William Riker, "Political Science and Rational Choice," in *Perspectives on Positive Political Economy*, ed. James E. Alt and Kenneth Shepsle (New York: Cambridge University Press, 1990), 180–81.
2. As Milner undoubtedly recognizes, there is innate ambiguity in her sensible approach. For example, she appears to exclude environmental and human rights issues. But the externalities from general economic production and their amelioration look like IPE to me, especially given the enormous domestic and international distributional stakes involved. Similarly, while all of international human rights may not be IPE, rights assigned to labor, including child labor, seem to me just as inseparable from the economic system as most externalities. Northern solicitude is widely seen in the South as largely motivated by protectionism.
3. Robert Gilpin, *U.S. Power and the Multinational Corporation* (New York: Basic Books, 1975); Stephen D. Krasner, *Defending the National Interest: Raw Materials, Investments, and U.S. Foreign Policy* (Princeton, N.J.: Princeton University Press, 1978). In her essay in this volume, Lisa Martin notes the increasing rejection of this overall framework in recent years. Marxism may have faded as a compelling approach as both its global political importance and its general academic attraction diminished, the concerns of domestic pluralism and international liberalism became increasingly suffused with rational choice, and realism's preoccupation with security reduced its apparent relevance.
4. Robert T. Kudrle and Davis B. Bobrow, "U.S. Policy toward Direct Foreign Investment" *World Politics* 34, no. 3 (1982): 353–79.
5. A nation is defined by Yael Tamir as "a community whose members share feelings of fraternity, substantial distinctiveness, and exclusivity.... They thus seek to secure for themselves a public sphere where they can express their identity, practice their culture, and educate their young." Yael Tamir, "The Enigma of Nationalism," *World Politics* 47, no. 3 (1995): 425.
6. A typical citizen's physical safety can often be assumed after capitulation to a foreign power, and such defeat need not lead to a decline in the material standard of living.
7. As a practical matter, however, states have not consistently pursued wealth maximization even when such behavior cannot be rationalized as service to the other goals. In contemporary policy this can typically be construed as a distortion impelled by special interests. Some current and much past policy, however, has been guided by a faulty understanding of the efficacy of various measures for generating greater wealth.
8. Autonomy and standing are thus quite distinct; the former focuses on a group's view of its own situation, independent of the views of others.
9. Even in the 1980s only Norway consistently made an aid transfer of more than 1 percent of its national product.
10. Davis B. Bobrow and Robert T. Kudrle, "Mid-Level Power Strategies for Changing International Niches: Experience in the Old World Order," *Journal of East Asian Affairs* 5, no. 2 (1991): 237–70. For example, Fin-

land paid a clear autonomy price with the Soviet Union for security gains during the cold war. The United States traded prosperity for security during that period, while Japan appears to have pursued policies resulting in synergy between them at modest cost in autonomy.

11. Edward P. Lazear, *Economic Imperialism*, NBER Working Papers Series, no. 7300 (Cambridge, Mass.: National Bureau of Economic Research, 1999).
12. See Duncan Snidal, "The Limits of Hegemonic Stability Theory," *International Organization* 39, no. 4 (1985): 579–614; Joanne S. Gowa, "Rational Hegemons, Excludable Goods, and Small Groups: An Epitaph for Hegemonic Stability Theory?" *World Politics* 41, no. 3 (1989): 307–24.
13. Anthony Downs, *An Economic Theory of Democracy* (New York: Harper and Row, 1957); Mancur Olson, *The Logic of Collective Action: Public Goods and the Theory of Groups* (Cambridge: Harvard University Press, 1965).
14. Peter J. Katzenstein, "International Relations and Domestic Structures: Foreign Economic Policies of Advanced Industrial States," *International Organization* 30, no. 1 (1976): 1–45.
15. See Robert H. Bates, "Comparative Politics and Rational Choice: A Review Essay," *American Political Science Review* 91, no. 3 (1997): 703.
16. Douglass C. North, *Structure and Change in Economic History* (New York: Norton, 1981).
17. Robert T. Kudrle, "Good for the Gander? Foreign Direct Investment in the United States," *International Organization* 45, no. 3 (1991): 399–424; Robert T. Kudrle, "Markets, Governments, and Policy Congruence across the Atlantic," in *Balancing State Intervention: The Limits of Transatlantic Markets, a Rand Study*, ed. Roger Benjamin, Richard Neu, and Denise Quigley (New York: St. Martin's, 1995), 101–43; Robert T. Kudrle and Stefanie Ann Lenway, "Progress for the Rich: The U.S.-Canada Free Trade Agreement," in *Progress in International Relations*, ed. Emanuel Adler and Beverly Crawford (New York: Columbia University Press, 1991).
18. For example, Judith Goldstein and Robert O. Keohane, eds., *Ideas and Foreign Policy: Beliefs, Institutions, and Political Change* (Ithaca, N.Y.: Cornell University Press, 1993).
19. For example, Lisa L. Martin, *Coercive Cooperation: Explaining Multilateral Economic Sanctions* (Princeton, N.J.: Princeton University Press, 1992).
20. For example, Helen V. Milner, "Industries, Governments, and the Creation of Regional Trading Blocs," in *The Political Economy of Regionalism*, eds. Edward D. Mansfield and Helen V. Milner (New York: Columbia University Press, 1997), 77–106; Walter Mattli, *The Logic of Regional Integration: Europe and Beyond* (Cambridge: Cambridge University Press, 1999).
21. This concern is treated in Gary King, Robert O. Keohane, and Sidney Verba, *Designing Social Inquiry* (Princeton, N.J.: Princeton University Press, 1994).

22. For a fine introduction to the former see James D. Morrow, *Game Theory for Political Scientists* (Princeton, N.J.: Princeton University Press, 1994).
23. See Sam Peltzman, "The Handbook of Industrial Organization: A Review Article," *Journal of Political Economy* 99, no. 1 (1991): 201–17; Stephen M. Walt, "Rigor or Rigor Mortis? Rational Choice and Security Studies," *International Security* 23, no. 4 (1997): 5–48.
24. Robert D. Putnam, "Diplomacy and Domestic Politics: The Logic of Two-Level Games," *International Organization* 42, no. 3 (1988): 434.
25. Anne-Marie Slaughter, "Governing the Global Economy through Government Networks," in *The Role of Law in International Politics: Essays in International Relations and International Law*, ed. Michael Byers (Oxford: Oxford University Press, 2000).
26. See Helen Milner, ch. 42 in this volume.
27. James E. Alt, Jeffry Frieden, Michael J. Gilligan, Dani Rodrik, and Ronald Rogowski, "The Political Economy of International Trade: Enduring Puzzles and an Agenda for Inquiry," *Comparative Political Studies* 29, no. 6 (1996): 689–717. This article extends James E. Alt and Michael Gilligan, "The Political Economy of Trading States: Factor Specificity, Collective Action Problems, and Domestic Political Institutions," *Journal of Political Philosophy* 2, no. 2 (1994): 165–92.
28. Raquel Fernandez and Dani Rodrik, "Resistance to Reform: Status Quo Bias in the Presence of Individual-Specific Uncertainty," *American Economic Review* 81, no. 5 (1991): 1146–55.
29. Kyle Bagwell and Robert W. Staiger, "An Economic Theory of GATT," *American Economic Review* 89, no. 1 (2000): 215–48.
30. The fact that this rationale is broadly consistent with the operation of the GATT, of course, does not itself overturn the traditional explanation.
31. See Martha Finnemore and Kathryn Sikkink, "International Norm Dynamics and Political Change," *International Organization* 52, no. 4 (1998): 887–917.
32. For example, B. Douglas Bernheim, "A Theory of Conformity," *Journal of Political Economy* 102, no. 5 (1994): 841–77; Gary S. Becker and Kevin M. Murphy, *Social Markets: The Marriage of "Economic" and "Social" Forces* (Cambridge: Harvard University Press, 2000).
33. Lawrence Lessig, "Social Meaning and Social Norms," *University of Pennsylvania Law Review* 144 (1996): 2181–87.
34. Finnemore and Sikkink, "International Norm Dynamics and Political Change," 914.
35. Bates, "Comparative Politics and Rational Choice," 702.
36. Bruno S. Frey, "The Public Choice of International Organizations," in *Perspectives on Public Choice: A Handbook*, ed. Dennis C. Mueller (New York: Cambridge University Press, 1997).
37. See Oliver E. Williamson, *Markets and Hierarchies: Analysis and Antitrust Implications* (New York: Free Press, 1975); Oliver E. Williamson, *The Economic Institutions of Capitalism* (New York: Free Press, 1985); Oliver E. Williamson, *The Mechanisms of Governance* (New York: Ox-

ford University Press, 1996). The quotation is from R. C. O. Matthews, "The Economics of Institutions and the Sources of Economic Growth," *Economic Journal* 96, no. 4 (1986): 6. See also Oliver E. Williamson, "The New Institutional Economics: Taking Stock, Looking Ahead," *Journal of Economic Literature* 38 (September 2000): 595–613. A "new" institutionalism can be found in a variety of other social science disciplines beyond economics and political science. For an extended discussion, see Robert E. Goodin, ed., *The Theory of Institutional Design* (Cambridge: Cambridge University Press, 1998), ch. 1.
38. Williamson, "The New Institutional Economics," 597.
39. For the latter see Daniel A. Farber and Phillip P. Frickey, "Positive Political Theory in the Nineties," *Georgetown Law Journal* 80 (1992): 452–76.
40. Douglas Irwin and Randall Kroszner, "Interests, Institutions, and Ideology in Securing Policy Change: The Republican Conversion to Trade Liberalization after Smoot-Hawley," *Journal of Law and Economics* 42, no. 2 (1999): 643–73.
41. It concludes that the interactions of institutional change with changing interests explain shifts in the Republican position, while ideologically-related explanations do not.
42. Robert H. Bates, Rui J. P. De Figueiredo Jr., and Barry R. Weingast, "The Politics of Interpretation: Rationality, Culture, and Transition," *Politics and Society* 26, no. 2 (1998): 221–56.
43. Barry Eichengreen, "Dental Hygiene and Nuclear War: How International Relations Looks from Economics," *International Organization* 52, no. 4 (1998): 1012.
44. Mancur Olson, "Toward a Unified View of Economics and the Other Social Sciences," in *Perspectives on Positive Political Economy*, ed. James E. Alt and Kenneth Shepsle (New York: Cambridge University Press, 1990), 212–31.
45. The amount of really formal work in most of political science remains quite modest. For some content analysis, see Lisa L. Martin, "The Contributions of Rational Choice: A Defense of Pluralism," *International Security* 24, no. 2 (1999): 74–81.
46. For a discussion in the context of the new institutional economics, see Williamson, "The New Institutional Economics," 604ff.
47. The failure of economists to predict such major recent developments as the stagnation of the Japanese economy in the 1990s or the U.S. rate of growth and deficit reduction in the late nineties comes immediately to mind.
48. Walter Mattli, "Sovereignty Bargains in Regional Integration," *International Studies Review* 2, no. 2 (2000): 148–80.
49. Davis B. Bobrow and Robert T. Kudrle, "Hedging: A Neglected Aspect of Regional Integration" (prepared for the eighteenth world congress of the International Political Science Association, Quebec City, August 1–5, 2000).
50. As perhaps first famously noted by Jean-Jacques Servan-Schreiber, *Le défi américain* (Paris: Editions Denoel, 1967). Of course, subnational

groups also pursue international standing, as soccer competition illustrates. This simply suggests the obvious point that a single individual may identify with groups of varying aggregation for different activities.
51. Robert T. Kudrle, "Does Globalization Sap the Fiscal Power of the State?" in *Coping with Globalization*, eds. Aseem Prakash and Jeffrey Hart (New York: Routledge, 2000).
52. Bates, De Figueiredo, and Weingast, "The Politics of Interpretation."
53. Dani Rodrik, "How Far Will International Integration Go?" *Journal of Economic Perspectives* 14, no. 1 (2000): 177–89.
54. Rodrik calls it the "augmented trilemma" by analogy to the economist's "impossible triple" of fixed exchange rates, capital mobility, and independent monetary policy.
55. John F. Helliwell, *How Much Do National Borders Matter?* (Washington, D.C.: Brookings Institution Press, 1998).
56. NAFTA does have an as-yet unrealized agenda of greater commonality in some areas, notably competition policy, but that agenda is very modest by European standards, and the failure to address it so far suggests lack of urgency.
57. Kudrle, "Does Globalization Sap the Fiscal Power of the State?"
58. From an economic viewpoint, each newcomer's contribution to the welfare of persons already in the jurisdiction turns on economies and diseconomies of scale and net fiscal impact: the contribution to the provision of pure public goods and the difference between the individual's tax payments and the value of exhaustive goods and services provided by governments to that person. By this measure, unskilled immigration appears to lower welfare, at least in the United States. In nonmarginal amounts, it also increases inequality in the before-tax distribution of income.
59. For an exhaustive discussion of the problem and a review of possible policies, see Reuven S. Avi-Yonah, "Globalization, Tax Competition, and the Fiscal Crisis of the Welfare State," *Harvard Law Review* 113 (May 2000): 1573–1646.
60. Although the United States does not control immigration effectively, this appears to result more from special interest pressures and a widespread view of illegal immigration as a victimless crime than from technical impossibility. Mercosur claims to envision open labor markets as a goal, but nothing has been done to implement the rhetoric. Given the dramatic differences in living standards and differences in size, it is impossible to imagine open migration from Brazil to Argentina for the foreseeable future.

INTERNATIONAL POLITICAL ECONOMY
From Paradigmatic Debates to Productive Disagreements
Lisa L. Martin

In their instructions to the millennial reflections panel participants, the organizers of these panels suggested that they were necessary, in part, because of the increasing diversity of subfields and sections in the International Studies Association. They wrote that this diversity "has made increasingly difficult the crucial task of identifying intra-subfield consensus about important theoretical and/or empirical insights." In this essay, I take issue with the organizers' claim.

International political economy (IPE), perhaps in contrast to the field of international relations (IR) more broadly, is today characterized by growing consensus on theories, methods, analytical frameworks, and important questions. This is not to say that scholars in IPE all agree with one another—disagreement is as prevalent as ever. However, disagreement today generally takes the form of productive, theoretically and empirically motivated claims, rather than the paradigmatic clashes that characterized IPE as an early field of study. Scholars typically see alternative approaches as complementary or applying under different, specifiable conditions. Or disagreements might take the form of debate about relative weights that we should attribute to alternative explanatory variables. These types of disagreements are the hallmark of a mature, productive field of research. In this essay I elaborate my claim, illustrating it with examples drawn from the study of international trade.

The Development of IPE as a Field of Study

IPE is a relatively young field. In its early years, it developed as a subfield within IR. Its questions, methods, and theories were drawn from the study of international relations, not from economics. Thus, Robert Gilpin's characterization of IPE as divided into three paradigms—realism, liberalism, and Marxism—emphasized the links between IPE and IR more generally.[1] These three paradigms characterized the teaching and study of IR quite accurately, and IPE was seen as fitting into the mold defined by IR. Books published in the major series in IPE, at Cornell University Press, as well as articles published in the major outlet for IPE, *International Organization*, confirm the utility of Gilpin's designation until recent years.

Yet, even while the threefold paradigmatic framework proved useful, hints of its inadequacy were apparent. Many authors and arguments did not fit neatly into any of the categories. Certain kinds of arguments did not fit into this categorization at all. Consider, for example, an argument about IPE that focused on the role of domestic institutions. Such an argument would not be liberal, since it concentrates on the state more than domestic interests. But it would not be realist unless national security concerns were paramount in those institutions, and it would not be Marxist unless the institutions were captured by capitalist interests. Thus, one of the more promising lines of research in IPE could not be captured by Gilpin's typology.

Over time, an alternative organizing device has emerged for the study of IPE. It takes the familiar form of a 2 × 2 table.[2] On one dimension, we ask whether the argument concentrates on the explanatory role of interests or institutions. On the other, we ask whether the major explanatory factors in the argument are located at the domestic or international level. This framework has proven more useful for arranging various works in IPE relative to one another, allowing us to identify precisely where various arguments differ from one another and where they agree. Nearly all major approaches in IPE fit fairly well in this framework, with the exception of works that consider the interaction of domestic and international levels, or the interaction of interests and institutions. I will discuss these points shortly. An additional valuable aspect of this organizing framework is that it has facilitated dialogue between political scientists and economists, which in itself is one of the more remarkable and progressive developments in IPE over the last decade or so.

If IPE had its roots in IR, over time IPE scholars have recognized that they must have a firmer grasp of the economics underlying the phenomena they study. At the same time, economists have begun adding political factors such as collective action and government institutions to their models. The result is an increasing overlap in the work of political scientists and economists, and the emergence of scholars who can talk comfortably to both groups. This dialogue with economists, and the fact that works in IPE must now confront the economic foundations of the policies they study, has made IPE a highly productive area of research in recent years. Increasingly, the theoretical apparatus used to study IPE has less in common with IR and more in common with political economy more generally.

Economics and Politics in International Trade

These general points can be illustrated by work on the politics of international trade. IPE scholars initially approached this topic with a focus on either the domestic or international level. On the domestic, E. E. Schattschneider's famous study of the Smoot-Hawley Tariff provided the framework for thinking about free-trade and protectionist interests.[3] Protectionist interests—primarily import-competitors—were concentrated and politically powerful. Free-trade interests, consumers and to some extent exporters, were more difficult to organize and not politically powerful.

Those working on domestic explanations of trade policy also noted that U.S. institutions seemed to matter a great deal for trade policy. Until the 1940s, according to this analysis, trade policy was made by Congress, which was responsive to narrow protectionist interests and encouraged logrolling. The result was inefficiently high levels of protection that hurt U.S. consumers and had negative effects on the international level. Only after Congress delegated trade policy to the president, through the Reciprocal Trade Agreements Act (RTAA) of 1934, could policy reflect diffuse free-trade interests.[4] Thus, another important aspect of domestic-level analysis was the emphasis on institutions. However, more recent institutionalist analyses have noted the weakness of earlier analyses of the RTAA. The logic of why Congress delegated authority, and why this delegation made a difference, often did not stand up to close scrutiny, relying on assumptions of naive constituents, members of Congress who acted against their own interest, or ideologically driven presidents. Douglas Irwin and Randall Kroszner (economists) have shown that congressional voting patterns do not fit the predictions of these explanations of the RTAA.[5]

On the international level, two sorts of analyses of trade dominated. Comparativists such as Peter Katzenstein and Peter Gourevitch contributed to the growing IPE literature by concentrating on how a state's role in the international economy influenced its trade policies.[6] In work that has largely stood the test of time, they demonstrated how and why small, trade-dependent states adopted a package of policies that combined economic openness with high levels of government spending to protect individuals who were put at risk by exposure to the international economy.

Another influential line of analysis on the international level, hegemonic stability theory, identified the distribution of power as the key factor explaining levels of openness in the international economy. Stephen Krasner elaborated the argument that the presence of a hegemonic state was a necessary condition for openness, resting his argument on an analysis of the interests of states of different sizes in maintaining an open international economy.[7] He presented some empirical evidence to back up this claim but also argued that the rather weak fit between economic openness and patterns of hegemony suggested a certain amount of inertia in the international economy. Economic historians, notably Charles Kindleberger, were also active in developing versions of hegemonic stability theory.[8] It has continued to have an impact today, for example in David Lake's more complex analyses of the incentives facing states with different levels of power.[9]

Economic interests did play a role in these important contributions to the development of IPE as a field. Yet, when one reads these works today, it is difficult not to be struck by the lack of contact between the new IPE field and the field of economics. With some exceptions, few references to the economics literature appear. Economic models or standard bodies of economic theory do not make an appearance. Methods commonly used by economists, such as statistics, are largely absent. While the economic interests of actors play an important role in the IPE literature during this period, few authors found it necessary to delve very deeply into economics to determine exactly what these interests were.

The result was a deep divide between IPE and international economics, crossed only in part by figures like Kindleberger. Economists had little use for debates about realism versus liberalism, and political scientists had little interest in how assumptions about factor mobility mattered. In stark contrast, the field of IPE today is characterized by intense interaction between economics and political science. Undergraduate IPE readers and graduate syllabi in IPE feature nearly as many publications by economists as by political scientists. New research in IPE has little chance of publication or influence if it does not draw appropriately on economic theory and results.

In the area of international trade, the introduction of economics to IPE has been dramatic. Beginning in the late 1980s, studies of the politics of trade began drawing explicitly on economic theory. Ronald Rogowski's application of the Stolper-Samuelson model to explain the pattern of coalitions through history stimulated both work building on his insights and vigorous responses drawing from alternative economic models.[10] Stephen Magee's famous "Three Simple Tests of the Stolper-Samuelson Theorem" illustrated the convergence between economic and political approaches to IPE.[11] In order to determine whether Stolper-Samuelson provides an accurate model of coalitions on trade policy, Magee examined patterns of lobbying before Congress on trade bills. This approach is identical to that used by political scientists in testing other models of interests on trade, for example, Helen Milner's study of how exporters and multinational corporations have changed trade policy.[12] Economists increasingly draw on political data to test their arguments, and political scientists use economic models of actor interests.

Much of the debate today over interests on trade policy revolves around applications of Stolper-Samuelson versus the Ricardo-Viner model and questions the conditions under which these different models apply. The key difference in assumptions between the models is the level of factor specificity assumed. Stolper-Samuelson assumes that factors are mobile, easily shifted from one use to another. Ricardo-Viner, in contrast, assumes specific factors, where the costs of moving to the next-best use can be prohibitive. The two models predict very different patterns of coalitions on trade policy and demands for policy. Determining whether trade politics is best explained by one model or the other has generated an active research agenda. Even more productive, perhaps, are efforts to develop measures of factor specificity that will allow us to specify the conditions under which one or the other model will fit best.[13]

On the analysis of domestic institutions, we again see substantial improvement in the sophistication of the models of institutions being used, as well as contributions from both political scientists and economists. The analysis of interaction between Congress and the president in the United States has moved away from the problematic assumptions underlying earlier assessments of the RTAA. Rather than vague invocations of "learning," self-abnegation, or inattentive constituents, recent analyses of institutional choice allow for strategic politicians and parties, and active, demanding constituents. For example, Susanne Lohmann and Sharyn O'Halloran argue that a combination of partisanship and economic shocks explains patterns of congressional delegation to the president.[14] Michael Bailey, Judith Goldstein, and Barry Weingast argue that the institutions for trade policy reflect electoral considerations and the benefits that can be realized from negotiating with other states.[15] Michael Gilligan argues that institutions matter to the extent that they "empower exporters."[16]

On the international level, some work on the effects of the distribution of power continues. For example, Edward Mansfield has subjected hegemonic stability theory to more rigorous empirical tests.[17] Joanne Gowa works along complementary lines, analyzing how security relations influence patterns of trade.[18] However, the most active areas of research today focusing on interests on the international level draws from new economic theories. Strategic trade theory, models of intrafirm trade, and analysis of how investment and trade interact are setting the new agenda for research in this area.

Studies of the role of international institutions in trade have also grown, again exemplifying contributions by both economists and political scientists. One particularly active area of research is in regional trade agreements, where economic and political factors interact in especially intriguing ways. Kyle Bagwell and Robert Staiger have developed a series of models of international trade negotiations and institutions, beginning to provide economic microfoundations for studies of these areas.[19] Research on the World Trade Organization is also taking off, although this is one area in which the contributions of economists remain modest. Instead, legal scholars have made more of a contribution to the study of the WTO's institutional features, such as its dispute settlement mechanism.

The Future: Getting to Interactions

As this brief survey of research on trade indicates, the interests/institutions and domestic/international organizing framework continues to prove useful for categorizing active research agendas. Productive research is taking place in all four of the boxes defined by this framework. It also illustrates the extent to which paradigmatic clashes have disappeared from the bulk of research, and the degree to which a good understanding of economic principles is today essential for scholars working on IPE.

All of these developments are, in my opinion, positive ones. IPE is a mature, exciting field of inquiry. However, being mature does not imply that the field is becoming dry or played out. Our understanding of interests and institutions is still quite primitive, with massive room for new work. Current research agendas provide the tools and point the way; but a multitude of challenges remain.

One of the major remaining challenges will involve breaking down the barriers between interests and institutions, and between the domestic and international levels of analysis. In other words, as the field progresses, our fourfold typology may become less useful. Research on the interaction between interests and institutions, and between the domestic and international levels, is just beginning and is essential. Helen Milner, for example, has developed a model of the interaction between domestic interests and institutions that provides a rich set of testable hypotheses.[20] She also brings another state into the model, suggesting a way to begin integrating the international and domestic levels of analysis. In the area of monetary politics, Lawrence Broz's analysis of exchange rate regimes is an example of how domestic and international factors interact in determining actors' interests.[21] Studying interactive effects is complex and difficult, but the building blocks seem to be in place. Overall, our assessment of the development of IPE over the last forty years has to be highly positive, indicating an exciting and tractable research agenda for the future.

Notes

1. Robert Gilpin, *The Political Economy of International Relations* (Princeton, N.J.: Princeton University Press, 1987).
2. This framework is identical to that suggested by Jeffry Frieden and David Lake in the introduction to the newer editions of their IPE reader, except that I refer to "institutions" instead of the "state." Jeffry A. Frieden and David A. Lake, *International Political Economy: Perspectives on Global Power and Wealth*, 4th ed. (Boston: Bedford/St. Martin's, 2000).
3. E. E. Schattschneider, *Politics, Pressures, and the Tariff: A Study of Free Private Enterprise, as Shown in the 1929–1930 Revision of the Tariff* (New York: Prentice Hall, 1935).
4. I. M. Destler, *Making Foreign Economic Policy* (Washington, D.C.: Brookings Institution Press, 1980).
5. Douglas Irwin and Randall Kroszner, "Interests, Institutions, and Ideology in Securing Policy Change: The Republican Conversion to Trade

Liberalization after Smoot-Hawley," *Journal of Law and Economics* 42, no. 2 (1999): 643–73.
6. Peter Katzenstein, *Small States in World Markets: Industrial Policy in Europe* (Ithaca, N.Y.: Cornell University Press, 1985); Peter Gourevitch, *Politics in Hard Times: Comparative Responses to International Economic Crises* (Ithaca, N.Y.: Cornell University Press, 1986).
7. Stephen Krasner, "State Power and the Structure of World Trade," *World Politics* 28, no. 3 (1976): 317–27.
8. Charles Kindleberger, *The World in Depression, 1929–1939* (Berkeley: University of California Press, 1973).
9. David A. Lake, "Beneath the Commerce of Nations: A Theory of International Economic Structures," *International Studies Quarterly* 28, no. 2 (1984): 143–70.
10. Ronald Rogowski, *Commerce and Coalitions: How Trade Affects Domestic Political Alignments* (Princeton, N.J.: Princeton University Press, 1989).
11. Stephen Magee, "Three Simple Tests of the Stolper-Samuelson Theorem," in *Issues in International Economics*, ed. Peter Oppenheimer (London: Oriel, 1980), 138–53.
12. Helen V. Milner, *Resisting Protectionism: Global Industries and the Politics of International Trade* (Princeton, N.J.: Princeton University Press, 1988).
13. See, for example, James E. Alt et al., "Asset Specificity and the Political Behavior of Firms: Lobbying for Subsidies in Norway," *International Organization* 53, no. 1 (1999): 99–116; Michael J. Hiscox, "Class versus Industry Cleavages: Inter-Industry Factor Mobility and the Politics of Trade," *International Organization* 55, no. 1 (2001): 1–46.
14. Susanne Lohmann and Sharyn O'Halloran, "Divided Government and U.S. Trade Policy: Theory and Evidence," *International Organization* 48, no. 4 (1994): 595–632.
15. Michael Bailey, Judith Goldstein, and Barry Weingast, "The Institutional Roots of American Trade Policy," *World Politics* 49, no. 3 (1997): 309–38.
16. Michael Gilligan, *Empowering Exporters: Reciprocity, Delegation, and Collective Action in American Trade Policy* (Ann Arbor: University of Michigan Press, 1997).
17. Edward Mansfield, *Power, Trade, and War* (Princeton, N.J.: Princeton University Press, 1994).
18. Joanne S. Gowa, *Allies, Adversaries, and International Trade* (Princeton, N.J.: Princeton University Press, 1994).
19. Kyle Bagwell and Robert Staiger, "An Economic Theory of GATT," *American Economic Review* 89, no. 1 (1999): 215–48.
20. Helen V. Milner, *Interests, Institutions, and Information: Domestic Politics and International Relations* (Princeton, N.J.: Princeton University Press, 1997).
21. J. Lawrence Broz, "The Domestic Politics of International Monetary Order: The Gold Standard," in *Contested Social Orders and International Politics*, ed. David Skidmore (Nashville: Vanderbilt University Press, 1997).

About the Contributors

Davis B. Bobrow

Davis B. Bobrow is a professor of public and international affairs and political science at the University of Pittsburgh. He has been president of the International Studies Association, a member of the Defense Science Board, a councillor of the Peace Science Society (International), and an official in the Office of the Secretary of Defense. His recent writing deals with international futures, alternative security perspectives, regional integration arrangements, East Asia in international affairs, and policy design.

Michael Brecher

Michael Brecher is the R. B. Angus Professor of Political Science at McGill University. Educated at McGill and Yale (Ph.D., 1953), he is the author or coauthor of eighteen books and eighty-five articles on India–South Asia, international systems, foreign policy theory and analysis, international crises, conflict and war, and the Indo-Pakistani and Arab-Israel protracted conflicts. Since 1975, he has been director of the International Crisis Behavior Project.

His most recent books are *Crises in World Politics* (1993) and *A Study of Crisis* (1997, 2000, with Jonathan Wilkenfeld). He has received two book awards: the Watumull Prize of the American Historical Association in 1960 for *Nehru: A Political Biography* (1959) and the Woodrow Wilson Award of the American Political Science Association in 1973 for *The Foreign Policy System of Israel: Setting, Images, Process* (1972). Among his other awards are the Fieldhouse Award for Distinguished Teaching, McGill (1986); the Distinguished Scholar Award of the International Studies Association (1995); the Leon-Gerin Prix du Québec for the human sciences (2000); and the Award for High Distinction in Research, McGill (2000). He has been a fellow of the Royal Society of Canada since 1976 and has held fellowships from the Nuffield, Rockefeller, and John Simon Guggenheim foundations. He has been a visiting professor at the University of Chicago, the Hebrew University of Jerusalem, University of California, Berkeley, and Stanford University. In 1999–2000 he served as president of the International Studies Association.

Frank P. Harvey

Frank P. Harvey is director of the Centre for Foreign Policy Studies at Dalhousie University. He is also a professor of political science at Dalhousie. His current research interests include ethnic conflict in the former Yugoslavia, NATO military strategy and peacekeeping, and national missile defense.

His books include *The Future's Back: Nuclear Rivalry, Deterrence Theory, and Crisis Stability after the Cold War* (1997); *Conflict in World Politics: Advances in the Study of Crisis, War, and Peace* (1998, coedited with Ben Mor); and *Using Force to Prevent Ethnic Violence: An Evaluation of Theory and Evidence* (2000, with David Carment). He has published widely on nuclear and conventional deterrence, coercive diplomacy, crisis decision making, and protracted ethnic conflict in such periodicals as *International Studies Quarterly, Journal of Conflict Resolution, Journal of Politics, International Journal, Security Studies, International Political Science Review, Conflict Management and Peace Science, Canadian Journal of Political Science,* and several others. Professor Harvey is currently working on his next book, *Coercive Diplomacy and the Management of Intrastate Ethnic Conflict*.

Ole R. Holsti

Ole R. Holsti has been on the faculties of Stanford University, the University of British Columbia, and, since 1974, Duke University as George V. Allen Professor of International Affairs. He is a former president of the International Studies Association and has received career awards from the ISA, the International Society for Political Psychology, and the American Political Science Association. He has also received two university-wide teaching awards. Holsti's most recent book is *Public Opinion and American Foreign Policy* (1996).

Edward A. Kolodziej

Edward A. Kolodziej is a research professor of political science and former head of the Political Science Department at the University of Illinois, Urbana-Champaign; director of the Ford Foundation Interdisciplinary Seminar on the World Society; and cofounder and first director of the Program in Arms Control, Disarmament, and International Security. He received a Ph.D. from the University of Chicago. He is the recipient of grants and awards from the Ford, Rockefeller, and MacArthur foundations, the National Science Foundation, the National Endowment for the Humanities, NATO, the Woodrow Wilson Center, Fulbright, and the U.S. Institute of Peace.

He has written or edited ten books on security and foreign policy including *The Uncommon Defense and Congress: 1945–63* (1966); *French International Policy under De Gaulle and Pompidou: The Politics of Grandeur* (1974); and *Making and Marketing Arms: The French Experience and Its Implications for the International System* (1987). The latter was cited by *Choice* as one of the major contributions to political science in 1987. Professor Kolodziej has also contributed more than one hundred articles to professional journals as well as chapters to edited volumes. His latest major publication is an edited volume, *Coping with Conflict after the Cold War* (1996), which develops global strategies for reducing armed conflict. He is currently working on three projects: a theory of global governance, a critical evaluation of contemporary security theory, and an edited volume on the global politics of human rights.

Louis Kriesberg

Louis Kriesberg (Ph.D., University of Chicago, 1953) is currently doing comparative research on reconciliation and the changing accommodations between ethnic, religious, and other communally identified groups. He is a professor emeritus of sociology, the Maxwell Professor Emeritus of Social Conflict Studies, and the founding director of the Program on the Analysis and Resolution of Conflicts at Syracuse University. His writings include *Constructive Conflicts*

(1998); *International Conflict Resolution* (1992); *Social Conflicts* (1973, 1982); and numerous chapters and articles. He coedited *Intractable Conflicts and Their Transformation* (1989) and *Timing the De-Escalation of International Conflicts* (1991).

Robert T. Kudrle

Robert T. Kudrle is a professor of public affairs and law at the Hubert Humphrey Institute of Public Affairs and the Law School, University of Minnesota. He studies industrial organization, public policy toward business, and international economic policy. He has served as associate dean for research at the Humphrey Institute and as director of the master's degree in public affairs. Kudrle has consulted for many organizations including the Antitrust Division of the U.S. Department of Justice, the Internal Revenue Service, the Urban Institute, the Canadian Department of Consumer and Corporate Affairs, the UN Center on Transnational Corporations, the Overseas Private Investment Corporation, and the Agency for International Development.

His work has appeared in such journals as *World Politics, International Organization, Journal of Conflict Resolution, Transnational Corporations, Public Finance, Journal of Law and Economics,* and *Canadian Journal of Economics.* Kudrle is past coeditor of *International Studies Quarterly* and serves on its editorial board. He also has been on the editorial boards of *Journal of Health Politics, Policy and Law, International Interactions, International Political Economy Yearbook,* and *Minnesota Journal of Global Trade.* A Rhodes scholar, Kudrle holds a master of philosophy degree in economics from Oxford University and a doctorate in economics from Harvard University.

Lisa L. Martin

Lisa L. Martin is a professor of government in the government department at Harvard University. She is a member of the executive committee of the Weatherhead Center for International Affairs. Her areas of teaching and research include the impact of institutions upon states' abilities to make credible commitments, the European Union, U.S. foreign policy, and legislatures in international cooperation. She has recently presented the following papers: "Agency in Delegation in IMF Conditionality" (with Devesh Kapur); "Governance Patterns in Tourism: The Leverage of Economic Theories";

and "An Institutionalist View: International Institutions and State Strategies."

Linda B. Miller

Linda B. Miller is a professor of political science at Wellesley College and a senior fellow of the Watson Institute at Brown University, where she edits *International Studies Review* under the sponsorship of both institutions. She previously taught or held research appointments at Barnard College, Harvard University, Princeton University, Columbia University, and the Woods Hole Oceanographic Institution. She has published widely on American foreign policy, international organizations, European politics, and the Middle East in a variety of U.S., British, and Israeli journals and monograph series on grants from the Council on Foreign Relations, the Rockefeller Foundation, NATO, the Sloan Foundation, the Pew Charitable Trusts, and the Tami Steinmetz Center for Peace Research at Tel Aviv University. Her books include *World Order and Local Disorder: The United Nations and Internal Conflict* and *Ideas and Ideals: Essays on Politics in Honor of Stanley Hoffmann*.

Helen Milner

Helen Milner has been a professor of political science at Columbia University since 1995. She was a research fellow at the Brookings Institution, 1983–1984, and held an advanced research fellowship in foreign policy studies at the Social Science Research Council, 1989–1991. She has been editor of *Review of International Political Economy* from 1996 to the present. Her research interests include international politics, international political economy, and West European politics.

Her publications include *Interests, Institutions, and Information: Domestic Politics and International Relations* (1997); *The Political Economy of Economic Regionalism* (1997); *Internationalization and Domestic Politics* (1996); *Resisting Protectionism: Global Industries and the Politics of International Trade* (1988); "Democratic Politics and International Trade Negotiations: Elections and Divided Government as Constraints on Trade Liberalization," *Journal of Conflict Resolution*, 41, no. 1 (1997); "Trade Negotiations, Information, and Domestic Politics," *Economics and Politics*, 8, no. 2 (1996) (with B. Peter Rosendorff); "Resisting the Protectionist Temptation: Industry and the Making of Trade Policy in France and the U.S. during the

1970s," *International Organization*, 41, no. 4 (1987); and "International Theories of Cooperation among Nations: A Review Essay," *World Politics*, 44, no. 3 (1992).

J. David Singer

J. David Singer teaches in the Department of Political Science at the University of Michigan. Much of Professor Singer's work falls within the Correlates of War Project, which he began in 1964 and which continues to the present day. His research interests include world politics/international relations, peace research, research methods, public policy and administration, and comparative government and politics. He has many publications including *Nations at War: A Scientific Study of International Conflict, 1816–1990* (1998, 2000, with Daniel Geller); "Militarized Interstate Disputes, 1816–1992: Rationale, Coding Rules, and Empirical Patterns," *Conflict Management and Peace Science* (1997, with Stuart Bremer and Daniel Jones); "The Correlates of War," in *Encyclopedia of Violence, Peace, and Conflict* (1998); "Armed Conflict in the Former Colonial Regions: From Classification to Explanation," in van de Goor et al., eds., *Between Development and Destruction* (1996); "Patterns of Alliance Commitment and the Risk of Armed Conflict Involvement," in Schneider and Weitsman, eds., *Enforcing Cooperation* (1997, with Volker Krause).

Yaacov Vertzberger

Yaacov Vertzberger is a professor of international relations at the Hebrew University of Jerusalem. He held visiting teaching and research positions at Stanford University; McGill University; the Institute of International Studies at the University of California, Berkeley; the East-West Center, Honolulu; Tel-Aviv University; the IDF College of National Defense; the Rockefeller Bellagio Center; the Swedish Institute of International Affairs, Stockholm; the Graduate School of International Relations and Pacific Studies at the University of California, San Diego; the Netherlands Institute for Advanced Study; and the United Nations University, Tokyo. He was also a member of the Mershon Center's Research and Training Group on the Role of Cognition in Collective Decisionmaking at Ohio State University.

Vertzberger is the author of numerous articles and books on decision making, policy formation, international conflict, and Asian security and politics. Among his books are *Misperceptions in Foreign Policymaking: The Sino-Indian Conflict 1959–1962* (1984); *The World in Their Minds: Information Processing, Cognition, and Perception in Foreign Policy Decisionmaking* (1990); and *Risk Taking and Decisionmaking: Foreign Military Intervention Decisions* (1998).

Stephen G. Walker

Stephen G. Walker received a Ph.D. from the University of Florida in 1971. He has held academic appointments at the University of Florida, University of Minnesota, and Arizona State University, where he is presently a professor of political science. He has served as vice president of the International Society of Political Psychology, coeditor of *International Studies Quarterly*, and on the editorial boards of *Political Psychology* and *International Interactions*. His research on the operational codes of political leaders as they relate to problems of crisis management has been funded by the National Science Foundation.

He has published in several academic journals, including *World Politics, International Studies Quarterly, Journal of Conflict Resolution, Journal of Peace Research, International Interactions, Political Psychology*, and *Journal of Politics*.

Jonathan Wilkenfeld

Jonathan Wilkenfeld (Ph.D., political science, Indiana University, 1969) is professor and chair, Department of Government and Politics, University of Maryland. He is director of the ICONS International Simulation Project and the Conflict and Negotiation Project at the University of Maryland and codirector with Michael Brecher of the International Crisis Behavior Project. He is a specialist in foreign policy decision making and crisis behavior, as well as simulation and experimental techniques in political science. He is the author of numerous articles and seven books, the most recent *A Study of Crisis* (1997, 2000, with Michael Brecher) and *Negotiating a Complex World* (1999, with Brigid Starkey and Mark Boyer).

His research has been supported over the years by the National Science Foundation, the U.S. Department of Education, the U.S. Institute of Peace, Sun Microsystems, NCR, and IBM, among others. His current work focuses on the combined use of aggregate and experimental techniques to study the mediation process in international crisis negotiations and how decision makers learn from previous crisis experience.